Christian Sebastian (Sebastian):

 I'm sorry for not making you a priority in my life. I was a bad father to you, Sebastian, and there are no excuses. I wasn't there when you needed me the most. If you could ever forgive me, I would like to know the man you are today. I love you, Sebastian!

Rhesa Elise & Asher James:

 Within the pages of this book is the truth! I have tried to continuously contact the both of you time and time again. Every Christmas! Every birthday! I have called asking your mother if I could talk to you both and visit you, as well as sending numerous texts and video messages. I have saved every single text message, video text, court document, and recorded every phone call that I have had with your mother. I look forward to one day showing you both everything. Nothing excuses the way I was, but not being in your life these past six years is not something I have enjoyed, nor is it of my own doing. I love you both! I miss you both more than you could possibly understand! Rhesa, you are my daughter! Asher, you are my son! You are my children! I am your father!

Steven F. Gray Sr.:

 Dad, I love you so much more than you could ever know! You never walked away from me, even when you wanted to. You were consistent in my life. You were always there when I wanted you, there when I didn't want you, and a pillar in my life whenever I needed you. You loved me unconditionally. I could never repay you. I love you with all my heart! (Sorry, Dad, but John Lennon was the greatest Beatle!)

Jeannie Gray:

You were the only mother figure I ever had. I never had to worry if you were going to punch me, slap me, kick me, stab me, make me go hungry, force feed me food that would make me puke, call me names, or fear for my life. I was never scared to come home. I was never terrified to go to sleep, never wondering if fear awaited when I woke up. You will never understand how much that meant to me, ever! I'm sorry for the way I was. I love you, Jeannie! Thank you!

John Cooper of Skillet:

Jesus Christ used your music to help bring me out from the dark thoughts that consumed my life for so many years. Thank you, John!

Kevin Young of Disciple:

Your lyrics are second to none!!! God has used your lyrics, and the heavy way you bring them to life, to build a dream in my life and turn positive thoughts into action. Your songs, "Radical" & "Dear X", are my life songs and what I choose to live by today. Thank you, Kevin!

Genaveive Linkowski:

You will never understand how The LORD used your voice in my life. Through it, I feel peace. Through it, I feel God's presence. Through it, Christ changed my heart. Through it, The Holy Spirit is teaching me to love. Thank you, Genaveive!

Pastor Jeff Chaves:

You were the spiritual leader I always needed. You never ceased to point me to Jesus Christ in every situation. You taught me that God is always in control.

No matter how much I thought He wasn't, He was. I learned that from you! I love you, Pastor Jeff! Thank you!

Special Thanks To My Editors:

Pastor Jeff Miller and his lovely wife Cheri Miller!
of
(City Lights Church. St. Louis MO)
Thank you both so much for your hard work, dedication, attention to detail, and for the kind way you both treated me and my book!
(Cheri: thank you for burning the Midnight Oil!)

Crawling To God

(...and my toxic relationship with myself)

Have you ever just sat and watched a baby crawl around? Have you ever wondered why the baby seems to be crawling around aimlessly? Have you ever wondered if the child even knows what it's doing by crawling around? All the child is doing is trying to get from one place to another, like so many of us do in life. This is exactly what I have done most of my life. There are no questions in the baby's mind other than, "I wonder what's over there." There are no thoughts other than, "I'm going to get there, somehow, someway." It's never worried if there might be something that could try to stop it, get in its way, or even hurt it. The child never thinks that far ahead, but God does.

This is how I have lived just about my entire life. I was never worried about anything, oblivious to whatever could happen along the way. When I look back on my life, I see a baby. I see a child in a man's body, well into my adult years. Life was definitely not easy for me as a child or an adult for that matter. Growing up I experienced pain of every kind, but we will get into those details later. What really tears me to pieces more than anything is a child's painful upbringing. Is it ignorant to wonder, or even ask God, why these things happen, then blame Him when they do? I have always been one to say, "You can't blame everything on what's happened in the past", and, "You just need to get over it." The more life goes on, the more I wonder what would happen if I took a slow walk throughout my entire life. What would happen? Would there be feelings I would again try to escape? Would I stop trying to remember? Would I be afraid of what I found? To be honest with you, I don't know. I know one thing though: I would see God in and around my life.

God was with me from a baby, to a toddler, to a young unbelieving man, and finally, to a man at the foot of the cross, broken, bruised, beaten, bloodied, and begging Him to take control. God has been in and around me for my entire life. The sad part is that I almost never knew it, and when I did notice He was there, I chose to turn around and walk the other way. I was *that* child, the child who just wanted to get there no matter what. Nevertheless, there was God, watching me, blocking this path or that path, opening this door or that door. He let me live my life and make my own choices, as well as my own mistakes. He watched me and let me do what I wanted, when I wanted, and how I wanted. He allowed me to do all these things but would not allow satan to take my life. The LORD knows I've been in some life and death situations. What I see now is God looking at me. He sees me as a child, a child crawling to Him--

Crawling To God!

8

Chapter One

-Psalm 22:10-11-
I was cast upon You from birth. From My mother's
womb You have been My God. Be not far from
Me, for trouble is near; for there is none to help.
(NKJV)

As you take this walk me, please keep in mind that this is the first time I have taken this walk, also. Although this is my life, I have stayed away from trying to remember anything about it.

Is it the right thing for me to do, taking this walk? I don't know what to say except I believe in my heart that God wants me to do this. I'm scared. I've thought extremely hard about what to say. Some of this you may relate to, some of it you may not. I have learned in life that it doesn't matter what tough things you may have gone through as compared to the tough things I have gone through. That sick feeling we get in our stomachs when something bad happens is pretty much the same for all of us. To you, it may be the absolute worst thing you can think of. To me, some of these things make me feel the same way: that sick to the stomach feeling. Somewhere out there someone is going through something they feel they'll never get past. Someone always has it worse. The only way for me to say anything is to just start writing and be as honest and as transparent as I possibly can.

My earliest memory was when I was three years old. My biological mother, Colleen, thought it would be funny to see if she could get her three-year-old son to smoke marijuana. What was she thinking? My first memory in life is that of me smoking pot at the age of three. Drugs were a huge part of my life and a huge part of what that household had to offer. I remember that night well, actually. Colleen was sitting in the kitchen, as she had so many other nights, with some of my aunts, uncles, and her friends. They were all sitting there getting high, drinking, and laughing. I had seen this all before many times over, so it wasn't like it was anything new. At the time, I had no idea what they were doing, but I knew it was wrong. Strangely, even at the age of just three, I found myself completely drawn to it. They were joking around and laughing hard. They seemed to be having a great time. Why couldn't I be a part of that? As I had done so many other nights, I was at the bottom of the stairs, peeking around the corner, when I heard Colleen call out to me, "Steven, come here."

Was I in trouble? I remember having an uneasy feeling as I walked over to her at the kitchen table.

"Yes?" I said.

"What are you doing over there?"

"Nothing, I was just looking." I could feel everyone staring at me now. Then she said something to me that no matter how hard I tried, I would never forget.

"You want to get high?" She said giggling. What else would a three-year-old say to that.

"Okay." Then everyone at the table started laughing.

"What is it?" I asked.

"Just get over here."

She was holding a cup upside down in one hand. In the other hand she was holding a joint at the open end of the cup, letting the cup fill up with the smoke from the joint. When the cup was full, I watched as she put her lips to hole at the top of the cup and inhale quickly. She coughed, blew the smoke out, and simply said, "Do it just like that."

She repeated the process again and held the cup down for me. I put my lips on the hole and tried to breathe it in. All that happened was I started coughing really bad. Everyone thought it was funny and started laughing. I do not believe I actually got high, but I do remember wanting to continue to make them laugh. That was all I remember of that situation. Colleen, a woman in her late twenties, was trying to get her three-year-old son high on marijuana in 1979. That will always be my first memory of my life. Thank you, Colleen.

The next morning, I was swinging on the playground inside the projects and saw my Aunt Gail walking by on her way to my house to see Colleen. Very proudly, I yelled, "Aunt Gail, I smoked pot last night!"

The look on her face made me know right away that what I just yelled out was not cool. Not long after that I heard, "Steven! Get in the house! NOW!"

It was Colleen, and I knew I was in trouble. I got yelled at pretty bad. She was so close to my face I could smell her breath. She wasn't just trying to scold me; she was trying to put the fear of herself into my life. As always, it worked. Why was it okay to do something that was not ok to talk about?

As a little boy, I had a difficult time making it to the bathroom on time. I had an 'accident' almost every day. I was afraid to tell her I had to go. I was afraid of Colleen, period. Well, one day I had an accident, and she could smell it.

"Hey, poopy pants, did you just poop in your pants?" Colleen asked me.

I was embarrassed and filled with shame. Very quietly, all I could muster was "Yes."

"Do you want me to put a diaper on you and make you walk around the projects?"

Immediately, I started to cry. I didn't want that. I would be made fun of, and she knew it. It was all about control. I was sobbing uncontrollably and could hardly get the words out.

"No! Please don't make me do that. I'm sorry. I won't do it again. Please?!"

She called me names that I cannot write in this book, names you should just never call a child. My cries and please would do nothing to stop her from making me walk around the projects with a diaper on. She went and got a diaper, made me put it on, and also transferred the poop that was in my underwear into the diaper. Some of it had gotten on my leg, and I believe, in my heart that she did that on purpose. I was trying to grab on to the door to stop myself from being pushed out the door.

"Now get out there and walk around the courtyard before I give you something to cry about!"

What kind of a mother does that to her child? Why was she doing this? I just wanted her to hug me. All I wanted from this woman was to tell me everything would be okay. I knew that if I didn't get out of the house though I would get a beating. I started to walk down the steps and up the first stretch of courtyard. As I expected, everyone started to stare. They were all laughing at me and calling me names. I can still hear the laughter...

"Ha! Ha!"

"Steven pooped his pants."

"Poopy pants, poopy pants."

"Steven's a little baby!"

"Steven wears a diaper!"

I just continued to walk around the inner part of the projects with my head down, the tears rolling down my face in a silent cry. They were already making fun of me, so why feed into it by crying aloud, right?

It wasn't until I made the left at the end that I could see her standing in the doorway, arms crossed, looking at me with disgust. Why was she still mad at me? It didn't matter. I just put my head back down and continued to walk. It was at this point I realized that, one day, I would do my best to put the fear of death into her eyes. As I walked by my grandmother's apartment, I looked up and saw her looking down at me. She had a sad look on her face and just nodded at me and said, "It's okay, Steven. Don't you worry; you're almost home."

That seemed to make everything a little better. I didn't hear all the kids making fun of me anymore.

My grandmother, I found out later in life, kept saying that I needed special prayer. Nanny was always a believer in Jesus Christ.

Not many things ever felt safe growing up. I was always afraid of getting beat or yelled at. What hurt the most was being called degrading names.

One time, Colleen borrowed a dish from my Aunt Gail. She was going to return it, but I wanted to be the one that brought it back to her. I wanted to prove I was worth something, that I could be trusted. I wanted to feel useful.

"Mom, can I take the dish back over to Aunt Gail's for you?" I asked.

"No, you'll just drop it."

"No I won't. I can do it. I won't drop it."

She glared at me and said, "Fine, take the dish over to Aunt Gail's. Do not be an idiot and drop it."

I knew I wasn't going to drop it. I just wanted to prove I could do it. I was walking down the same path to return the dish as I did when I had the diaper on. I was concentrating so hard on the dish, holding it with both hands, when it slipped and fell to the ground, breaking into three big pieces.

"Oh no." I was in so much trouble.

I picked up the pieces and began walking back to my house. Coming in the door with the broken dish and my head down, fear running through my mind, I said, "I dropped it."

She just started yelling at the top of her lungs.

"What, are you an idiot!?"

"I didn't mean to. It just fell."

"Shut up! You have an excuse for everything, don't you? You can't do anything right. You're just like your damn father, a loser!"

I stood there crying and waited for the slap to come.

"It just fell," I said again.

Then the slap came. I could feel the blood in my mouth. She continued to yell at me and call me names like: stupid, loser, worthless, and no good.

I remember her saying that I was just like my father. I didn't care though. I was curled in the fetal position on the kitchen floor waiting for the next hit, slap, or punch. I was dragged by my arm, up the stairs, and off to bed with no dinner. I just wanted my dad to call me. I wanted someone to tell me they loved me. I knew my dad loved me.

That was just one of many nights that I had gone to bed without dinner. Most times I didn't care though. She never cooked anything I liked anyway and would frequently take pleasure in force-feeding me food that would make me puke. That's just the way life was. Get used to it. That was the fear…

I can still hear Colleen crying upstairs in her room. She had just found out that she was pregnant with my little sister Rhonda. She got pregnant from a guy who was married to another woman, who, of course, she was having an affair with and was twenty-six years her senior. It was a real, genuine, hearty cry too. All I could think of was what it was I did wrong. His name was Jack, and he came down stairs and told my older sister Belinda and I to sit still on the chair and not to make a sound. Who was this person? Belinda and I just sat there, scared.

I knew life shouldn't always be like this. I dreamed of a life were things were good. A life with no fear or pain. I dreamed of a life with my dad and wondered why she didn't like him. I wondered why she always talked bad about him. I had a very real and genuine fear of Colleen, and she knew it.

…The smell of vodka.

…The glaring eyes.

…The beatings.

…The countless weeks and months of being grounded in my room with nothing but the hope that maybe tomorrow will be different.

It seemed as if the littlest thing would get me in trouble. I was always sent to bed early while the other kids were outside playing. Even my two sisters at the time, Belinda and Rhonda, would still be outside playing.

"But it's still light outside." I would say.

"Too bad." Fear and control.

At least sleep would come without getting hit, right? There was no yelling, name-calling, or food I didn't like when I was sleeping. What I liked most about going to bed was that it was time without Colleen.

———————

Have you ever seen the movie *Seabiscuit*? It's really interesting because the movie is centered around an underdog of a horse that had no chance of winning. They tried to train the horse to win by keeping the second horse a little further ahead with the hopes that Seabiscuit would try harder and eventually go faster to try to win. What they didn't realize was they were training Seabiscuit to lose.

This is exactly what I feel like. I trained to lose. As a very young child, I was trained to lose the battles in life. Why keep trying to go for the gold, the trophy, or the finish line when it's something that you have been shown and taught is unreachable?

It wasn't until they realized that they were training him to lose that they realized they had to retrain him to win. Had they spent too much time going the other way? It would take a lot to retrain Seabiscuit to be a winner. That's what we all need to realize. Unfortunately, I didn't figure this out until later in life. I was a very well trained loser! I would have to try to allow God to retrain me.

Have you ever seen that guy on the corner begging for money for food, but when you try to buy him something to eat he doesn't want it because he just wants the money? What about the guy who just robbed a store and is on the run and now facing jail time? What about the homeless person walking down the street in the wintertime with a blanket over his body and a blank look on his face? How about the person you stand next to in line that hasn't showered in a while? Or, how about the man who is so high on drugs that he can't stand still, his face is pale, and looks like he literally might just die right there on the spot?

I have been that person in each and every one of those situations. In one way or another we're all trained to lose at some point in our lives. Look again at these lost sheep next time and think to yourself: if they had the proper upbringing, a solid home, people they knew cared, knew how to love and be loved, and were taught to have a relationship with Jesus Christ, these same people could have been and could very well one day become:

...a volunteer
...a pastor
...a counselor
...a cop
...an usher at your church
...a father
...a husband
...a provider
...A MAN OF GOD

Now, turn the situation around. The people I just mentioned, if they had been trained to lose, they may very well have been that person you couldn't stand next to because you're afraid he might rob you or his smell might get into your clothes. I believe that if I have been trained to lose, then I can be trained to win. All I need is God in my life and a willingness to follow Jesus Christ.

"They don't have an awareness of where they are in their lives, primarily because they don't have a clear picture of where they have been."
T.D. Jakes
(So You Call Yourself A MAN?)

When I read that in T.D. Jakes' book, I was floored. "That's me," I said to myself. So many times I get to a point where I just don't know where I am in life. This could be because I have no clear picture of where I have been. Maybe that's why I am doing this. I'm still crawling to God. God is still waiting for me to come home.

I know I can produce a harvest for God! I want to. I feel I need to! I want my children to remember their Dad as someone who walked the line with the devil, was delivered by Christ, and let God change his life. The only way I can figure out how to do that is to see where I have been and let God retrain my life.

-Psalm 83:16-
Fill their faces with shame, that
they may seek Your name, O LORD.
(NKJV)

Why would God want to cover my face with shame? To turn my face towards Him! It would be a long time for me to understand or even believe this, but it's true. I have trouble fully understanding that to this day. It's weird, because when things are going well, I tend to forget what God has done for me.

When things are going bad and not as I have planned, my face is lifted up to Him.

———————

It's my birthday and there is a knock at the door. I drop absolutely everything and run to the door to answer it. It's my dad! As he opens the door, I jump into his arms.

"Daddy!"

I hugged him so tight. I remember it like yesterday. His brown leather jacket, his beard on my face, and his Chaps cologne. He is my dad. For my birthday that fourth year of my life, he got me the best present I could ask for: an all-black Huffy bike with a padded banana seat. It was so cool. There was a pink one for my older sister Belinda. He was here to pick us up for the weekend. I only got to see my dad four times a year, no more than that. I would ride the bike later. For now, I just wanted to sit on his lap. That's the only place I ever felt safe. Nothing else mattered. I don't remember much about that day other than just sitting in his lap and waiting for him to tell me it was time to go have fun for the weekend. That meant a hotel, a movie, the arcade, holding his hand everywhere we went, and eating food I wasn't afraid to eat.

His name is Steve Gray Sr., and he is my dad!

<u>Chapter Two</u>

*"Sometimes it can be so difficult to figure
out how easy it is to follow The LORD."*
<u>(Ryan Omlie)</u>

I wasn't in kindergarten yet, I know that much, but I remember the counseling appointments with Colleen. I must have been about three or four years old at the time. My little sister Rhonda was just a baby and she would take all three of us kids to the appointments. She was always crying to the counselor about her life, and so much of it focused on me. I could not for the life of me figure out why this was happening or what it was that I was doing so wrong all the time.

"Why did you do this?"

"Why did you do that?"

"Why do you act this way?"

"Why can't you behave?"

"Why do you want to go live with your father?"

"Why do you put your father on a pedestal?"

"Why are you asking me all these questions!?" is what I wanted to say. I just wanted to color. I didn't know what I did to have to talk to a counselor at that age. Why? What had I done by age four to:

1) Be in counseling
2) Actually realize I was not wanted
3) Be told that I was the problem

4) Not feel loved

-Ephesians 5:1-
Therefore be imitators
of God as dear children.
(NKJV)

The other day Sabrina was going through a box full of things that she'd collected over time from her past. I must have heard the word "Wow" a million times. I remember wondering what could really make her all that interested in just some old things she found in a box from her life. There were letters, pictures, and things like that, mementos she called them. I never understood what a memento was.

"This is from…"

"Wow, this is when I…"

"Steve, these are…"

To be honest with you, I really didn't care. I just couldn't see anybody getting excited over some stuff from their past. I had just gone through a suitcase full of things from when I was in rehab. There was and old journal, an A.A. book, a bible, a newsletter from an old job that I had gotten fired from for testing positive for drugs, and stuff like that. Nothing I wanted to dwell on. I'm not exactly sure what it was I said, but Sabrina turned to me and said, "You know what, Steve? You don't care, because you don't have any positive memories from your childhood." She was right. Her comment hit me like a ton of bricks. She didn't say it rudely, but she was right on the money.

Some choices you make...
Some choices you don't make...
Some choices you deal with...
Some choices you live with...

-Romans 5:3-5-
And not only that, but we also glory in tribulations, knowing that
tribulation produces perseverance; and perseverance, character; and
character, hope. Now hope does not disappoint, because the love of
God has been poured out in our hearts by the Holy Spirit who was given to us.
(NKJV)

I remember the trailer park we lived in when I was five years old and in kindergarten. To go to school I had to walk up a one-quarter-mile steep hill. My sister Belinda, took a different bus. We had one of those plastic clocks that you see at a barber-shop or something that said, "Be back at this time." Belinda would set the time for me that I would have to start walking up the hill so I wouldn't miss my bus. Colleen would get us up, but she was out the door with Rhonda before I had to leave for school. I was five and had to get dressed and keep a very close eye on the plastic clock sitting next to the real clock so I wouldn't be late. I didn't even watch television. I just sat in a chair and watched the clock. I was excited to go to school then. My first crush was in kindergarten, and her name was Allison Messing. I sat across from her, and I just knew that one day we would get married.

I enjoyed school at that age because I did not have to be at home. The trailer we lived in was a scary place. My room had a door that went directly outside and I always thought I heard someone trying to break in. We had these inch-long black and orange caterpillars that would crawl up the side of the trailer. If we didn't sweep them off, they would crawl on the windows and eventually into the trailer. That was a pretty good motive for wanting to sweep them off every day.

Like everywhere else we lived, I spent most of my time in my room, grounded. I didn't know what it was I was doing wrong all the time, but being in my room was a very real thing. It was around this time in my life that I started to think that if I was always going to be grounded, why not actually do things that would get me into trouble. At least I wouldn't be confused about why I felt like I was hated and in trouble. What it did was get a reaction and that was what I was looking for. I was looking for a reaction instead of the confusion I felt.

-Galatians 5:10-
I have confidence in you, in the LORD, that
you will have no other mind; but he who troubles
you shall bear his judgment, whoever he is.
(NKJV)

I can still remember the drugs and alcohol and the big part they played at that time. I can still see the bonfire going in the backyard while I was in my room. I wasn't allowed out because it was grown-up time, as Colleen called it. The music was loud. My aunts and uncles were out there yelling, screaming, and having a good-time. They were drinking alcohol, smoking weed, and God knows what else. The party started earlier in the day and they couldn't wait to get us kids to bed.

By this age, I already knew what pot smelled like. Colleen would take one of her records, de-seed her pot on it, and roll her joints while having a few vodka and cranberry juices. I knew what she was doing when she said she was going to her room to relax. Most of the time, she smoked her pot and drank in front of me. I would stare at her, but I seemed to be invisible to the woman who gave birth to me.

She would play her old Richard Pryor records and get high. I would hear every foul word that came from those speakers. Children should never hear things like that, but for me, it was as normal as brushing my teeth. She would giggle, laugh, and eventually pass out. That's who Colleen was.

I knew that smoking some of her pot was completely out of the question, but her cigarettes were another story. I knew it was wrong, but I didn't care. Early one morning, I noticed her cigarettes were on the kitchen table. "Why not," I thought. I took one, lit it, coughed a couple of times, and then ran some water over it. My older sister was with me and we both lit another one. We continued this and acted as if we were adults, pretending to be mature. I must have lit about six or seven cigarettes, taking only a drag or two from each before putting it out. I lit the last one, started to walk to the living room, and walked directly into Colleen. I felt the hit on the side of my face and was knocked to the ground.

"What do you think you're doing!?"

I couldn't think straight because of how hard she had just hit me, but I remember looking up and seeing my older sister with a look of terror on her face. She began to cry immediately. She was looking directly at Colleen, fearing she was next. She picked me up by my throat and slammed me on the kitchen counter. Her grip on my throat was so tight that I couldn't breathe.

"You want to act like an adult? What the hell are you doing smoking my cigarettes? I can't even sleep without you going through my things." She began slapping me repeatedly.

"Stop your crying! Now you're going to smoke until you throw up."

She sat Belinda on the counter next to me, put a cigarette in each of our mouths, then lit them. "And you better inhale!"

She sat at the kitchen table and lit a cigarette herself while she made us smoke. Belinda threw up right away and was told to go to the bathroom and clean herself up. I, on the other hand, was going to be as defiant as I could. I inhaled little bits at first and blew out the smoke so she could see that I was trying to challenge her, not because I wanted to, but because I didn't want to give her the satisfaction she wanted. She would win though. She always did.

Colleen made me smoke until I finally did get sick. I tried to hold back as much as I could, but eventually I threw up. That was all it took for her to be satisfied.

-Matthew 11:12-
And from the days of John the Baptist until
now the kingdom of heaven suffers violence,
and the violent take it by force.
(NKJV)

———————

Like I said before, you can't blame your life on things that have happened to you in the past. At some point, we all know right from wrong. We all choose our own path.

Sabrina went to go to the store the other night and my daughter Rhesa wanted to go with her. But if I'm home, she would prefer to take only my son Asher. Two small children like that is a lot to handle in a store. So anyway, Rhesa figured out that she was not going and began to cry. She turned away from me and put her face to the closet door with her head down. This tore me in a way I couldn't understand. I picked her up, hugged her, and told her that I loved her and that Mommy would be back soon. I tickled her stomach, and she bounced right back to her bubbly self. This is important and relevant to me because our children should never think that their parents do not want them. Now, if she was having an attitude and wanted to stand at the closet door, then by all means, knock yourself out. This was different though. She felt like Mommy didn't want her at that moment and that couldn't have been further from the truth. Rhesa needed to know that she is, and always will be, wanted and loved.

Now, just like the walk up the hill to catch the bus to go to school by myself, I would have to get off that same bus at the end of the day and walk down that same hill. I always came home to an empty trailer. The only kind of supervision I had was a phone call to my Nanny that I had gotten home safe. She would then give me my directions on what I was supposed to do. She would try to keep me on the phone for as long as possible. Sometimes when I called, she would answer it, "Hello, Steven!"

"Hi Nanny! It's me, Steven! How did you know it was me?"

"Because, God told me!"

I truly did love Nanny, God rest her soul. Later in life, some thirty years after, I found out she would always say that I needed special prayer.

This day though, there would be no phone call. I had fallen asleep on the bus ride home, and when I woke up, I knew something was wrong. The bus was parked with a bunch of other busses. I got up to look around but couldn't see anyone. I got up and walked to the front of the bus, but I was too scared to get off. I sat in the front seat and began to cry because I knew I was in trouble again. I just wanted to be back in my classroom, sitting next to Allison and eating my paste. Maybe I would fall asleep again, wake up in the morning, go back to school, and no one would ever notice. I sat there for a while, scared. Finally, it was just about dark and now I was too scared to stay on the bus.

-Psalm 12:5-
"For the oppression of the poor, for the sighing
of the needy, now I will arise," says the LORD;
"I will set him in the safety for which he yearns."
(NKJV)

I managed to get off the bus to try and find someone. After what seemed like hours of walking, I heard, "Hey kid!" I turned to look, and there was a guy walking toward me.

"Hey kid, what are you doing here? Are you ok?" I started to cry.

"I fell asleep on the bus."

"Are you okay?" The man asked me. Again, all I said was, "I fell asleep on the bus."

"Come on, it's okay. We'll get you home. Where do you live?"

"I live in a trailer."

He asked me my name and for some other information. He made some phone calls and soon we were on our way in a small yellow bus to my house. Come to find out, he was a bus mechanic for the school. He asked me if I wanted anything to eat and told him no. I lied. I was so hungry, but I was also scared about what would happen when I got home. I hoped that Colleen would be happy to see me, but I knew different. He brought me to my front door and dropped me off. Colleen was all smiles and hugs. She thanked the guy repeatedly and walked him to the front. I thought everything was okay, that she was happy to see me, but when she came back inside, she slammed the door shut and started yelling at me.

"Are you freaking stupid?! What happened?"

"I fell asleep on the bus." I started crying again.

"You never called Nanny! You scared her and you scared me! You can't even stay awake on the bus?!" I couldn't stop crying. Why was she mad at me?

"Are you an idiot?" She asked me.

"No. I'm sorry."

"Get your stuff off and go to bed!"

She pushed me down the hall to my room and slammed my bedroom door shut. A little while later, I came out and told Colleen that I was sorry and that I was hungry. I asked if I could get something to eat. She shook her head no and ignored me. I went back to bed hungry and confused. I just could not wait to fall asleep.

We never had much money, and there were periods when there wasn't always food for us to eat when we were hungry. Nanny was watching us one day and asked if we were hungry. I said yes and wanted to know when we could eat, what we would have, and how long it would be until we ate. I remember her asking us what we wanted, but none of us had an answer. She started to go through the refrigerator and cupboards when I vividly remember her saying, "My God!"

There was a whole frozen chicken and a quarter box of pancake mix. There was no other food whatsoever in the entire house. "When did you eat last?" She asked us.

"At school," I said.

"You guys are hungry, huh?"

Only Belinda and I were old enough to understand the conversation. We stood there, bug eyed, like dogs waiting for a treat.

"Don't worry. You guys go in the living room and watch television. I'm going to make you dinner."

And we didn't worry, because Nanny's word was, well, Nanny's word!

-Matthew 25:35-
for I was hungry and you gave Me food;
I was thirsty and you gave Me drink;
I was a stranger and you took Me in;
(NKJV)

Nanny made the biggest pot of chicken and dumplings I ever saw. I could smell it cooking the entire time and couldn't wait to eat. She knew we were hungry and let us sip the broth while it cooked. Then we sat, we ate, and we were satisfied. I fell asleep at the table that night with a full stomach. This is truly one of my fondest memories. I feel blessed to have this memory. That night, while I was in bed sleeping, I heard Nanny talking to Colleen.

"Colleen, you can't live like this. You have to feed those kids. There's no food in this house. You have to get on welfare. Go to a food pantry. Do something! You have to get some food in this house for those kids."

Colleen continued to drink and do her drugs though.

At school one day, we made helium balloons and put our school name, classroom, teachers name, our name, and something about what we were doing inside our balloon, and let them go in the air in the playground. We had all these bets as to whose balloon would be found first. We couldn't wait to get to school every day to find out where our balloon landed. We would think of all these exotic places like Florida or Oregon and hope it landed there. Wouldn't you just know it? Everyone's balloon was found except for mine. Just perfect.

One day, Colleen stayed home from work and told me to get in the car. I thought she was taking me to school when she said, "Do you want to stay home from school today?"

I felt like something was wrong because she was being extremely nice to me.

"Okay," I said.

We went to a few food pantries that day to get food. To me, it was a supermarket, and I could not be happier. One woman was really nice and was giving us all this food, toothbrushes and soap, and food, food, food. There were snacks, donuts, chips, and all this food! Was I just a pawn to get this food with? At the time, it was just nice to know that we were coming home with food, and I couldn't wait to eat it all.

When we got home, she began putting all the food away and I asked if I could get something to eat. She told me that she would make me a bowl of

Top Ramen. She said it was cheap and that I could have that. I told her that we had all this food and I started naming all the things we had. She just looked at me and said, "You can have some soup and like it. Or you can have nothing!" Really?

The next day when I went to school, my teacher told me that I missed school the day my balloon was found. Really? Par for the course.

Christmas was a sad time. It always has been for me growing up. Christmas is supposed to be about the birth of Jesus Christ. We have to teach this to our children from a very young age for them to understand. There is a selfishness about Christmas that kids have that, I believe, they deserve to a point. It's supposed to be a happy time, a family time spent laughing and giving and receiving, but I don't have a memory of that kind of Christmas. It was made known, every year, that money was tight, and presents would be few. I have never once been so excited for Christmas morning since the first Christmas I can remember at five years old. One time I can remember getting a piece of black charcoal in my stocking. Colleen told me it was because I was bad. Another time I got an empty box wrapped in Christmas paper that she thought was the funniest thing and said it was a joke. I never saw the humor in it. I thought it was cruel.

It was okay though, because my dad would be coming soon with a bunch of Christmas presents for me. That's what I was thinking, and I was right. He showed up at the door with Christmas presents for me and my sister Belinda. We each had our own black bags filled to the brim with presents. I ran past the bag and into my dad's arms. I couldn't wait to get away for the weekend. My dad knew it and so did I. We shared an unspoken love that I would not trade for the world. We still do.

When he had to drop us off after the weekend, he had to park at the top of the hill because of the ice. When we got in the house, Colleen was cooking something on the stove and seemed extremely mad. I asked her why she was mad, but she ignored me. I looked at my dad, and he looked at me. He bent down and kissed me and said, "I love you Steven. Hang in there."

"I love you too, Daddy. I want to come live with you."

"I know you do."

Colleen was making him feel very unwelcome, so he left and I watched him walk up the hill, and eventually, away.

"Why are you mad at me?" I asked Colleen. Nothing…"Are you mad at me?" I asked again. Nothing….

"What did I do?" Still, not a word. She just glared at me until I turned away and went to my room.

It's not that everything was always bad all the time. It's just that there are really very few memories that I would sit and tell my children about.

I remember sitting outside my classroom at five years old and the look on her face when she had to come and pick me up. I didn't care though. I knew I was going to get a beating, but the crying that would come afterward would have me so tired that I would pass out and be at peace. The name-calling didn't even bother anymore; I had become immune to it. I was hurt all the time. My feelings hurt. My body hurt. My mind hurt. I was hurting inside. All I wanted to do was hurt her back.

One morning while she was sleeping, I took her lighter and lit the butter dish on fire on the kitchen table. I don't know what I was thinking. I could have burned the house down. It did, however, catch the table, curtains, and wall on fire. I got so scared that I ran to my room and hid under the covers. The fire department never came out. Colleen was able to put the fire out with water from the kitchen sink. I had almost killed her and my two sisters. I got beat so bad that I stayed home from school.

-1 Timothy 5:15-
For some have already turned aside after satan.
(NKJV)

At what point do we willingly walk away from God? When do we choose to follow satan? I know kids that love God. My wife has a friend from church whose daughter got baptized at eight years old. Her mother is a believer and does her best to instill in her daughter that Jesus is our Savior. That kid spends a lot of time at church, and most of her mother's friends are true believers. What we do, our children will also do. I know this girl, and I know that she has a relationship with Christ.

I never had the privilege of a parent showing and teaching me who Christ is. I knew what bad things were. I knew what good things were too. I chose the bad things.

Satan got a hold of me at a young age, and I accepted him with open arms. He gave me a taste, and I liked it. I chose to do wrong and follow the enemy from a very young age. The good news is that God can use evil for good. Where was God though? He was there, guiding me, allowing me to experience life on life's terms so that when I did find out who He was, I could know how good it feels to be truly loved. Good things are great, but for me, good feels even better when I know what bad has felt like.

What if Colleen had given her life to Christ? What if she loved God? Children almost always do what their parents do. Would I have given my life to Christ as well? What if I had learned that loving God was a normal thing and allowed Him to work in my life? There are two things that I'm absolutely sure would have happened:

> 1) I would have never experienced the things I had or have the painful memories I hold today.

> 2) I would have never experienced God working in my life the way He is doing now.

-Exodus 9:16-
But indeed for this purpose I have raised you up, that I may show My power in you, and that My name may be declared in all the earth.

(NKJV)

_____

We soon moved out of the trailer and into another set of projects. I was in first grade. My sister Belinda and I would have to walk about a mile to go to school. Colleen made sure we got up, but she was gone before we left. Belinda had to wear the house key around her neck because, of course, I could not be trusted, per Colleen.

My first grade teacher was Mrs. Straight. I was having problems doing my school work and getting things done on time. Her assistant was Ms. Fanny. I had a huge crush on her, and even she couldn't get me to do my work. I just never paid any attention. It really wasn't so much that I was not listening; it was that I started to become disconnected with life at this age. I remember wondering if life would always be like this. I started more and more to want to go live with my Dad. I don't think I was suicidal yet then, but I know that there were times when I didn't want to be alive anymore. I was always grounded and in trouble.

…Always being yelled at.

…Always getting hit for something.

At that age, I couldn't think about being an adult and getting away. I thought that life would always be this way. I was a very unhappy child, and at only six years old, thought there was no hope in the world.

-Deuteronomy 31:6-
"Be strong and of good courage; do not fear nor be afraid

of them; for the LORD your God, He is the One who
goes with you. He will not leave you nor forsake you. "
(NKJV)

I walked with my head down most of the time. At school, I kept my head down all the time. I couldn't seem to shake the feeling that I was being haunted by some unseen monsters. I couldn't explain it to you then, but I know now that the enemy had his hands around my life. I was yelled at and grounded nonstop. I brought home my report card to be signed one time. When I showed it to Colleen, I was hit back and forth in my face with my report card.

"What are you, freaking stupid?" she yelled.

I wasn't sure if I should cry so she would stop hitting me, or if what she wanted for me to do was cry. I didn't want to, and I usually held it back pretty good, but eventually the tears came, which was followed by, "Stop crying! What are you, a freaking baby?" Then a few more slaps and it was off to bed without dinner again.

I was given extra time at school to get my work done. When everyone was at recess, I was trying to finish. At the end of the day when all the kids were getting ready to leave, I was trying hard to finish the day's work. If I finished on time, I was given these little gold stars with a note to give to Colleen letting her know that I got my work done that day. If there was no note with a gold star, I was in trouble. A few times Mrs. Straight gave me the note anyway, even though I had not finished my work. I wondered if she knew how much trouble I would get in without it.

After school, Belinda and I would walk home. Our next door neighbors would watch us until Colleen got home. They were not nice people at all. They would yell at us for moving the least little bit, and we had to sit on the couch and not move until Colleen got home. It was horrible. I kept trying to tell her that they were bad people and that they yell at us and tell us to just sit there, but she would not listen.

One morning I was having a bowl of cereal, and the guy that lived next door came over and started talking to Colleen. They were talking and standing real close to each other. Then they started kissing. They were kissing and touching each other in ways that children should never be allowed to see. I remember watching them and saying, "Stop!"

She just looked at me and went, "Mmmmmmmmmm!" And she continued what she was doing.

I couldn't take it anymore and finally stood up and yelled, "STOP IT!"

"Shut up, and mind your own business," she yelled at me. Then he came over and said, "Shut your mouth! Now!"

One day, Colleen said that we were moving because the people next door were crazy. To this day, I still wonder what happened to make her finally see that they were the wrong kind of people to be friends with. We packed up our things and moved back into the projects we first lived in were my Nanny lived. Things would be better now. Right?

-Psalm 88:18-

39

*Loved one and friend You have put far from
me, and my acquaintances into darkness.
(NKJV)*

Darkness became my closest friend. It was
not easy for me to make friends, and the friends I did
make were not the ones I should have been friends
with. I became loud and obnoxious. I wanted
attention, and I would do anything to draw it to
myself. The 'good kids' were lame in my eyes. It
was all about me and whatever I could do to get
noticed.

I again had trouble at school. I was constantly
seated in the back of the class because I was a
disturbance to everyone else. Second and third grade
came with a lot of hope that I would finally do the
right things. That did not happen. It came with a lot
of trouble, getting kicked out of class, and getting
sent to the principal's office. I just did not care.

One time when I was sent to the principal's
office for something I did and he yelled at me for a
while. I was young, and I remember him saying,
"I'm not going to tell your mother what you did,
because she'll probably just beat you again."

Instead of calling home to tell Colleen what I
did, he made me sit outside his office and write out
of a dictionary. I went home that day wondering if
there had been a surprise phone call I didn't know
about and I wound up telling on myself. I don't
know what it was that I did, but I remember saying
to her, "He said that he wasn't going to tell you
because you would beat me again."

Her face got cherry red and I was waiting for the slap to come, but it never did. She just yelled at me and said that what goes on in her house, stays in her house. I didn't understand this. Almost every beating I got produced a field of bruises, lumps, and scrapes for the world to see. I wanted to be taken out of that house. Of all the people I should have told what was going on, the one person I was afraid to tell was my dad. I was afraid to tell him for two reasons:

> 1) I didn't want to tell him and have him tell me that he just can't take me to go live with him right now.

> 2) I was afraid of the beating I would get.

I received plenty of beatings, but the one I would get if I told my dad had me so terrified that I didn't even think about it. I could only tell him everything if I wasn't living there anymore. I told my dad I wanted to come live with him plenty of times. I told him she was mean to me all the time. He always said that he just couldn't take me with him right now. He never knew how bad it really was. I prefer to believe that he would have taken me had he known the truth. I'll never know.

My Aunt Gail and two cousins lived in the same projects we did. There were five of us all together, and my Nanny watched us all. It was my two sisters, myself, and my two cousins, Monique and Ronnie. Colleen and Aunt Gail would drop us off at Nanny's before school. We had to take a city bus to school, and the bus would pick up a bunch of kids right in front of the projects and drop us all off in the same spot.

There was a crossing guard there and her son went to school with us. His name was Randy, and he liked to beat me up. The crossing guard was only there in the morning, so at the end of my day when we were dropped off, I would try so hard to be the first one off the bus because I had to try to run as fast as I could to get away from him. Sometimes I would get away; sometimes I couldn't. I would try to make it into the view of my Nanny's house. If she saw him beating me up, she would come outside to save me. Randy had a friend, Stephen, and he would usually be the one to catch me and hold me for Randy. Randy was a big kid. He was chubby and couldn't run very fast, but Stephen could. On the bus, Stephen would sometimes tell me that when he caught me, he would let me go just before Randy got me. I would always yell out at the top of my lungs, "I don't need you to let me go!"

What was I thinking? A free chance to escape a beating and I was already too prideful to accept help from someone. Was it in fact pride, or was I so used to getting beatings that it just didn't faze me anymore?

-Jeremiah 13:17-
But if you will not hear it, my soul will weep in secret for your pride; my eyes will weep bitterly and run down with tears, because the LORD's flock has been taken captive.
(NKJV)

I tried hard to be noticed, doing immature things just to get attention. This in turn, had gotten me picked on and made fun of. The only friends I had were the kids that nobody wanted to hang around with.

One day Colleen was giving me a haircut. She was using these clippers that wound up breaking while she was shaving the top of my head and left a big bald spot on the side of my head. I wanted her to shave all my hair off, but she wouldn't do it.

"I can fix it," she said.

She proceeded to use a piece of black charcoal to blacken in the bald spot. I felt so stupid. She rubbed it on as hard as she could. It hurt bad. I told her to stop, but she slapped me in the back of the head and told me to shut up and sit still. She thought it was funny and kept laughing. She did this as she drank vodka and smoked a joint. The next morning, I had to sit in the chair while I got all charcoaled up and sent off to school. As soon as I got to school, the ridicule started.

"Ha Ha!"

"You look stupid!"

"Your mom can't even cut your hair!"

"Look at Steven. You can see the bald spot."

I had enough trouble with kids picking on me as it was. Just another crappy day at school.

Colleen continued with her drinking and drug use. Nanny would watch us before and after school as I said, and most nights my Aunt Gail would be there to pick up Monique and Ronnie before Colleen came home. I could tell the look on Nanny's face to

Aunt Gail when she wondered why we were not at home yet. Most nights were late nights at Nanny's house. I don't know what time she would pick us up, but it was usually always late. She almost always smelled like alcohol, and her words were almost always slurred. One night was really bad. She came in Nanny's door stumbling and could hardly walk. Nanny was not happy. I know it was a Friday night because we didn't have school the next day. Nanny had had some words with her, and afterwards, Colleen walked the three of us kids across the courtyard to our apartment. I remember that she kept walking sideways like she was going to fall. I tried to keep quiet because I didn't want to get into trouble. We got in the house and it was time for bed.

"Mom, you're drunk," Belinda said.

I didn't want to have WWIII so I said, "Belinda, shut up!"

We were six and seven years old at the time, which made Rhonda three years old, and we were getting picked up by our drunk mother. All Colleen said to us was, "Shut up, the two of you! Get to bed!"

I hoped she would fall down the stairs and die. Everything would be okay then. What a sick way for a child to think. I really felt that I was justified feeling that way. I was six, and I wanted my mother dead. Colleen was simply a horrible person and an even worse parent.

The next morning when I woke up I was scared to get out of bed. I listened for a little while and the entire house was quiet. Belinda and Rhonda were sleeping, and I didn't hear Colleen either. I got out of bed and started to walk downstairs. Halfway down I stopped to listen; still nothing.

I was hoping she left or something. When I got to the bottom of the stairs, I looked around the corner and saw that she was passed out drunk on the couch. For a moment I thought she was dead, and a small feeling of peace came over me. Then I smelled the worst smell I had ever encountered in my life up to that point. She was alive and breathing. Damn! That's when I noticed that there was puke all over the place. There was puke on the coffee table, on the floor, and on the couch. There were also three big ashtrays, a cooking pot, and a small trash can all filled with puke. I looked at her for a while and felt sorry for myself.

"Mom, are you okay?" I asked. She started to move around a bit.

"Mom?" I asked again.

"Mom! Are you Okay?"

"Get the hell away from me! Leave me alone!" Ah, a mother's love…

I wanted to take her vomit and dump it on her, but I couldn't do that. Instead, I took it, dumped it down the kitchen sink, and turned the water on. She could clean herself up. I wanted to get the other things emptied out so Belinda and Rhonda didn't have to see it. Eventually she got up, had a cigarette, smoked a joint, and went back to sleep. Great parenting, Colleen! Top notch, all the way. Superb! Classic! Thanks for the life lessons!

-Leviticus 26:17-

*I will set My face against you, and you shall be defeated
by your enemies. Those who hate you shall reign over
you, and you shall flee when no one pursues you.*
(NKJV)

The bible says that God will never give you
more than you can handle. I didn't always believe
that. I believe it now, though. Sometimes it's so hard
to see the way out. I get so caught up with how bad
things are at times that I don't always see the path
He is trying to clear for me. No more than I can
handle right?

One morning Colleen told me to go to the
Hess gas station across the street to get her some
cigarettes. I was given $1.50 in dimes and a note
saying that I was to buy two packs of Kool cigarettes
for my mother. I was supposed to cross a busy street
(twice) to get Colleen cigarette at six years old, by
myself.

On the way back home I saw some kids
playing around with a ball. They were laughing and
having a good time. They were bigger kids and
looked like they were having a lot of fun. I stood
there and watched them for a while when one of the
kids noticed me and said, "Hey kid."

Wow, they were going to let me play too.
This never happened to me. I was so excited to play
with someone.

"Hey kid. Come here."

I started to walk over when I saw him wind up the ball to whip it at me. I turned immediately to run away but wasn't fast enough. The ball hit me square in the back. I screamed and started to cry. I ran home and tried to tell Colleen what happened, but I couldn't stop crying.

"What happened? Why the heck are you crying?"

Between my sobs I told her what happened.

"Oh jeeze, will you stop acting like a baby? Stop your damn crying!" She told me to grow up and said that I was just like my father who was an idiot.

I was a weak kid growing up and a very emotional child who cried easily. My cousin Ronnie would beat up from time to time. I couldn't tell you what we fought about, but we would get into these fights and I would wind up lying on the ground in the middle of the projects crying and waiting for someone to notice.

Ronnie had chronic nosebleeds, and the littlest thing would make his nose bleed non-stop. I would always aim for his nose, but could never get it. One day we were swinging a swing back and forth and I saw my chance. If I swung it back to him as hard as I could, maybe he would miss it, and it would hit him in the face and break his nose, so I decided that that was what I would try to do. It worked like a charm. It didn't break his nose, but he did miss catching the swing, and it hit him right smack in the face. He went down to the ground in a flash, and I had never seen so much blood. For a second I felt bad and was sorry for what I just did.

He looked up at me and I could tell he wanted to come after me. Instead, he just ran to Nanny's house.

No matter who you were, I was going to try hurt you before you ever got a chance to try to hurt me. The best way to do that was to never let anyone get too close to me. If you did get too close, I would hurt you in whatever way I could. It didn't matter if you were genuine or if you really wanted to be my friend or help me out. Someday, you might want to try to hurt me. Before that could happen, I was already planning what I could do to hurt you. Mix all that together and what you get is a dangerous child who is capable of anything. A child who cannot be trusted.

-Proverbs 25:28-
Whoever has no rule over his own spirit
is like a city broken down, without walls.
(NKJV)

I was about four or five when my great grandmother Aurora died. She was in her late eighties or nineties. Colleen was talking to Nanny about how she didn't have anyone to watch us kids so she could go to the funeral. She was also concerned about me seeing a dead body, but I made my case that she was my Great Grandmother.

"I loved her," I told them.

"You never even met her. You didn't know her," came the reply.

Anyway, I found out that we were going to be able to go to her funeral. I was excited because I wanted to see a dead body. I wanted to have that story to tell my friends. I just really wanted to see a dead person. I wanted to touch it and couldn't wait. I made sure I was the first one ready that morning. I was up, dressed, and ready to go before anyone else. I was told time and time again that I would have to kneel down in front of her and pray. No problem there. Just show me the dead body already.

When we got to the funeral parlor I wanted to be the first one in, but there was a line. I kept trying to peek around the corner to get a quick look. When it was our turn, my little sister went up to the casket with Colleen and I went up with my sister Belinda. I knelt down and just looked at my Nanny's mother. She was pale and lifeless. Not much to it really, but I kept on staring. I don't know what I was thinking or what I expected. She seemed to be at peace. I wanted the peace she had in her face as she lay there lifeless. She had lived in an old age home. I remember all the times that my aunts and uncles would talk about how they needed to go see her but were too busy with this or that.

"She has Alzheimer's and won't even know that we came to see her." That's what I remember people saying about her. I realized that my great grandmother must have been lonely.

———————

-Isaiah 65:8-
Thus says the LORD: "As the new wine is found in the cluster,
and one says, 'Do not destroy it, for a blessing is in it,' so will I do for My servants' sake, that I may not destroy them all."
(NKJV)

We are born into sin, right? I believe that The LORD would be justified in destroying us all. Speaking for myself, though, I know I'm worthy of Him destroying me. I was born into sin and grew up learning new sin and that it was okay. God can plant His seed in us, and if we water and feed ourselves with the word and stay connected, we will grow in the love that Christ has for us, and our love for Him will grow stronger. Maybe there is something inside this rock that God could be pleased with.

-Joshua 17:14-
Then the children of Joseph spoke to Joshua, saying, "Why have
you given us only one lot and one share to inherit, since we are a
great people, inasmuch as the LORD has blessed us until now?"
<u>(NASB)</u>

I believe that I have come such a long way from where I was, but I have such a long way to go to be where I need to be. Because of how far I have come, I sometimes feel that I'm due more than I have.

I've worked for it, right?

I've done this, right?

I've done that, right?

I have to check myself at times, because I still wonder why things are tough and why some things are still the way they are.

The other day I got mad at my (now) ex-wife because I was trying to write and she sat my kids in the room with me while she did some laundry. My daughter was trying to get on my lap while trying to play with my son, who also was sitting on the bed and needing attention. They were both making noise and laughing, and I got really mad and let my Sabrina know how I felt about it. She took the kids and tried to perform the tasks of laundry lady, soother to the kids, monkey bars, and wife. I thought for a minute and truly left like God showed me that instead of living in a shelter or being homeless and on drugs that:

    … I was at home,

    …with the television on,

    …with my kids who want to play with their Daddy,

    …have a wife who does my laundry,

    …and makes my lunch for work,

    …a bed to sleep in and a blanket to cover myself with,

    …a job to go to in the morning,

    …food in the refrigerator,

    …clean dishes to eat from,

    …a church to go to,

    …the ability to fly three thousand miles to see my son Sebastian,

    …a life with hope,

How dare I think I'm owed more than I have. What I should have been thinking about is what it is that makes God smile. I already know some of the things that make Him sad, even cry. God has emotions. He created them.

I think I was in the second or third grade when one day I just did not want to stay in school any longer that day. I went to the nurse's office and told her that I wasn't feeling well. She checked me out and said that I looked fine and that I should probably just stay in school for the rest of the day. She told me to lay down for a few minutes and see if maybe I would feel better. I lay on the bed that was in the nurse's office and held my stomach, with no pain in it, and said I really needed to go home. I knew she didn't believe me but she said that she would call my Nanny to see what she wanted her to do. Colleen was working and Nanny was the only one that I could have gone home to. The nurse asked if I was really sick. I said yes and that my stomach hurt really bad. I was fine. Nanny said that she would pay for a cab and would be waiting at her house for me. When I got to her house, she said I looked fine and couldn't see any reason why I needed to get out of school early. Not long after, the other kids from school were home and outside playing. I wanted to go outside as well, but Nanny said I could not go outside and play because I came home from school sick. When I kept persisting that I suddenly felt better and wanted to go outside to play with the other kids, she told me that I could sit out on the porch and wait for Colleen to get home. I could tell Nanny didn't believe me either. She was watching my every move. As time went by with me just sitting on the porch, I had a few thoughts:

1) I really wanted to go play with the other kids.

2) I was getting nervous about Colleen getting home and not looking sick.

3) How I didn't look this far ahead when I went to the nurses' station and said I needed to home.

A little later I heard Colleen come in through the back door. Nanny was telling her everything that happened, including that I suddenly felt fine and wanted to go outside to play.

"Oh really?" I heard her say.

The front door opened and Colleen came out and stared at me while I sat there with my head down and holding my stomach that didn't hurt.

"You're sick, huh?"

"Yeah, my stomach hurts," I said looking at the stairs.

"And you felt good enough to go play after you got here? You're a freaking liar." Then came the surprise slap. "What the hell is the matter with you?"

"I didn't feel good when I went to the nurses' station. I had a stomach ache."

"Come here!" She grabbed me by my neck, dragged me across the porch, and threw me through the front door into my Nanny's kitchen. She began to slap me and hit me in the face while she called me a liar. She was right about being a liar, but being slapped around like that I thought was a bit much.

"All right, Colleen, that's enough!" Nanny yelled.

I was curled up in the fetal position on the floor and didn't want to get up. Maybe there would be another surprise slap when I got up. There usually was. Colleen loved the surprise slap.

"Get your butt up off the floor, and get your rear end home. Now!"

I got up and we walked over to our house where I was sent to bed without dinner, again! I was grounded for a while, and grounded for me meant that I was in my room from the time I got home from school until I was ready to leave for the bus stop in the morning. I never did that again. What did pique my curiosity was the lying part that got me out of school. It made me wonder how far I could take my lies. I would eventually practice lying, getting better at it in years to come.

-1 Kings 22:23-
"Therefore look! The LORD has put a lying spirit in the mouth of all these prophets of yours, and the LORD has declared disaster against you."
(NKJV)

Do I believe the Lord decreed disaster for me? Yes, I do! Looking at it now, though, it was His loving arms around my life. Sounds strange, doesn't it? We can learn from a disaster, can't we? I believe The LORD decreed disaster for me as a way of His goodness and love being able to shine through me many, many years later. The enemy had to have thought that he was winning. How do I explain love like that? I look at my kids, and although I would and will let them make mistakes so that they can learn from them, I would not willingly let any three of my children make a mistake so huge that it could ruin their lives.

-1 Samuel 10:26-
And Saul also went home to Gibeah; and valiant
men went with him, whose hearts God had touched.
(NKJV)

His letting me make a mistake so huge as trying to live my life as a lie would eventually bring me to my lowest of lows. Instead of trying to climb out myself, the only thing on this planet that would give me another chance would be God Himself. It was because He saw the potential in me. He sees it in everyone. He doesn't say that He'll help this person but not that one. There is no favor like that with God.

-Psalm 57:4-
My soul is among lions; I lie among the sons
of men who are set on fire, whose teeth are spears
and arrows, and their tongue a sharp sword.
(NKJV)

"Do as I say, not as I do," is something I've heard my entire life. It really didn't matter what the situation was. I saw so much as a child that I was confused as to why it was okay for other people to do it but not myself. I longed for attention and just wanted to be noticed in any way that didn't include a beating.

My dad picked Belinda and me up one weekend and we were just driving around and talking. I don't know how the conversation came up, but we started talking about what we wanted to be when we grew up. I was sitting in the back seat, listening to what my dad and sister were talking about when I blurted out, "I want to be a robber when I grow up!"

My dad just looked at me through the rear view mirror. He didn't say anything. He just looked at me. I don't even know why I said that. I never expected my life would turn in that direction.

I wanted to be involved in things with other kids, but I was never allowed. My Aunt Gail was talking to Colleen one night in the kitchen while my cousin Ronnie and I were in the living room watching television. I had my ear tuned in to the conversation in the kitchen, and Aunt Gail was saying that she was going to put Ronnie in little league baseball in the spring and asked if I would be able to play also. My heart leaped for joy as I waited for the reply.

"Yeah, I was thinking of putting Steven in little league, too."

Wow! I really couldn't believe my ears. I was going to be able to play baseball. I could catch, swing, hit, pitch, and ground the balls as well. At least that's what I told myself. I couldn't wait. I could not believe that Colleen was actually going to let me do something fun.

"Are you really going to let me play little league?" I yelled out.

"Shut up, and mind your business!" she said.

I didn't care. I was going to play baseball and couldn't wait for spring to come. Spring finally did roll around and Ronnie was in his baseball uniform ready to play little league. Guess what? No baseball for Steven, though. If I wasn't in trouble, I got to go with my Aunt Gail to Ronnie's games and put the numbers on the scoreboard. I watched the other kids play and got mad that I couldn't. Actually, I'm not sure what I was more mad at: not being able to play or the fact that I knew Colleen was never going to let me play in the first place. I only went twice to put the numbers up because I wanted so badly to play and be someone. I got tired of the other kids having a good time.

I remember being in third grade, getting into trouble constantly and always being sent to the principal's office where I would have to write out of a dictionary. We had something going on in class one day, and there were prizes that everyone got. The big prize was a king-size Snickers candy bar. My team won, and we were all going to get one, but, as Mrs. Russell was passing them out, she came by my desk and said loud enough for everyone to hear, "You don't get one!"

I remember feeling like garbage, but I didn't want anyone to know, so I just shrugged my shoulders and said, "So! I don't care!"

I don't know why I feel that is even relevant, but it's one of those things that have stuck in my head all these years.

It wasn't long after that that one night Colleen had a nervous breakdown. Maybe it was all the drugs and alcohol, but I'll never know. The cops came with an ambulance and fire department to take Colleen to the hospital. Nanny tried to comfort us kids, but I wanted nothing to do with it. I wouldn't dare say it at the time, but I was truly hoping that she was either dead or going to die. I didn't need comforting from anybody. I was thinking how happy I would be to get to go live with someone else. Nanny stayed to watch us while she was gone, and she kept telling us that everything would be okay. I kept thinking that, no, everything wouldn't be okay if she was all right and got to come home. Nanny told us that she needs to feel as if she's wanted and loved. I wanted to burst out in a fit of rage and tell her that, "I NEED TO FEEL LOVED TOO, NANNY! I NEED TO FEEL LIKE I'M WANTED!"

What about me?

What about me!

WHAT?! ABOUT?! ME?!

I was getting old enough now to understand that I was treated differently. I didn't want anything to do with this family or this life. It was time to start acting and doing things that would get me out of this damn house of hers.

-2 Samuel 22:5-
"When the waves of death surrounded me,
the floods of ungodliness made me afraid.
(NKJV)

It wasn't long before we moved again. It seemed as if we moved a lot, and it always came with the hope that we would move somewhere nice. This time it was a duplex house where the landlord lived upstairs. The place wasn't bad, and there was a big backyard with a creek at the end of the property.

We only lived about a mile from the school, and my older sister and I would walk there in the morning. Things did not get any better for me at school. I started making more of the wrong kind of friends and was kicked out of class more often.

There was this girl in my class, Amy Yetto, and she was the first girl I ever kissed. There was this hiding spot in the closet to kiss her and do things I really shouldn't have been doing. Amy and I would pretend we were married, but being married comes with a divorce. I told her that we could get divorced the next day. She came over to my house and told Colleen what I had said about getting a divorce. She looked at me for a very long moment. I wasn't sure what to do, so I just put my head down, and then all of a sudden the surprise slap came. She slapped me so hard that I almost fell off the porch. She told me to get to my room and stay there. I didn't mind though, because I didn't want to cry in front of Amy. The slap really hurt and left a big red spot on my face for the rest of the day.

I didn't understand what just happened. We were just kids playing around. Marriage comes with a divorce, right? That's what I thought back them. All my aunts and uncles were divorced. Most of Colleen's friends were also divorced. It seemed normal. I remember the conversations they all had about being divorced and how they all hated their ex-spouse. I was so embarrassed about getting hit in front of Amy. Once again, I was grounded, sent to my room, and deemed not worthy for dinner.

Going to school meant that I would be free for a little while. I couldn't wait for the next day to come so I could go to school, but I couldn't seem to be able to control my outbursts. I wanted to be noticed, so I acted out. I thought it was cool. I can still see the look of restlessness on my fourth grade teacher's face when I came into class every day. I did what the other kids did who didn't pay attention. I blew spit-balls in class and interrupted whenever I could.

-Psalm 69:20-
Reproach has broken my heart, and I am full of heaviness; I looked for someone to take pity, but there was none; and for comforters, but I found none.
(NKJV)

I'm not looking for pity. What has happened in the past has happened. It's time to break the cycle. These verses I put in here are what God is giving me in direct response to what I was feeling at the time these things happened in my life.

Yes, I wanted comfort.

Yes, I had a broken heart.

Yes, I was in despair.

Yes, later in life I made wrong decisions.

Yes, I am angry at these things.

———————

Around this time I remember Colleen starting to date more and more men. It always came with drinking, partying, and lots of pot smoking. She got a CB radio for her car and went by the handle Sea Breeze, the name of her drink of choice, vodka and cranberry juice. How perfect is that? No matter how hard I try to forget it, I can still smell the vodka on her breath.

-Jeremiah 4:22-
"For My people are foolish, they have not known Me. They are silly children, and they have no understanding. They are wise to do evil, but to do good they have no knowledge."
<u>*(NKJV)*</u>

The men came and went. Colleen kept saying she wanted to find a good father figure for us. I couldn't understand her thinking because the guys she was dating were not good people. They never wanted to talk to us. They just wanted to go out and not have us around when they came home. Not to mention, I didn't need a father figure. I already had a father who loved me.

One night she brought home one of her many men and we were all going to a drive-in movie. On the way out the door I said to the guy, "I like you a lot more than the other guy that came over last week."

Colleen was mortified. She gave me this look in which I knew meant a beating was coming when we got home later that evening. That wouldn't be until way later, so I just continued.

"Yeah, she dates lots of guys. She's trying to find a father figure for me."

Again, the look I got said everything. He just kept smiling at me and nodding his head. We went to the movies, and as sure as the sun rises, I got a good one when we all got home. I got slapped around pretty good for making her look stupid and embarrassed.

"What goes on in my house, stays in my house! You have no right to say anything that goes on in my house! Your job is to keep your mouth SHUT! That's it!"

One night we were driving around aimlessly. She said that she was testing out her new CB radio and wanted to see how it works. It was just the three of us kids and her driving around in the middle of the night. We stopped at a truck stop and parked for a while. Some guy was being rude and using foul language over the CB to her. Some other truck driver stepped in over the radio to 'protect' Colleen, and things just went on like that for a while. He asked if we were okay and she told him yes. Then she asked him, "Do you need a place to sleep tonight?"

Of course, his answer was "Yes."

She told the truck driver what car we were in and told him that he could follow us to our house. He parked his rig down the road a ways, and we picked him up in our car and drove back to our house. When we got home, she told him where the shower was, gave him a towel, and told me that I had to sleep on the dining room floor because the truck driver was going to sleep in my bed. I told her I didn't want him sleeping in my bed, but I was told, "Shut your mouth, and do as you're told to."

I asked to sleep on the couch, but that answer was also no. Her excuse was that the living room was right next to my room and she didn't want me disturbing him. I was given a blanket and pillow and sent to the dining room floor. When she thought I was sleeping, I saw her go into my room, and she stayed there for a while. I heard some noises coming from my room and became extremely enraged. I remember wanting to get a knife to kill them both.

What a thought for a kid to have, and to have it towards his own mother. Colleen's room didn't have doors, and I assume that's why she wanted to use my room. I can only guess. Why was I always the one to get the short end of the stick? The next morning when I woke up, the truck driver was gone and there was a twenty dollar bill on the coffee table from him with a note that said, "Thank you for last night."

-Colossians 3:8-
But now you yourselves are to put off all
these: anger, wrath, malice, blasphemy,
filthy language out of your mouth.
(NKJV)

My rage began to take form in the shape of wanting to hurt people. I felt like I couldn't control myself, but I knew what was right and wrong. All I wanted to do was hurt you. The scary part is that it felt good to hurt people. It felt good to be angry. It felt safe.

Colleen had worked for the state at this time. I don't know exactly what she did for them, but she drove a state vehicle and was very proud of it. It had the state seal on both front doors, so the following night, I went outside with a knife and slashed all four of her tires on the car. She had recently gotten into a fight with my Aunt Gail's boyfriend Dave, so she thought he slashed her tires. The cops came to the house along with my Nanny. They tried to calm the three of us kids down, but I needed no comforting. I was very pleased with myself. I was enjoying the confusion I just created and wondered how I could create this again. I wanted to scare Colleen.

Things did not get any better. I became more defiant. I got into fights at school, always being the one that got beat up of course, but I didn't care. Not long after we moved into that house, Colleen sent me to go live with my Nanny for a while. She looked at me and said that what she wanted was the best for me, and she wanted to know why I acted this way. I wanted to scream out:

...it's the beatings I get.

...it's your drinking.

...it's not feeling loved.

...it's the parties you take us to and getting drunk in bars with us.

...it's the drugs.

...it's being kicked to the side.

...it's YOU!!!

My Nanny tried to talk to me and asked me what was going on in my head, but I had no answer. She tried her best to talk to me about the love of God and Jesus Christ. Nanny would just look at me with a lost look, as if she almost knew how bad I was mistreated. I think maybe she wanted me to tell her, but I never did. I wanted to be in trouble. I wanted to be in trouble because I would get my beating and then be left alone. I couldn't hurt my Nanny though. I just wanted to go back home, because I wanted to start more trouble. I wouldn't dare do the crap I did at Nanny's house that I would at Colleen's. Nanny was, well, Nanny! She didn't hate me the way Colleen hated me. I wasn't mistreated at Nanny's house.

It wasn't very long after that, after all her dating, that she finally met the guy she would very soon call her husband, and I would very soon, unknowingly, turn to the enemy for help. And then, one day she brought him home. His name was Dan Pera. He didn't like me; I didn't like him either, and I wasn't afraid to let him know. This is when a permanent hatred filled my mind, body, and soul.

-Lamentations 1:20-
"See, O LORD, that I am in distress; My soul is troubled;
My heart is overturned within me, for I have been very
rebellious. Outside the sword bereaves, at home it is like
death."
(NKJV)

The very first time I met Dan, I did not like him. It wasn't the average, "That's my mom you're trying to be with," because to tell you the truth, I really didn't care. I wasn't the son that was trying to show how he was the man of the house. It was a whole lot more than that. I could see right through him and all of his bull-crap lies. I truly believe he knew I saw right through him. He knew I knew.

Dan was more than twenty-five years older than Colleen, and just like most of Colleen's other men, Mr. Dante Pera was also a married man. This was the guy that she said I needed in my life to show me how to be a man. He was always very nicely dressed and friendly to all of us, but when he would look at me, there was this coolness in his eyes that made me want to show him just how full his hands were going to be with me.

Rhonda's father had just passed away, so for her, it was easy to latch right on to him. He showed her a fatherly love too. Rhonda genuinely loved him as a dad, and he genuinely took her in his arms as a loving father should do and treated her as if she was his real daughter.

Colleen never stopped with her slander about my dad, making it a point of always telling us the bad things that he did:

...how he didn't love me,

...how he didn't come out to see me that often,

...that he loved his new kids more than he loved me,

...how we were just a burden to his new life and family.

So it wasn't all that hard for him to show my older sister that he was in it for keeps and how much he loved her, too. Mind you, he was still married, still living with his wife. As for myself, I knew it was all for show.

I had a dad. He was real, and no matter what anybody would say or do to try to show me differently, I KNEW BETTER! As for all the things that Colleen would say about my dad, I never, not once, believed what came out of her mouth. She was an abusive drunk, drug addict, and borderline hooker in my eyes!

Dan would spend a lot of nights at our house, way too many for my liking. As they did before, the noises would drive me crazy that came out of her bedroom. This woman, who was supposed to be a loving mother, had absolutely zero respect for her children.

One night we had to drive him back to his house an hour away. We pulled into his driveway and sat there for a few minutes. His wife was looking out of their living room window at our car, and Colleen said, "I can't kiss you because your wife is looking out the window."

I was wishing that she would kiss him so his wife could see and come out and start some trouble. Time and time again, I would tell her that I didn't like him, that he was mean to me, and that he didn't like me either.

"So what! He's my choice!" she would say.

One time I yelled out to her, "He's freaking MARRIED!!! He's cheating on his wife! YOU'RE WRONG!"

The slaps and punches came continuously. I had gotten hit plenty of times; that didn't bother me. This was the first time that I can remember that she started to punch me, and I wasn't even ten yet. The hits, slaps, and punches came and seemed to never stop. In the middle of it all, she grabbed me by my throat, pulled me up close to her face, and screamed at me, "THIS IS MY LIFE! HE IS MY CHOICE! YOU, MIND YOUR OWN DAMN BUSINESS!"

More slaps and punches to my side came after that, and then she pulled me up close to her face again and said, very softly, "When it comes between you and Dan, you will lose EVERY SINGLE TIME!"

I lay there on the floor, wondering what just happened. I could hardly move a muscle.

The next day I went to school and picked a fight with a bigger kid and wound up getting beat up by a girl that was with him. I ran home to tell Colleen what had happened, but when I got there, Dan's car was still there. I looked through the window, and she ran to her room naked. Not long after, she came out and I told her what had happened. She yelled at me to get back to school and called me a pussy.

A couple months after that, I came home from school to hear,
"Dan and I are getting married, and we're moving out to the country."

Of course we were.

<u>Chapter Three</u>

-Micah 4:10-
Be in pain, and labor to bring forth, O daughter of Zion, like
a woman in birth pangs. For
now you shall go forth from the city, you shall dwell in the
field, and to Babylon you shall go.
There you shall be delivered; There the LORD will redeem
you from the hand of your enemies.
<u>(NKJV)</u>

At one time, I really did love my Sabrina. She would read about my life as I wrote and would be shocked at some of the details. She always encouraged me to push on. She knew I had a rough upbringing, but to see it on paper, I think has added some clarity for her as to the person I am on the inside.

———————

I was very much in agony at this point in my life about how I was treated and misused. This hell I was in would last another twenty-five years or so before ever allowing the LORD to work in my life, and He would do it, faithfully.

We made many trips out to the piece of property where the house was being built. The house was in the middle stages of construction and took forever. Dan told Colleen that he owned a construction company, but he was really a private contractor who never had much work. So in turn, the house took a very long time to come together. She loved taking us kids up there on the weekends, because she could spend time with Dan, and he would have less explaining to do to his wife.

The house was unlivable, so we stayed in a fifth-wheel trailer that was less than fifty square feet. It was very tight. Still, it didn't bother her to take us three kids there. We usually had to stay outside while she and Dan stayed in the trailer during the better part of the day having sex. The three of us were left alone in the middle of a country that we didn't know.

There was nothing to do, and I couldn't stand the fact that we had to amuse ourselves outside while she had sex with Dan. I roamed around and tried to mess up the process of the house as much as I could. I would take the nails and hammers and throw them in the woods. I would try to kick the beams out of place and try to saw some of the wood in half. It was all very pointless, because this was where we were going to live, whether I liked it or not.

At the end of the school year that year, we packed up all our things and moved into that tiny fifth-wheel trailer. I was not happy. We could have stayed at our old house and waited for the new house to be completed, but Colleen wanted to spend as much time with Dan as possible. It just did not matter that he was not only still married, but also still living with his wife who thought everything was fine! His being married had no effect on her whatsoever. She thought he had money, and that was her motivation. He would come by, spend some time with her, and then say, "Duty calls." Then he'd leave.

Colleen would say, "Soon, you won't have to worry about all those duty calls, right?" And he would just smile and laugh.

-Proverbs 26:26-
***Though his hatred is covered by deceit, his
wickedness will be revealed before the assembly.***
(NKJV)

I often wondered why a guy who owned a construction company spent so little time working. He would spend his days at our little trailer, then his "Duty Calls" at night would take him away to his wife. I didn't figure out until later that his "Duty Calls" meant he had a wife waiting at home. No work seemed to ever get done on the house. There were always issues with workers not showing up as scheduled, as he would say, or there was a problem with this and a problem with that. I felt as if I could see through all his bologna, then why couldn't she? It wasn't that hard.

I couldn't stand staying in that trailer either. I hated trailers. I had had my fill of them. My two sisters got the roll out bed by the door, and Colleen got the roll out bed at the other end at the back. I got an installed cot right above her bed that was less than eighteen inches from the ceiling.

The toilet was another issue. We had to buy water to flush it at first, and most of the time, I was told to go to the bathroom outside. I hated that trailer. We spent the entire summer and a couple of months into the school year in it.

Colleen took us clothes shopping for school that year, and what I really wanted was a button up shirt and tie. I don't know why, but that was what I wanted, and she bought it for me. I was so excited to wear it for the first day of school. I would look good, and things would be different for me this time. No one knew me, so this was my chance to be a new me, not make enemies, get picked on, or get beat up anymore.

> *"It's time that we begin to challenge and confront ourselves about what we hold within ourselves."*
> **T.D. Jakes**
> **_(So You Call Yourself A Man?)_**

It's time to challenge and confront myself about what I hold inside. Keeping it in all these years has done nothing for me except keep me angry at the world. It's not just this one incident that I'm talking about; it's my entire life I have to confront. I have gone through my whole life never dealing with anything that has ever made me mad or angry. I cannot live like this. For me to be able to walk closer to Christ and have a deeper relationship with Him, I have to allow God to push me to challenge and confront my life.

I absolutely love the *Rambo* movies. The *Rambo* movies are a man's man kind of movies. In the final one, John Rambo had finally allowed himself to get in touch with reality. He was sent to

Vietnam but never returned home after the war. One of the missionaries asked him if he was ever curious to go home and see how things have changed. His reply was, "You have to have a reason for that." Was there really not a reason, or was he just not seeing the reason? In the end, he wound up going home.

"You've got to have a little Rambo in you!"
T.D. Jakes
(So You Call Yourself A Man?)

So now, between what I read in scripture today, my T.D. Jakes book, prayer group, and my own personal prayer time, what God wants me to do is to open up and be completely vulnerable to Him, in His arms. Doing that, I take myself out of my comfort zone and allow Him to show me His awesome power in my life.

My fight lies mainly in my past. He is challenging me to finally deal with it. There are other fights in my life, such as trying to be a man of God and fighting for my family's spiritual growth.

-Psalm 118:17-18-
I shall not die, but live, and declare the works
of the LORD. The LORD has chastened me
severely, but He has not given me over to death.
(NKJV)

I was ready for school that morning, and I could not wait for the bus to pick me up. I was so excited to make new friends and not get picked on. I could possibly hang out with the cool kids, the popular kids. I never had before, but I knew I could be cool. I had my yellow oxford button up shirt on with my blue striped clip-on tie. The bus came up the hill to pick up my sisters and I, and we got on the bus. I sat down by myself with my head down as always. Some of the kids on the bus were talking about the trailer in the front yard. Already I started to feel stupid.

To look at the property, it wasn't much. It needed a lot of work. The house was far from finished, and you could tell that it wasn't livable. What made the situation worse was the small aluminum trailer, right smack in the front. I could hear a couple of the kids talking about it, about how we must be on welfare.

We made it to school without too much trouble and I found my classroom. It seemed all the other kids were wearing their Bugle Boy jeans and nice new white sneakers. I started to think about how I was dressed, and all I could think of was how much of a dork I looked like. I didn't want to take my tie off now because I didn't want everyone to know that I was embarrassed to be wearing it.

My seat was in the front of the class, and I tried hard not to look around at anybody. I don't remember too much of the first day except for when we went to lunch and recess. Everywhere I went to sit in the cafeteria seemed to be saved for someone else. I had a hard time trying to find a seat so I could eat my lunch. Finally, I just went to a seat without looking around for any approval and sat down. Right away it started, "Are you the kid that lives in that tiny trailer who's on welfare?"

I explained the house was being built and not livable yet, but they didn't care about that. They didn't want me sitting there, but I was too afraid to move. They knew I was scared too. When we went outside for recess, I tried to hang out with whoever was there, maybe try to make some friends, but they all just told me to get away. Then they started to pick on me about how I was dressed, what a dork I looked like and that I was the poor stupid kid who lived in an aluminum trailer.

"Is that a clip on tie that you're wearing?" one of the kids asked me.

"No, it's a real tie," I lied.

"Why did you wear a tie to school? You look like a loser!"

Now, I couldn't tell them that I actually thought the tie looked pretty cool and that I thought it went really nice with my yellow oxford shirt, so I said, "My mom made me wear it."

As soon as I said that, I wished I never did. My mom made me wear it? What was I thinking? And I said it to a bunch of fifth graders. Fifth grade is when most boys start trying to talk and act as men, and I just told everyone in my class that my mom dresses me. That was my first day at my new school. The ridicule that was in place was now kicked into high gear. It just never seems to stop. I pulled off my clip-on tie, put it in my pocket, and walked away. I tried to find a spot where no one would notice me, but it didn't work. I was now the center of attention.

I started to believe that it was going to be the same no matter where I went or what I did. It stayed that way for me for a while. I tried to stay to myself. I couldn't ever seem to make any friends, and when I tried, I was pushed around and made fun of. I started to disconnect and wander in my thoughts.

My teacher, Mrs. Stickles, was at a loss with me also. I just didn't try. I don't know what I was looking for by not doing my work or not doing what I was told, but I just didn't care.

I was eventually put back into a lower level reading class with fewer kids. I was happy with that because it gave me the excuse to try even less, but it also came with more harassment from my classmates. Instead of trying harder to prove that I was worth something, I started to do the worst I could possibly do, on purpose. I didn't care; I was already the class idiot. My school life was just as miserable as my home life.

During spelling class we were called up to the chalkboard to spell words. I always misspelled my words on purpose. Even on the rare occasion when I was given a word I actually knew how to spell, I wrote it wrong anyway. This in turn drew laughs from the class. I actually knew that if I was wrong in front of the entire class I would get laughed at, but I did it anyway. I can't even tell you why I would do that to myself, but I did.

I don't know where my mind was, but it was a long way from where it should have been. I'm not talking about my mind being elsewhere at times. I started to lose touch with reality. I just was not all there in my head.

-Psalm 38:17-19-
For I am ready to fall, and my sorrow is continually before me.
For I will declare my iniquity; I will be in anguish over my sin.
But my enemies are vigorous, and they are strong; and those who hate me wrongfully have multiplied.
(NASB)

We were still living in the trailer when one day Colleen brought home a dog. She said she bought it at the pound and named him Loner, because while all the other puppies in the litter were trying to feed themselves on the mother, she kept kicking our dog away so he couldn't eat. How fitting, I thought.

I was happy enough with the dog. I had zero friends, and we lived in the middle of nowhere. The closest person I went to school with lived five miles away. I loved the name of our dog though. I was a loner too and thought our dog and I would be best friends. Unfortunately, I didn't love Loner as much as I loved his name. I never treated that dog right at all. I tormented him, and when no one was around, I would yell at him and back him into a corner. He would get up on his hind legs, growl, and show his teeth. At the time, I really thought it was amusing. The dog was still a puppy, so I was able to control it. When he showed me his teeth, I would grab him by his neck and squeeze until he whimpered. Sometimes I squeezed until he couldn't breathe.

Other times, I would just kick him around and slap him. I treated Loner the way Colleen treated me.

-Exodus 32:25-
Now when Moses saw that the people were
unrestrained (for Aaron had not restrained
them, to their shame among their enemies),
(NKJV)

I find it ironic now looking back at this situation. I had no control over my own life. None! I couldn't stand it. But I found that with our dog Loner being smaller and weaker, he was very easy to control and manipulate.

...Just like I was.

I distributed pain to that dog.

...Just as I had received.

I made him hurt.

...Just as I had been hurt.

I made it confused.

...Just as I was confused.

I made him angry.

...Just as I was angry.

I taught him never to trust.

...Just as I was taught never to trust.

This is so sad. It makes me want to cry. I had no control, so I took control over something that had no control over itself.

-Hebrews 6:4-6
For it is impossible for those who were once enlightened, and
have tasted the heavenly gift, and have become partakers of
the Holy Spirit, and have tasted the good word of God and the

powers of the age to come, if they fall away, to renew them
again to repentance, since they crucify again for themselves
the Son of God, and put Him to an open shame.
(NKJV)

For me, I have to be extremely careful, because when I dwell on a verse, not meditate, dwell, especially one like this that is so convicting. The enemy can sneak his way in and speak into my mind what he wants it to mean for me and not God. Do I really believe Christ died for me? Do I have what it takes to follow Him? Can I be the man God wants me to be? Have I committed too much wrong? Does love reside in my heart? Am I really even saved?

-Hebrews 5:12-
For though by this time you ought to be teachers, you need
someone to teach you again the first principles of the oracles
of God; and you have come to need milk and not solid food.
(NKJV)

I didn't get it right away. I read my bible and text verses every day. What is it that God is trying to tell me? I still couldn't get my mind off the Hebrews chapter six verse. I turned my head to the television to catch some of the Red Sox game that was on. My daughter Rhesa and I just sat and watched the game. The bases were loaded with Adrian Gonzalez up to bat. I prayed for a Grand Slam, but he hit a three-run RBI double.

(To me, the Red Sox are THE GREATEST baseball team in the history of the game.)

Then David Ortiz comes up to bat and I asked my daughter to pray with me for 'Big Papi' to hit a home run.

"God…Please…Let…Big…Papi…Hit…A…Home…Run"

STRIKE 1.

So I said to Rhesa, "Rhesa! We forgot to say, 'In Jesus' name. Amen!'"

"In…Jesus'…name, DADDY!…Ameeeen!" my daughter Rhesa yelled.

BANG, home run!!! I couldn't believe it! Wow! I just had one of the biggest moments I will ever share with my daughter. First, she prayed with me for my Red Sox a specific prayer and showed me that she is not ashamed of me or my God.

Second, God used her to show me what He wanted to show me about the two verses. In Hebrews 6:4-6, for me, He is telling me that with the little knowledge I have about Him, if I walk away from Him, it will be detrimental to my life here on earth for my family and for my afterlife. Am I really willing to walk away from what I know is good? Satan has fought me every step of the way in trying to write this.

God used my daughter to show me how simple it is to trust and get in touch with my childlike faith. Daddy loves you, Rhesa! Forever and always! You're my favorite girl! Daddy loves you too, Asher! Forever! You're my favorite boy!

Math was fun and the only subject that would get me out of class. The two fifth grade classes were split in two for math. One was for those who were at the grade level they should be at. The other was for those who were doing less than what they should be doing. I was in the lower level and sent across the hall to another classroom. For me, it was a time to get away. I was happy to go because I wasn't picked on. Most of the kids in that class were like me in the sense that they just didn't want to do their work. I never did my homework. Mr. Muller, my math teacher, would shake his head when he came by my desk daily to check who had done their homework or not. I was determined to do as little as possible and try even less. When he came by our desks, he would have his grade book with him, and if we did our homework, we got a hundred. If we didn't do our homework, we got a zero. He told us at the beginning of the year that if we did our homework every night, we would pass his class. I was defiant and determined to do things my way. I wanted to control my own life, and nobody was going to tell me what I would or would not do.

"Why are you not doing your homework, Steven?" Mr. Muller asked me one day.

"Because I don't want to," I responded.

He looked at me with a hopelessness in his eyes, no doubt, one that he had given many kids in his class before. He went on to explain our homework for the night, telling us what we had to do, when I said, loud enough for the entire class to hear, "This sucks!"

"What did you say?" he said.

"This sucks!" I repeated.

He looked at me again and said, "I'm going to speak to your mother."

"So, I don't care." I wanted to sound tough and cool for the other kids. I wanted to sound as if I had no fear and would do whatever I wanted, whenever I wanted, and however I wanted.

Colleen quit her job with the state and started driving a bus for the school district. She would get someone to take her drug tests for her or buy a detox agent to pass the tests. This was almost twenty-five years ago, and back then, they told her when her drug tests would be.

Anyway, when she came pulling into the driveway after we got home from school, she almost ran from her car to the trailer and came inside with a note in her hand. I was scared and knew what it was about.

"I just had a meeting with your math teacher, Mr. Muller. Any idea what it was about?"

"I don't know."

She showed me the note in her hand, and in my teacher's handwriting were the words "this sucks."

"This sucks!?" She grabbed me by my throat and started to punch me in the side of my head repeatedly.

"Who do you think you are? I'll frigging kill you!" She stopped punching me, and with her hand still around my throat, began to bang my head off the bathroom door of the trailer. She did that for about ten seconds and then began to slap me in the face repeatedly. Out of breath, she still managed to throw me on the floor.

"You ever tell a teacher again, 'this sucks,' and I kill you right where you stand."

Please do, I was thinking.

Pretty soon the time came for us to move into the house. I was happy to get out of the cramped trailer. It was nice to have my own room and heat. We moved into the house in October. I know this because it was Dan's birthday. We were given instructions that while they showered, we were to get ready the cake she bought for him and then lay out the gifts she had gotten him. We had to hurry though, because he had to leave soon so he could go back home to his wife to spend his birthday with actual family members. His wife thought he was here working on the house.

I had nothing to do with setting everything up for him at all. I just watched in shock as my two sisters did it all. They actually seemed happy to be doing this. I was trying to think of a way to spit in his cake without my sisters seeing.

I don't remember what the little things were that she got him, but next to the wall was some kind of a table saw that was bigger than I was. It supposedly did all these things, and he just had to have it. I wondered if he would use it for his non-existent business. Another thing I thought about was the price. It cost Colleen $1,200.00 in 1986. She made sure to tell us exactly how much it cost her. I wondered how she got the money for it, because she

83

always said that she had no money and things were always 'tight.' Every birthday, every Christmas, every Easter, every whatever always came with the explanation that there just isn't money for this or that. But of course, there was $1,200.00 to spend on a saw for your fiancé who was still married to another woman. Great freaking parenting, Colleen.

-Deuteronomy 28:28-
The LORD will strike you with madness
and blindness and confusion of heart.
<u>(NKJV)</u>

Madness is a scary thing. I look back and see a child who is mad at the world. I see a child who was uncomfortable with just being alive. I'm not just talking about not wanting to be alive in the situation. I mean not wanting to be alive at all. Wishing I was dead. I thought a few times about suicide, literally. I wondered what would cause me the least amount of pain.

I thought about cutting my wrist with a razor blade..., but what if I didn't die?

I thought about jumping off the top of my school..., but what if I survived?

Dan got Colleen a twenty-two caliber rifle, and I thought about using that. I knew where she kept it, so I took it one day and tried to see if I would be able to use it properly. I put the barrel in my mouth, but with the rifle being so long, I couldn't reach the trigger. I used my big toe to press the trigger, but nothing happened. Dan and Colleen would occasionally shoot the gun in the backyard.

The next time they did, I would watch to see how it was loaded and used so I could shoot myself in the head if I ever wanted to.

The principal of my school, along with my teacher, Mrs. Stickles, had many talks with Colleen about my behavior and grades. It was obvious I wasn't trying, and they began to think it went deeper than that. In a way, they were right, because I just didn't care at all about life, never mind school. I did poorly on purpose. I never gave them or myself a chance to see what I could really do. I knew I wasn't stupid and that I could get decent grades if I tried, but I just didn't want to. Colleen constantly told me, "You're going to fail! What's wrong with you! Don't you care?"

"It's too hard." That was all I ever said.

I was pulled into the principal's office one day, and we had a long talk about my grades.

"Do you think that you would do better if you were in the fourth grade?"

Wow! Now that was music to my ears! I knew I had to play it cool and not let on that that was what I wanted. I did want it, but I wanted it for all the wrong reasons.

"Yeah, I think that would help me a lot."

He wasn't stupid either. He tried to give me every reason not to go down a grade. The decision was ultimately his, so I just played dumb the entire time. Never once did I let on about the beatings I was getting at home. I did want to tell him that Colleen did drugs and drove a bus for the school and that he should do a surprise drug test on her, but I was so afraid of what would happen. The talks continued over the next couple of weeks, and one Friday I was told that on Monday morning I was to report to Mrs. Wank's class to repeat the fourth grade. I was so happy. I would be on the other side of the school, and my lunch and recess time would be different as well. I would be older than the other kids and would already know some of the school work. I wouldn't have to try real hard to be able to just get by. That probably meant less time grounded in my room.

Truth be told, I just didn't want to get picked on or made fun of anymore. It was hard for me to do really well, but I would never find out what I could have possibly achieved if I had tried. The second it got hard, I quit doing the work.

-Psalm 10:9-10-
He lies in wait secretly, as a lion in his den; He lies in wait to catch the poor; He catches the poor when he draws him into his net.
So he crouches, he lies low, that the helpless may fall by his strength.
(NKJV)

It's amazing to look back on this situation as an adult. What sheer terror it is to see a child waste away in the hands of demons like that with no one to truly help him. I would grow up to make my own, very educated decision, to walk away from God. This is something completely different though. Right now, I want to reach out to myself, try to save myself from a world of hurt. I'm so angry to see myself this way. Not long ago I asked myself, at what point do we willingly walk away from God and choose to follow the enemy?

———————

"This is going to hurt, Steven. I love you, and I always will, but right now, you are going to start to suffer more than you already have, and it's only going to get worse as time goes on. Your next thirty years are going to be filled with more pain, hurt, and suffering than most people go through. Your happy times will be few. There is a reason I am going to allow this. One day you'll figure it out, but that won't happen for a very long time. I have a purpose for you that only you can fulfill. I'll never be far away from you. This is going to hurt me too, but I already see the end. You will need to learn to call on My Name. I love you!" -God

From this point on, I lived in a complete state of rebellion. I was out to hurt you and destroy as much as I could. It was enjoyable for me. I can tell you that I knew I was walking away from something very powerful. I cannot tell you why, but I knew it was something very, very powerful. My Nanny had told me about God. I was mad at Him, and I wanted to hurt Him, too, for giving me the mother He gave me and for making me go through what I had already gone through by the age of ten. I knew I was walking towards something very dark. I may not have known completely what all this entailed, but I tell you what, I knew I wanted evil.

For me, I willingly walked towards the enemy at that point. The ramifications for doing that would take years to learn, years to unfold, and years to realize what I was doing to myself. The enemy was about to enjoy every moment of it.

-Jeremiah 50:22-
A sound of battle is in the land,
and of great destruction.
(NKJV)

Guns and Roses came out with an album in the late 80s called *Appetite For Destruction.* This summed it up pretty well for me at the time. I loved the name of that album. To me, it was exactly what I had inside of me, an appetite for destruction. I began to isolate in my room, even when I wasn't grounded, and just listen to my tapes. Whatever message the band was trying to get across to kids, I couldn't tell you. I interpreted whatever I heard into whatever I wanted to hear. Then another band, Skid Row, came out with a song called "Youth Gone Wild." This band would become my favorite band of all time, and that song being my way of life. I even wound up getting the words Youth Gone Wild tattooed on my arm later in life. I wanted to be Sebastian Bach. He was more than an idol I looked up to. He was my god. I took the music and the lyrics way too seriously. I was impressionable and thought destruction and being wild was too cool and the way to be. I didn't know how to care or love anything.

-Matthew 18:14-
Even so it is not the will of your Father who is in

heaven that one of these little ones should perish.
(NKJV)

God was too involved in my life to let me just go and be lost forever. He didn't leave me to just go wander off somewhere. He was there. He was in my life. He was watching me, waiting for me to come crawling home to Him.

Things at school went from bad to worse. I had begun to be openly disrespectful to everyone in a position of authority. My blatant and open disrespect for any and all people grew by the day.

Our house was far from finished, but at least we were living in it. The walls still needed to be painted and doors needed to be hung on the bedrooms and bathroom. Dan was now living full time with us. He told his wife that he was going to be with Colleen and her family. What a treat! I'm not sure of the specifics of what had happened, but I was getting in trouble for something. I'm sure I had an attitude, and I remember yelling back at Colleen. I had on shorts, boots, and a t-shirt, nothing else. It was winter and very cold outside. She grabbed me by my arm and threw me out of the front door of the house.

"Get out of my house!"

It was dark outside and extremely cold. The wind was bitter, and we had at least two feet of snow. I began to beat and pound on the door so I could go back inside where it was warm.

"Let me in! Let me in! Let me in the house! It's cold outside!" I was crying. I heard her coming to the door and I thought she was going to let me in.

She opened the door and threw out my jacket.

"Get the hell off my property!" she yelled at me.

Get off her property? Where was I supposed to go? I put the jacket on and stood there for a few minutes thinking. Was she really kicking me out of the house when it was this cold? I began to kick and punch the door trying to see if she was going to let me back in, but all she did was turn up the volume on the television.

I stood there and had no clue what to do. There was a creek down the road, so I figured I would take a walk down there. I could cover myself with some leaves and try to go to sleep. I started to walk down the road when our dog came running up to me. I was so happy to see him. I thought he was going to come to the creek with me, but he just stood there and barked.

"Come here, Loner," I said in between crying. "Come here boy! Come on Loner. Come on! You want to come to the creek with me?"

He just looked at me, barked again, and ran back to the house. I started to walk towards the creek again and thought about jumping off the bridge into the creek so maybe I would die. The bridge was only twenty to thirty feet high. The water was, at best, twelve inches deep. I did not want to live in pain. I was lost, but I wasn't stupid. The further down the road I went, the more scared I got. I was in the middle of nowhere with woods all around. Every sound made me jump. Who was I kidding? I couldn't go down to the creek by myself, so I started to make my way back home. I got to the edge of the property and looked at the house. I just wanted to burn it to the ground, with Colleen and Dan in it.

I got to the front door and, instead of knocking on it, I began to kick and beat it as hard as I could. Colleen and Dan were watching television with my two sisters.

"Let me in the house!" I yelled.

I continued to beat and kick the door. I was committed to breaking it down if I could and was going to try to do exactly that. I was cold and crying.

"Let me in the (expletive) house now!"

The door flew open, but I couldn't see who it was through all my tears. That's when I felt the massive hand around my neck and got thrown into the living room where they were all relaxing. It was Dan.

"Who the hell do you think you are?" he said.

He picked me up by my neck again and dragged me to my room. Before he threw me into my room, he smacked my head off the door jam for good measure.

"How do you like that?"

He tossed me into my room, and I thought it was over, but he followed me in and began to punch me in the head and the rib cage.

"You don't treat your mother like that, you understand me?"

"You aren't my father!"

He continued to beat me. I tried to cover my face with my hands, but when I did, he would start punching me in my side. When I covered my side, he would slap and punch me in the head and face again. Finally, I went limp. He had knocked me out cold! I wasn't out long, because I opened my eyes to see him walking out of my room.

"I'm sorry, Colleen, but that kid needed a beating."

"Hey, don't worry about it. I agree. Do whatever you need to do," was her reply.

I laid there with tears rolling down my face and afraid to move. I didn't want them to know I was awake. No one came to check on me that night.

-Jeremiah 22:28-
"Is this man Coniah a despised, broken idol –
a vessel in which is no pleasure? Why are
they cast out, he and his descendants, and
cast into a land which they do not know?
(NKJV)

For many years, all I ever wanted was attention. Just a little attention was all I needed. To not always feel like I was being kicked to the side. Was that too much to ask? Now all it seemed like was that I was always the center of attention. I was made a spectacle of. I was a punching bag. I was someone to kick around. This is how I felt, and I didn't like it one bit. Attention? I wanted to scream out, "Please starve me of your attention. I don't want it anymore!" Again, I ask, Why does God do the things He does? I just don't understand.

-Esther 8:6-

> *For how can I endure to see the evil that will come to my*
> *people?*
> *Or how can I endure to see the destruction of my*
> *countrymen?*
> *(NKJV)*

I won't eat food I don't like. I won't even eat food that I think I may not like, and that was very frustrating for my ex-wife. She did her best to cook for me and to try to make new things occasionally, but if I even thought for a second that I might not like it, I wouldn't go near it, and that upset her. I used to love her. She was the absolute greatest woman God had ever given me up to that point in my life.

> *-Philemon 1:15-*
> *For perhaps he departed for a while for this*
> *purpose, that you might receive him forever,*
> *(NKJV)*

When I was a kid, Colleen would make me eat things that I didn't like. I couldn't stomach mashed potatoes, peas, or liver. Now, the mashed potatoes were probably just me not liking the way she cooked them, but the liver and peas would literally make me gag and throw up. I would gag at just the smell of it. All kids have issues with eating certain foods at certain times in their lives, but this was different.

Dan loved liver and onions with peas. I could not stand them. It makes me sick to this day. I still believe in my heart that, although Colleen may have actually enjoyed eating liver, she took great pleasure in forcing me to eat it. I remember going to the grocery store and her plopping the liver in the cart and saying, "Mmmmm, liver."

I would just look at it and my stomach would already be in knots. I would ask, "When are we going to eat that?"

"Soon," she would say, with a very sly smile.

"Do I have to eat it?"

"Yup. You'll eat what I put in front of you, or you can have nothing!"

Having nothing is what I would have preferred, but that never happened. I would remind her while she cooked it that night, "You said that if I didn't like it, then I could have nothing."

"You're going to sit there and not move from that table until you eat it. All of it! And I don't care how long it takes!"

Most times I just played with it until I got yelled at and slapped. I would try to put little bits of it in my mouth and swallow it with milk or Kool-Aid. I was given one glass to drink, and I had to try to make that last through the entire meal of liver, peas, and onions. Every time she cooked that for dinner, it would take three to four hours for me to finish, at least! It didn't matter to Colleen that the food would actually come back up in my throat, that I was fighting extremely hard not to puke. It didn't matter to her that I truly couldn't stand liver, onions, and peas. Most of the time, I fought hard to swallow it all, including what came back up in my mouth. I had no choice. It was either that or a beating. I got hit and grounded enough to not want anything else to

94

fuel the fire. It seemed as if we had liver a couple times a month, just so she could mess with my mind.

Finally, I had had enough. I just couldn't stomach it anymore. She cooked it again one night, and I was determined not to touch it. I just sat there at the table and didn't touch a thing. She saw the defiance in my eyes and said with a smile, "You're going to eat that. Whether you like it or not, you are going to eat everything on that plate. You wait and see."

We would wait and see, because I was not going to touch one thing on that plate. I wasn't asking her to make something else. I was asking to go to bed without dinner. I'd been sent to bed plenty of times without dinner that this made no sense to me. That's how I knew she enjoyed this. It was either having power over me or not liking me. Either one, I could not have cared less. Colleen just didn't like me at all. I just sat there and watched everyone else finish their dinner and didn't touch a thing. A few hours went by, and then the yelling started. I didn't want to hear it, so I just sat there. I don't know why, but I just started to cry.

"Eat your dinner now!"

"I want to go live with my dad. He wouldn't make me eat this. I hate you!"

This made her so mad that I thought I was going to get the worst beating ever. She went into the kitchen, got the bottle of Ajax dish soap, and began hitting me with it in the head repeatedly. I didn't care, because it didn't hurt all that bad.

"Eat your damn dinner!" she yelled.

"I want to go live with my Dad! I hate you!"

"Your Dad doesn't want you!"

She stopped hitting me with the soap bottle, called my Dad, and handed me the phone. I was crying and trying to tell him that she was hitting me because I wouldn't eat my dinner.

"Just listen to her, Steven," he said.

That was all I can really remember about that phone conversation. When I got off the phone, she grabbed me, threw me towards my room, and said that she was going to bring the leftover liver, onions, and peas to school and make me eat it for lunch. I really didn't think she would do that, but she did. She truly enjoyed messing with my mind, causing me pain, and having power over me.

I really didn't worry too much that day leading up to lunch time. I thought it was an empty threat. At lunchtime, we went to the cafeteria. I was only sitting down for a couple of minutes when Mr. Booth, the principal, came in and asked me to come to his office. There was no wondering why. I knew right away. Halfway to his office, he said to me, "Your mother is here. She said you gave her a hard time last night and wouldn't eat your dinner. She brought it in for you to eat for lunch. You can eat it in my office, so your friends don't have to see what's going on. We warmed it up for you."

She drove a bus for the school so what could I do? I just kept my head down and wondered when this would all end. He didn't know the truth and I didn't want to tell him. It was useless. I walked into his office, and Colleen was sitting at a table smiling at me.

"I brought your lunch," she said.

"And I want to kill you," I was thinking.

I didn't want to play any games, and there was no getting around it. I tried hard and fought the gag reflexes. She would win again.

"I told you that you were going to eat it all," she said as she left, smiling.

I remember thinking that it was so easy for her to go from all smiles to such an evil person in the blink of an eye. I left Mr. Booth's office to go to recess and threw up in the bathroom. When I got outside, Mr. Booth asked me, "Did you eat all of your lunch?"

I just looked at him without responding and walked away.

-Micah 7:8-9-
Do not rejoice over me, my enemy; when I fall, I will arise; when
I sit in darkness, the LORD will be a light to me. I will bear the
indignation of the LORD, because I have sinned against Him, until He pleads my case and executes justice for me. He will bring me forth to the light; I will see His righteousness.
(NKJV)

———————

Nothing is more satisfying to God than when you can turn your life away from the enemy. To be able to allow God in my life is something I have not only fought dearly to avoid, but I never understood how to do it in time of need. I know that God is the answer to all things. I can even explain this to people when they may be hurting. But when the need arises, even now, I find it so difficult to call on His power to help me. I know that He can, but I usually question if He will.

Prayer is the single most powerful tool that we have as Christians. It's a gift, but I'm learning that I have to believe in what I am praying. There is a big difference between just saying, "God, please help me. I am in need of Your help. Please take care of this situation for me. I know you can. In Jesus' name. Amen."

Or maybe a prayer like this, "Father, I need Your help. You are the only one who can guide me today through my trial. I need You to show me what to do with my life. I am having trouble in this area that only You and I know about, and only You have the power to change. Father, help me find Your will for my life today. I know You can help me. I know that you will help me, if it's a part of your will, and if it will glorify You. Help me to pray about all things, Father, not just when I have a problem. Help me to love You. Help me to see Your will for my life. Help me to see things through Your eyes! Help me to make decisions that will be pleasing to You. Help me, and show me how to be a man. Build a fire in my soul that burns for You! Thank you Father for the answer that You will give me. In Jesus' name I pray. Amen."

I have prayed both of these prayers at different times in my life. When I'm praying a prayer like the second one, I cannot only feel God's presence in my life, but He is quick to bring me peace of mind, and whatever His answer may be, I know it's the right one and it's easier to accept.

I'm not perfect. I have to keep trying over and over. I do fall, but I get back up and try again. The enemy does rejoice when I fall, but he is defeated when I choose to get back up and try one more time. The LORD is my light in the darkness. I just have to find Him. He's always there. The enemy is powerful. When I resist the enemy and get back up again, the LORD reminds me of this.

-Jude 1:9-
Yet Michael the archangel, in contending with the devil, when he disputed about the body of Moses, dared not bring against him a reviling accusation, but said, "The LORD rebuke you!"
(NKJV)

The enemy, I've learned, is to be respected on all levels. I have to fight against the devil and his demons every day that God breathes life into me, but make no mistake, you need to respect his power. I once told the devil that I was ready to fight him, that I could fight him off and fight against everything he had for me. That was the day that I walked out of rehab with over a year of sobriety. It didn't go so well.

My point is this: God loves me, and He is fighting for my life. He wants me to respect everyone and everything in my life. If He is all about love, why would He want me to disrespect the enemy? He wouldn't! Tough lessons learned.

Like I said, my fight is for my spiritual growth and my family's spiritual growth as well. I am supposed to be the leader. The time is now! It is time to be free from all the things that have held me back all these years: all the hate that has filled my life, the lies that I have believed, the fear that has torn me apart, and the deception of thinking that God won't do it for me also.

"If we are to avoid the quicksand, we must wise up to the schemes of the enemy."
Steve Farrar
(Point Man)

One of the schemes the enemy uses in my life is to keep me locked up in the prison of my childhood. Why? Because if I'm stuck there, then I am no good to anyone, because of what it brings out in me. I will be no good to my family, no good at my church, no good for myself. I would just be that same angry, rage-filled person just trying to fake it.

-2 Thessalonians 1:6-7-
Since it is a righteous thing with God to repay with tribulation those who trouble you, and to give you who are troubled rest with us when the LORD Jesus is revealed from heaven with His mighty angels.
(NKJV)

Towards the end of the summer one year, I wanted to grow a pumpkin patch. I had some pumpkin seeds and wondered if I could actually grow a pumpkin. I asked Colleen if I could try to grow a pumpkin patch in the backyard.

"No. You won't be able to get anything to grow," she said.

"Yes I can. It'll work. Can I at least try?"

To my disbelief, she responded with, "Fine, go right on ahead. But it won't work."

Like anybody else, when I put my mind to something, amazing things can happen. I took the hoe, the little pitch fork, and a crow bar, and I dug up the ground in the backyard. I turned the soil upside down and sideways to make some good planting ground. It was about twenty feet long and six or seven feet wide. I was pretty proud of myself. I even wet it a little a few times to get it to break up better. I could remember seeing farms on television, so I made long lines in it to put the seeds in and be able to cover it up with the remaining soil. I worked extremely hard on it. I laid the seed down in the trenches of the soil I made and covered it all back up with dirt and waited. Every day when I got home from school I watered it. On the weekends, I pulled out whatever weeds I saw that were coming up. I took excellent care of my pumpkin patch.

In about a month or so, I could see the beginnings of life start to come up from the ground. It was lush and green. I was proud of what I was doing. I remembered thinking, "I did it!" I can't remember the exact timeline of when it happened, but I saw the first pumpkin taking form. It would be the only pumpkin that would come up. I looked and looked for others to start to blossom, but they never did. That was okay with me, because one was all I needed to make me feel like I had accomplished something on my own. Me! It was a good thing for me to realize that. I had needed to realize that I could accomplish something if I set my mind to it. It also made me think that I didn't need anyone's help for anything.

-2 Chronicles 26:5-
He sought God in the days of Zechariah, who had
understanding in the visions of God; and as long
as he sought the LORD, God made him prosper.
(NKJV)

It was just a couple of weeks before Halloween, and I was bringing my pumpkin into the house when Colleen started to yell at me, "Get that pumpkin out of my house!"

"Why? What did I do?"

"I said get that pumpkin out of my house, now!"

"Where am I supposed to put it?"

I was devastated and confused. I didn't understand what was going on. I went outside and walked to the end of our property line and put my pumpkin just beyond it in the woods, but that wasn't good enough either. She came outside and continued to yell at me, "Get that pumpkin off my property! Get it out of my sight!"

I tried so hard to find a spot to put my pumpkin that would not aggravate her, where it would be okay, but there was no use. I could not find anywhere to put it that was suitable enough for that damn woman who gave birth to me. I just circled the property line and came up with nothing. Finally, I just walked back to the house with my pumpkin in my hands, but she grabbed me, threw me out of the house again, and told me not to come back until the pumpkin was gone. It was almost dark outside, and I figured it would be easy to stash my pumpkin until tomorrow. I found a spot for it and just continued to walk around the property when I started to get rocks thrown in my direction. I was scared it was something or someone I didn't know. Then I realized it was Dan. He was throwing rocks in my direction to scare me. It was working well. Great choice of men, Colleen. Again, truly superb! Thank you so much!

"Stop throwing rocks at me!" I yelled out, but that only made the rock tossing more fun for him. A couple of times they almost hit me.

"Stop throwing rocks at me!"

It would eventually stop, but it fueled my hatred for this house and this life.

-Psalm 139:22-
I hate them with perfect hatred;
I count them my enemies.
(NKJV)

If ever there was a perfect hatred for someone, I held it in my heart. Completely! Every bit of it aimed at Colleen and Dan.

One of the few luxuries I was given were my drum lessons. I enjoyed them immensely, but even they were stopped time and time again. I would do this or that, and it was no more drum lessons, because I didn't deserve them. My drum teacher couldn't even keep me on pace with the other students because I was always in and out of class for periods at a time.

Dan liked to eat London Broil. He really did have a fantastic way of cooking it. He marinated it overnight with Italian dressing, then slow-cooked it the next day. He would then thinly slice it at a forty-five degree angle. Always pink on the inside, but not raw. We were at the table one night all ready to eat. I was anxious for two reasons. It was London Broil, and it seemed we never had anything I truly enjoyed. I was excited, so I reached for the tongs to grab my London Broil, and Colleen stabbed me in the hand with a fork. Not enough to draw blood, but hard enough to scrape my hand and leave some marks.

"You don't grab your food first! Let your sisters go first! You can go last now."

Whatever! I actually found some humor in it. I always went last anyway. Nothing changed. It did seem to me that she looked at me while she grabbed the really good pieces. I could be wrong. It was a long time ago, but I don't think I am.

I started to steal whatever money I could find around the house. Usually it was just change, but a couple of times I stole a twenty dollar bill. I thought I was lucky, because Colleen just blamed Dan for going into her purse again, because of course, his construction company suddenly didn't have any work right after they got married.

At this point, they fought almost nonstop, and I found it pleasing. I used the money I stole to buy my lunch at school. We were on the free lunch program, so there was a certain lunch I had to get. With the money I was stealing, I was able to buy what I wanted. I felt if I had to deal with the food I was given at home, then I deserved to eat what I wanted at school.

It wasn't long before I got caught. I got out of school one day and saw Dan there to pick me up. I was surprised, to say the least. He didn't look too happy. As I walked up to him, he hit me in the middle of the entire school. There was no talking beforehand, no knowing that I was about to get a beating.

"You're stealing money from me and your mother?"

I couldn't even think straight at the moment. I don't even think I heard what he said. He just hit me a few more times and then threw me into the back of his little Mazda pickup truck, slammed the tailgate, and sped off with me flying around in the bed of his truck. All my friends had seen what just happened. So did Colleen, because she was one of the bus drivers. Some of the teachers witnessed this too, and they all just looked at me and then went about their business.

"Wait until your mother gets home."

Whatever!

———————

I have wondered a lot lately if writing this book is a good idea. I have wondered whom it may affect. I have no ill will intentions at all to hurt anybody or to make anyone feel bad about anything. What exactly do I write and how far into my life do I go?

-Haggai 2:9-
'The glory of this latter temple shall be greater than the former,' says the LORD of hosts. 'And in this place I will give peace,' says the LORD of hosts."
<u>*(NKJV)*</u>

I have said time and time again that I want peace. I can't get there until I deal with the hatred I live with every day. Doing this makes my house cleaner, and in doing that, more acceptable for Jesus to come live in. He is able to give me peace.

After we got home, I waited in my room until Colleen got home from work. She came straight to my room and gave me another one of her fantastic beatings, my second beating of the day, thank you very much! She yelled at me for stealing her money and going through her things.

"This is my house! These are my things! You have no things! Nothing! I let you dwell here! That's it!"

She told me I was grounded again, but no big surprise there. I literally lived in my room. Who was she kidding? She went into the laundry room to get something and a vase fell down from the top shelf and broke on her leg. It put a serious deep cut down her shin. Dan was outside in the yard and didn't hear it right away. She was screaming for a towel and was crying loud and hard. I casually walked to the linen closet, got her a towel, and tried to walk back as slow as I could to give it to her. Dan came into the house, and we all got in the car and took her to the hospital. On the drive there, she was crying and kept saying, "Why me?! Why me?! It hurts so bad! Why me?!"

Good, I'm glad it hurts, you freaking horrible woman! Stop your crying! I hope it's more painful than you can handle! You have no clue what pain is, Colleen! Little did I know, I was smack in the middle of a spiritual battle in my life with how I viewed things and how I wanted to live my life. I just couldn't see what was happening.

-James 1:13-15-
Let no one say when he is tempted, "I am tempted by God"; for God cannot be tempted by evil, nor does He Himself tempt anyone. But each one is tempted when he is drawn away by his own desires and enticed. Then, when desire has conceived, it gives birth to sin; and sin, when it is full-grown, brings forth death.
(NKJV)

For me, enjoying the pain someone else was feeling or dealing with would give birth to many demons in my life.

Right now in my life I am in the middle of, I believe, the worst spiritual battle I have ever encountered. The enemy is truly working on me. I find it extremely difficult to call on the Lord for help.

What if this…

What if that…
Why this…
Why that…

The truth is: I don't know the answer to those questions, and it scares me more and more each day. Not long ago I was reading a book from T.D. Jakes called *So You Call Yourself A Man?* When I'm reading my bible, I highlight and underline verses that I feel God is trying to speak into my heart. It's kind of like His way of talking to me. Well, I was at work and I didn't have my bible highlighter with me, so I grabbed a highlighter from my desk and highlighted a spot on the page in between paragraphs where there was no writing, so I wouldn't highlight something I didn't want to, just to see if it worked.

That morning, I was having trouble trying to understand what God was trying to say to me. I knew He was trying to tell me something, but I just couldn't figure it out. When I turned the page over in my bible, I saw that I had, accidently, highlighted the words, into fierce spiritual battle. The entire sentence reads, "Even under a strong anointing, some men find it difficult to enter into fierce spiritual battle."

The day before that, our prayer leader at church came up to me during prayer group and asked if he could pray over me, using anointing oil. Now was this a coincidence? I don't believe in that stuff. God was trying to tell me that I was about to go through one of the toughest spiritual battles of my life.

The battle I went through as a child was also tough, but I was unknowing and unbelieving at the time. It didn't make it any less effective though. Knowing and believing in Jesus Christ, and having to go through a spiritual battle, for me is faith shaking. I will tell you what that situation is as soon as I figure it out. For now, I need prayer, and I need to continue to do something the enemy doesn't want me to do, continue writing this book.

It wasn't long before I started to snort Cascade detergent. One night while putting some Cascade into the dishwasher, the dust from it had gotten on my face. It made me sneeze uncontrollably and I thought that it was one of the coolest things. Occasionally I would snort a little here and there so I could sneeze and feel the rush. It also made me feel a little lightheaded and I was starting to enjoy that too. I brought some to school and got a few of my friends to snort some also. Colleen kept telling me to stop it, but I thought it was funny. That was until one of my friends, who had an older cousin a couple of grades higher than I was, got mad and threatened to beat me up if I continued to let him snort Cascade. That cured me of bringing it to school, but I continued to snort it at home whenever I could.

Very soon after that episode, I was put into counseling for how I was behaving. It was everything I was doing that was the problem. I really was out of control. I started to play with matches again, and I was putting these little plastic skulls on light bulbs around our house waiting for someone to turn on the light so the skull would burn. Like I said,

I was out of control and was going to eventually hurt someone, or myself, in the process, so, counseling was the call.

The counselors tried all these tests on me. The ink blot, mind stuff, and things I can't remember. I never said how I truly felt or what was going on at the time. I was out of touch with reality while trying to feel the warmth of something that wasn't there. They never found out what the real problems were. To them, I looked like a kid that was from a good loving home who turned out to be a problem child. Why wouldn't they think that? My two sisters were very good kids with excellent grades who excelled in whatever they did. I looked like the kid that liked to cause trouble at every turn. They were right about the latter, but there were some dark secrets underneath it all. I felt I had a better chance of getting out of the house if I just shut my mouth and acted up. Little did I know, though, I was so lost in my own little world, that I really was "different."

Colleen had told me time and time again that every session cost her twenty dollars. She would ask me, "What's wrong with you? What can I do? Why do you act this way?"

Part of me thought, "Are you really serious right now?" I just wanted to slap her. She was looking like the concerned parent who cared. Another part of me felt like she was being kind going to the appointments, because she did not want me to spill the beans. When the first counselor couldn't figure out what the problem was, I was sent off to another one, a woman, because people thought that I would be able to connect with someone of the opposite sex better. That didn't work either; I despised women. I kept my mouth shut and acted the part of a problem child. Things at school got worse as well. I went from going backwards to full speed reverse.

My mouth…

My language...

My defiance…

I was growing very curious of girls by now, and instead of trying to talk to them, I started smacking all the girls on the butt. I had a counseling appointment after school one day, and Dan was going to pick me up and take me home afterwards. I was quiet on the ride home, because I knew it would only be a matter of a day or so, if not that day, that Colleen would be told of my actions at school. I figured I would wait in my room and see what happened when she got home, but her car was already there when we pulled into the driveway. My heart was in my throat as we pulled up to the house. I remember walking in the back door with Dan when Colleen came running around the corner, into the kitchen, grabbed me by the throat, and threw me to the floor. This would be, by far, the worst beating I would ever get. I can't even tell you what was said because I don't remember. I just remember the beating. I was kicked and punched by my own mother, and I'm not talking about like before. I mean that she was hitting me as if I was a full-grown adult male. I was punched in the face and stomach, thrown into walls, my neck squeezed until I almost passed out, and when I would go limp, I was pulled back up and punched some more. It felt like it went on forever. I couldn't seem to cover myself in the right spots, because wherever I tried to block myself from getting hit, I was hit in a different spot. I tried to cover my face but she pulled my hands away, held my wrists together, and slapped and punched me in the face over and over and over and over again. She threw me on the carpet, kicked me in the stomach, and walked out of my room. I heard her talking to Dan. I didn't even try to listen, because I was just glad it was over, but it wasn't. Dan came running in my room and punched me in my head while I was still on the ground. He pulled me up and began to punch me very slowly so I could feel each one. Too many quickly repeated punches in the same spot and I could go numb. He would wait a second or two, and then punch me again. He was punching me in the stomach and squeezing my throat so I couldn't breathe. I was gasping for air. Then he banged my head off my dresser and I almost passed out. He went to walk out of my room and picked up my nightstand, "Dan stop!"

But he threw the nightstand at me anyway and hit me directly in my head. I was out cold. When I woke up, my head and face were bleeding, my face was numb, my eye was swollen, my lip was split on the top and bottom with blood dripping out, I couldn't move my side, and my chest hurt. Why was all this happening to me? Why wouldn't I behave? Why do I have to stay here? Why do I do the things I do? I wasn't stupid. I just didn't care about much. I knew what would happen if I acted a certain way and did certain things, but I did them anyway. I knew the consequences for my actions. I was torturing myself. Were they wrong for the way they disciplined me? What comes to my mind is, if knowing this or that would happen, why would I knowingly try to bring it on myself? It was because I could control it that way.

Instead of doing things that would keep me out of trouble and still get beat anyway, I made people work for their money with me. It was control. I was trying to stop the surprise beatings or the surprise grounding. At least I would know when they were coming. It didn't work all the time, but enough to not be surprised all the time.

-Psalm 81:10-16-
"I am the LORD your God, who brought you out of the land of Egypt; Open your mouth wide and I will fill it. But My people would not heed my voice, and Israel would have none of Me. So I gave them over to their own stubborn heart, to walk in their own counsels. Oh, that My people would listen to Me, that Israel would walk in My ways! I would soon subdue their enemies, and turn My hand against their adversaries. The haters of the LORD would pretend submission to Him, but their fate would endure forever. He would have fed them also with the finest of wheat; and with honey from the rock I would have satisfied you."
(NKJV)

I don't think it was even a couple of months after that before I was sent off to my first residential home for troubled boys. I forget the exact circumstances, but I do remember a court date where I told the judge I did not want to live at home anymore. I never told him about the beatings. He didn't even need to know all that for him to place me in a troubled boys' home.

The residential home I went to was for a thirty-day evaluation to see what the problems were, if any, and to see if I would be a good fit for the home. Colleen was crying while the counselor drove us, but her tears meant absolutely nothing to me. I, on the other hand, couldn't wait to get there. I was scared, and there was a little knot in my stomach, but it was the uncertainty of the whole thing. Inside, I just really could not wait to get there.

I was dropped off and Colleen was told to leave. She continued to cry on her way out, and I wondered what pain she might be feeling. I remember thinking that she truly looked hurt and sad. As I watched her leave through the window, I became torn inside. I was torn about feeling happy that she was sad and in pain. I really wanted her to feel pain. I wanted her to feel the way about me that she felt at that moment, like she loved and cared about me. I almost felt like she loved me at that moment.

I tried to quickly push that thought from my mind, turned around, and took a big sigh of relief. Finally, I knew that for thirty days I would be free from being force fed food that made me puke, free from the surprise beatings at any given moment, and free from being called stupid, worthless, no-good, jerk and retard! I was nine years old, and this was the happiest moment in my life.

I was shown my room, where I would eat, and where I would go to school. The school was on the same property. Everything was, and we were not allowed to leave to go anywhere. I thought that there were going to be all these counseling sessions and brain pickers and tests, but there was none of that. The house I lived in was only for the kids undergoing the evaluation process. It was called the "thirty-day house."

In the house I was in, the boys lived on one side; the girls lived on the other. The two sides were split by a huge kitchen and living room. There was nothing to this place at all. It was kind of relaxing. We went to school, came back to eat, did some chores, and watched television. I only had one counseling session while I was there. They told me point blank that this thirty minute meeting we were going to have would allow them to decide if this was the right place for me to be long term.

They wanted to know what I thought the problem was, and I couldn't give them an answer. I just cried and told them that I didn't want to live at home anymore. They said I would know in about a week or so if I would be placed in their residential home or sent somewhere else to re-evaluated.

I thought I would have a better chance of being placed there if I started to act out, so that's just what I did. I began by being rude to my teacher, which would get me kicked out of class for the day. Upon returning the next day, I started to make sexual comments to her.

I had seen some of the other kids flip-out and get so out of control that they had to put them in a restraint room and strap them down until they calmed down enough to go back to class, so I tried that also. Surely, this would be enough for them to think this was the right place for me to be.

I remember thinking this place was filled with happy kids who were all troublemakers, who all wanted to be known as the worst of the worst. I was drawn to it. I wanted to live here more and more every day. There were no overnight visits allowed with our parents of any kind, for any reason, and I was just fine with that. I was, however, allowed permission to go to Colleen and Dan's wedding. I didn't want to go, but I was told it was the right thing to do and that it would be a healthy experience for me.

I waited for Colleen to pick me up outside that morning, and to my surprise, Dan drove in to pick me up instead. You've got to be kidding me! He didn't say one word to me on the one hour drive home. I had nothing to say to him either. We drove in complete silence. There's not much to really say about the wedding except that when Colleen said, "I do," I was thinking it would be really funny if she said, "I don't." I wondered how she could be duped so easily by this guy, but in that moment, it made complete sense. He was obviously a conman, and she didn't see it. She was a conwoman, and he didn't see it either. Only then was there a small sense of peace, because I knew for sure that both their worlds were going to crash right into each other's and

116

explode. I couldn't wait for that to happen. I smiled to myself and wondered if I would be given the pleasure to watch it happen. I got back to the residential home that night and was asked how everything went.

"Fine." I had nothing else to say.

I think it was a couple of days after that that I was told the boys' home was not the right fit for me and that I would be going home the following weekend. I felt as if I was just stabbed in the stomach.

Colleen must have known, because she waited for me to get home before she went on her honeymoon. Dan had already gone down to Florida and was waiting for her. My Aunt Gail told us that we were going to take her to the airport, and I said, "Maybe her plane will crash."

"STEVEN!"

-Romans 15:7-
Therefore receive one another, just as
Christ also received us, to the glory of God.
(NKJV)

I finally met a friend who accepted me for who I was, and I accepted him for who he was. His name was James DiStephano. James was paralyzed from the neck down, had to breathe via a machine, and was pretty much always home.

For some reason, James had plenty of friends at school. He was a very popular kid, but not many spent time with him outside of school. He couldn't do much. It wasn't his fault, and it wasn't their fault.

He was confined to a wheelchair. I had no friends to speak of, and he accepted me for who I was. We became quick friends.

His mother was a nice woman who knew of my troubles at home. She took me in whenever I wanted and would pick me up when I got kicked out of the house. She fed me and let me sleep over whenever I wanted. James and I spend a lot of time together. He knew I wasn't liked very much and had no friends, but that never stopped him from being my friend and sticking up for me at school.

Whenever I wasn't grounded, I was over at his house. One time, he wanted to buy a remote control car, so I suggested that we paint a coffee can white and put the words Multiple Sclerosis on it and go house to house to raise money. We could then keep the money and buy a remote control car. We only got to go to two house before his mother, Joanne, got a call and came to get us.

"What are you two thinking? Steven, I'm not going to tell your mother, because I know you'll get into trouble, but this is unacceptable." She made us go back and return the money.

Another time, James had some leftover firecrackers from the Fourth of July and was allowed to light them off. We lit a few, and then I had the brilliant idea of lighting one and sliding it into an empty one- gallon wine bottle we found. The first one went off fine with no trouble. The second one, though, exploded the bottle into a million little pieces. I couldn't understand how neither one of us didn't get cut, or worse. After the explosion, Joanne came running out of the house' "What are you two thinking? You guys could have killed yourselves! What if it sliced James' breathing machine? Steven, I'm not going to tell your mother, because I know she'll beat you senseless, but you have to use your head. You need to think about what you're doing."

I was truly sorry. She was right; I wasn't thinking of what could have happened. I never thought that far ahead.

Another time, we got some rubbing alcohol and decided to burn down the empty house next door to his. It was my idea, of course. I tried to get that thing to burn, but it just wouldn't go up in flames. A car had driven by the house slowly, so we got out of there as fast as we could. When we got back to his house, Joanne was waiting for us outside. She said that a neighbor had seen us and called her.

"Are you two crazy? You were trying to set a house on fire! Steven, I'm not going to tell your mother, because she will probably kill you, but I am going to take you home. I'll tell her that James isn't feeling well. It's probably a good idea that you two stay away from each other for a little while."

Pretty soon, they found a residential home for me to go to. I was told that I would be at the home for up to two years. What a sigh of relief. I felt like God had just given me one of the biggest blessings of my life. This home was just like the one I was in before it and had all the same rules. Only this home had about ten or twelve dormitories that held twenty-five to thirty kids each. There was even a private school for us a few miles away that had over one thousand kids attending. The school was where any judge would send a "troubled youth." Every one of us wanted to be known as the worst.

At this place there was no real counseling. Counseling was there for us to utilize when we felt we were ready. We were never pushed to talk about the things we felt troubled us. We never had scheduled appointments. If we wanted to talk about our life, then we had to request a meeting with our counselor.

Both the school and the home came complete with restraint rooms and padded walls. What this place was was a dumping ground for troubled kids. There was no real help, or hope, for us. We weren't pushed, or even told, that if we can try to heal, then there could be hope for us in the future. We were all there just doing our court-mandated time and waited it out. For most of us, that would come at the age of eighteen. I'm not saying all the parents of the kids were dumping their kids off, and that they didn't care. I don't even know how the court viewed it. But the place was exactly that: a dumping ground for troubled kids.

There were three to four of us to a bedroom, and our things got stolen all the time. In the morning, if I didn't get up by four o'clock, then I got a very cold shower. We all had chores to do every day and got paid five or six dollars a week for doing them without being told. We even got paid a little extra if we picked up other chores that needed to get done, so I asked for extra chores all the time. One week my allowance was $32.50, and in 1987; that was a lot of money for an eleven year old kid. I bought a carton of cigarettes and began smoking. I only smoked while I was at the home, never when Colleen and Dan were out for a visit.

We all started trouble with each other all the time. Mostly it was just words back and forth. One day I woke up in a room with a counselor sitting in front of me, asking me if I was all right and if I was able to remember anything.

"No," I said. I did not remember anything and kept wondering why I was in a small room with a counselor.

What happened, I found out, was that I got a little smart mouthed and cocky with one of the older kids and wound up getting knocked out cold. To this day, I can't remember what happened. I was told the older kid picked me up and slammed my head into the ground.

One weekend, I got to go home for a visit. My Aunt Gail came out to our house with my two cousins, Monique and Ronnie, and so did my Nanny. I had just gotten a brand new ten-speed bike, and my cousin wanted to race. There was a big hill in front of our house, and Colleen said Ronnie and I could race down that.

We started from the top of the hill. I was going so fast that I had put the gears in high and was still peddling fast when about half way down, right in front of our house, the front brake handle fell off the handlebars and got caught in the spokes of the front tire, launching me off the bike. The accident went in slow motion. I could see my front tire and the pavement coming up to my face. The next thing was trying my hardest to walk to my house, while I was swinging my arms back and forth. Colleen was standing at the front of the property yelling at me, "What are you, friggen stupid? What the hell did you do, numb nuts?"

All of a sudden I couldn't move my right arm and shoulder. I was finally aware of the pain that was shooting down my chest, arm, and shoulder. I couldn't move an inch, and the entire time, Colleen is calling me "stupid." Once again, great parenting, Colleen! Such love shown. Thank you!

What happened after the brake got caught in the spoke was that I flipped over my bike and hit the road, face and shoulder first. I slid on the pavement another fifty to sixty feet, while my bike flew in pieces another eighty to one hundred feet past that. I had broken my collarbone in half, separated the growth plate in my right shoulder, got a major concussion, and got road rash from my head all the way down to my feet, and all I did was get yelled at and called "stupid." I vaguely remember the ride to the hospital. The next day she told me to stand still while she took a picture with my crumpled bike in front of me and held my tire with my good hand.

"This is so you'll remember what stupid looks like," Colleen said.

Needless to say, I couldn't go back to the residential home because they were not set up to take care of someone who couldn't take care of himself. I needed help lying down and getting up. I was also on some powerful painkillers. I didn't have to go to school either. I took about four months to heal.

On another weekend that Aunt Gail came out with my Nanny and cousins, we had a sit-down breakfast, which was unusual. My older sister Belinda wanted more eggs, so she made some. She wasn't able to finish them all, so she threw out what she was unable to eat. When Colleen saw this, she went and grabbed her by her hair, yanked her head back, and began to slap her repeatedly in the face. She was extremely violent with her slaps. She was yelling at her about the food being hers and how Belinda had no right to throw it away. She called her a pig and told her that she was selfish. My Aunt Gail stepped in with, "Colleen! What the hell is the matter with you?! Knock it off!"

Then Nanny yelled, "COLLEEN!"

She stopped hitting her but looked at her like she was going to get it later when they left. I just looked at Nanny and Aunt Gail with an expression that said, "Now do you see?" I knew Aunt Gail genuinely felt bad for us. I also knew that there was nothing she would do either, her or Nanny. They never did crap to help. We were all just left there with satan's daughter to deal with it. I had it the worst. With Belinda, it was on and off. Rhonda never had to worry; she was Colleen's favorite. I was told over and over, "You just wait for Dan to get home."

She had challenged me my entire life, and I was done. I was now challenging her.

"You think you can stand up to me? You think you have the balls?" she asked me.

I looked her dead in her face and told her, "I don't need balls to kill you and Dan while you're sleeping." I walked back to my room. Colleen never came in my room that night. I was eleven years old. I had finally had enough. I was willing to sacrifice my life to stand up to her and Dan. I was done!

It was only about a month after that that something else had happened and I got another beating. I can't think of what it was, but after the beating, my sister Belinda and I were both kicked out of the house. We walked up the street to a payphone where she called her best friend and I called James. We each bought a pack of cigarettes from a vending machine and waited for our rides to come and get us.

When I got to James' house, I called my Dad and told him absolutely everything that had been going on. I held nothing back. He asked me where I was, and I told him. He told me to call him back in exactly ten minutes. I watched as the clock slowly ticked off the seconds. I called my Dad back and he said these words to me, "I'll be there tomorrow night to pick you up, Steven. You're going to come live with me."

I was scared, so I asked, "How long can I live with you?" I never wanted to go back to Colleen's house.

"Forever, Steven." I began to cry immediately. "You're coming to live with me for good."

124

Those words did for me almost what it was like when I gave my life to Jesus. Finally, the pain was about to end. I cry even as I write this. The very next day, as promised, my Dad, Steven F. Gray, Sr., made the four hour trip to pick me up to go live with him. I was never beat again. I was never called stupid or worthless again. I was never scared to fall asleep again! It would be years before I would ever see that evil woman again!

-1 Chronicles 22:18-
"Is not the LORD your God with you? And has He not given you rest
on every side? For He has given the inhabitants of the land into my
hand, and the land is subdued before The LORD and before His people.
(NKJV)

The other day I had a scary thought. I was wondering if following God was worth the pain. One of the things that writing this book has done for me so far is that I have stayed almost non-stop in the Word. This is not bragging; I'm trying to show you what the LORD is doing for me. God is healing me.

Chapter Four

-Psalm 18:25-27-
With the merciful You will show Yourself merciful;
With a blameless man You will show Yourself blameless;
With the pure You will show Yourself pure; and with the
devious You will show Yourself shrewd. For You will
save the humble people, but will bring down haughty looks.
(NKJV)

At this point in time right now, it's been a while since I've written anything. It's almost been a year. I'm just coming off of another relapse, and my ex-wife and I are currently going through a divorce. I would love to sit here and pass blame, but I can't do that. Sometimes people have just had enough and can't go any further. That's where Sabrina is right now. She has had enough of me. I literally just got out of rehab on Monday, and right at this very moment, I am sitting outside in a sober living house writing.

I've been trying to figure out where to pick up in my writing. I've been through all my notes and believe that I have everything organized to continue, but I'm feeling stuck. I knew what I wanted to write and I knew where I wanted to go with it. I felt like I knew what direction to take. I'm stuck, and I don't know exactly the reason why.

The reason is that, in all honesty, I couldn't continue to write like everything is okay. I can't just sit here and make it seem like everything is flowing naturally. There has been a big life shift since I wrote the scripture to start Chapter Four. The last time I

126

wrote anything was June of 2011. It is now June of 2012. That was one year ago and a lot has happened. Have you ever done, felt, said, or thought of something that made sense only to you at that exact moment?

"Some of us are fortunate enough, by God's grace, to experience a few moments on this earth when the preciousness of the Gospel manifests itself with life changing clarity. In those moments we realize that preserving and sharing the message of salvation is worth any cost, because its value is beyond any price."
John MacArthur
(Hard To Believe)

I want to tell my life story and share with you what God has done. I also believe in my heart that it will help me deal with my past and finally put my anger and hatred in the grave, where it belongs.

I want to reach out to other drug addicts and homeless people to show them the love that Jesus Christ has for them, show them that someone else with a rough history has been redeemed. I also want to show them that they can love and be loved.

I want to show other Christians that there are hurting people out there. There are people on the street who are hurting and eating out of dumpsters, that there are drug addicts who are willing to do anything to get their next fix. I want to show these other Christians that there is this entire other world that needs attention. I want to show them that this life is for everybody, not just for those who "have it together."

Now, one more thing I would like to touch on before I continue is my divorce. Now as some of you other Christians are reading this, you might be thinking, "You're supposed to be a Christian, and God hates divorce."

"Why didn't the two of you not persevere?"

"Why go through with a divorce?"

First of all, I didn't want to get divorced. Filing for the divorce and going through with it is not something of my doing. I fought it. I wanted to go to counseling. I wanted to try to make it work, but Sabrina just would not stay married to me any longer. Before you start blaming her, let me tell you that Sabrina tried to make this marriage work for a long time. It was me who wound up not caring anymore. By the time I saw the light, it was too late for her to want to care. She tried going to our pastors and even took me to marriage counseling, but all I ever saw was her trying to attack me, instead of her trying her to fight for me.

I became an abusive, angry, vile, hate-filled person. I know that even right now, at this very moment, God does not want her to continue with the divorce. He has spoken this into my heart. Haven't you ever been in a position where you are so hurt by someone else's actions that you couldn't see or hear what The LORD was trying to tell you? I know I have. If you have never experienced that, then you, my friend, are truly blessed. If you have, then you know exactly where she is coming from.

Was it entirely all my fault? No! Did she do some things wrong too? Yes, but this isn't about her. It's about the wrong that I've done. I can't sit here and blame her, because she has really fought hard up until now. For four years she fought. As the man and husband of the house, I just didn't try hard enough. I didn't fight for my family.

> **"Don't just say that this is ugly and immoral – of course it is – but ask yourself if it is not also your sin that such tragedies occur, that such Christian families are left alone, and are not helped by you who are free."**
> **Reverend Richard Wurmbrand**
> **(Tortured For Christ)**

> **-2 Timothy 2:10-**
> **Therefore I endure all things for the sake of the elect, that they also may obtain the salvation which is in Christ Jesus with eternal glory.**
> **(NKJV)**

Chapter Five

-Lamentations 3:56-
You heard my voice: "Do not hide Your
ear from my sighing, from my cry for help."
(NKJV)

I couldn't believe it; I was finally going to live with my dad. That was all I ever wanted. Ever since I was a little boy, that was all I ever dreamed about, and it was finally happening. I didn't want to fall asleep in case it was a dream and woke up to realize that I was back in Colleen's house, scared, waiting for the next violent beating that waited around the corner.

I didn't have that many friends, but the friends I did have, I made sure I told. The only thing I was going to miss at all was my friend James. His mother and he were the only people that ever knew what I was going through. It really was tough to say goodbye to them. This was the first time I ever felt the pain of losing someone special in my life. I would miss James.

Joanne, his mother, was extremely happy for me. I could see it in her eyes. She had tears of joy, and she was sure to remind me that this meant I was getting a shot at changing my life, in which I needed to change how I thought and acted. I was sure to tell her that I would do just that.

Other than that, I could not have cared the least little bit about leaving everything else behind. I did not care, nor did I think about it. I was leaving.

My attitude was literally, "Have a good one; see ya. So long and goodbye! Peace the frig out!"

When I got home from school that day, I packed all of my things and placed them on the porch. With a joyful heart, I walked around the house smiling. I never said one word to Dan either. A couple of times I had the thought of taking my baseball bat, and as I brought it outside to put it with my things, taking a nice crack at the back of his head. Dan just ignored me, and I returned the favor.

Colleen and Dan had their friends over that night. They were another couple that they hung out with from time to time. The wife was a Notary of the Public, and she was there because my Dad and Colleen needed to get something signed that said I was going to live with him. I told their friends a few times that I was going to go live with my Dad. I knew they knew, but I kept saying it anyway.

Dan would glance at me and give me a dirty look from time to time, but he never said a word. He knew better than to start some crap in front of people. Even he wasn't that stupid. It truly is sad because I wanted so badly for him to get smart with me. I wanted him to say something, because I had been practicing a good response all day. The second he opened his mouth, whatever it was, I was going to say, "Shut up. What are you going to do about it? Go ahead, hit me again and I'll stab you in the back of your friggin head." In some sick way, I wanted to catch one last beating before my Dad came. I wanted the cops to come for my Dad to see. I really would have stabbed him that night, thinking I was justified.

Colleen did yell at me, "Shut up! We all know your moving to your Dad's. You think the grass is greener on the other side? You'll see! But until your father gets here, you're still in MY house. So shut your mouth and get out of my sight! Go wait outside until your father gets here!"

My response?

"Or else what? I can't wait to get out of this house."

I waited for her response, but she never said anything. Dan never moved an inch or turned his head to look in my direction. Their friends were looking at Colleen, and Colleen was just staring at me.

"Get out of my house," she said.

We stared at each other until, eventually, I walked outside. On the way out, I slammed the door hard and sat down to wait for my Dad. I knew he was coming to pick me up because he said so. My Dad always kept his word. He never lied; that wasn't his style. There was still this small bit of fear in me that wondered if this might all be a dream.

-Deuteronomy 28:66-
Your life shall hang in doubt before you; you shall fear day and night, and have no assurance of life.
(NKJV)

What if he doesn't come to get me? What if this is all a joke? What if he decided that I can't go live with him right now? What if I still have to live in this house

132

And then I heard…..

-Matthew 14:31-
And immediately Jesus stretched out
His hand and caught him, and said to him,
"O you of little faith, why did you doubt?"
(NKJV)

...the most beautiful sound in the world!

It was the sound of the tires of my Dad's car coming up the driveway to pick me up. (Man, let me tell you, I am tearing up as I type this!) I ran off the porch to look, and sure enough, it was that old grey Chevy Citation with my Dad behind the wheel. I almost couldn't wait for him to get out. He got out of the car, and for the first time, he didn't wait for me to run up to him first. He came to me, and I jumped into his arms. He had tears in his eyes, for me.

I have never hugged him, or anyone else for that matter, so hard, and for so long, in my entire life. He just held me tight as I cried. Not much was said.

He whispered, "I love you Steven."

I tried to hold on tighter. After a couple of minutes, he set me down, looked at me with a smile and tears in his eyes and said, "Are you ready?"

I couldn't talk. I just looked up at him with tears rolling down my face and shook my head yes.

"Come on, let's get your things in the car and go home."

My body was weak, and I felt faint, but I started packing my things into his car anyway. He went into the house to sign some paperwork as I packed his car as fast as I could. At one point, I looked through the screen door to see what was going on. Colleen was talking and signing some paperwork, and I could tell that she was really pissed, and so was my Dad. He just stared at her while she was getting loud with him. Then I heard Colleen say, "You can have him; he's nothing but a foul-up anyway. He'll always be a foul-up."

After a few minutes, he came out and said, "Let's get out of here and go home. You ready?"

Smiling, I said, "Yes!"

I wanted to go inside to say goodbye to my sister Rhonda, but she was at one of her friend's houses. My older sister Belinda was in her room. I didn't know what to say to her. We never got along anyway. I just looked at her and said, "Goodbye, Belinda." She looked at me and nodded.

As I was walking past the living room to leave, I stopped. I don't know why. I didn't want to say goodbye to anyone. I didn't want to be there and was glad to be leaving. I hated her, and I hated Dan, but I stopped anyway. Everyone's heads were down. No one acknowledged me at all, except for Colleen.

"Get your ass out of my house."

I don't know what I was expecting, but those words hurt. Her remark did not surprise me. I almost cried, but I didn't. I got into my Dad's car and looked through the windshield down the driveway. I could feel my Dad looking at me.

"It's okay, Steven," he said.

I just nodded.

"You ready?"

"Yes."

"Let's go home. We'll stop and get something to eat on the turnpike."

"Okay."

As we pulled out of the driveway, I felt like I wanted to cry. I quickly buried that feeling and thought of a dream that had just come true for me. The dream of no more beatings or being talked down to. No more being grounded in my room for months on end. No more having to walk on eggshells. No more not feeling loved. The dream of going to live with my Dad had come true! I leaned my head back against the headrest and tried to understand Colleen. One day I will come back here and put the fear of God into the deepest part of her soul. I would mess with her mind like she messed with mine. One day I was going to come back and take her life.

"I thank God, in whom I don't believe that I have lived to this hour when I can express all the evil in my heart."
Reverend Richard Wurnbrand
(Tortured For Christ)

I was a very sad, angry, confused, heartbroken, tormented child, who didn't think there was a God to believe in.

I quickly pushed all those negative thoughts away from my mind and filed them nice and neat into my memory file. I thought of better days to come. I thought of peace. I thought of sleep and passed out before we were even five miles away.

-Psalm 55:18-
He has redeemed my soul in peace from the battle
that was against me, for there were many against me.
(NKJV)

"Steven, are you hungry?"

I opened my eyes to see we were at a Burger King on the Massachusetts Turnpike.

"Yes," I said.

We got out of the car and went in to get some dinner. As we sat down to eat, my Dad was asking me questions about what was going on in that house with Colleen and Dan. He wanted to know, in more detail, what had been happening. I really didn't want to talk about that now. I was tired, and the last thing I was trying to do was to relive a life I was trying my hardest to walk away from. I wasn't mad at him for wanting to know more; I just think my mind was physically beat down. I tried not to get into too much detail, but I did answer him. Unlike the conversation I had with him the night before, I was more candid about everything. More open. I told him in more detail about the beatings I received.

I remember the look on his face. He wasn't crying, but his eyes were moist. He looked extremely upset. I would be too if I ever found out that one of my kids had been getting treated that way. Then he asked the million-dollar question, "How come you never told me about any of this before, Steven?"

That was a tough question. It's a really easy answer, but a tough question. I didn't want him to think I didn't trust him. I didn't tell him, because I didn't want to hear anything like, "Hang in there, Steven."

"It will be ok." Or…

"I just can't take you to come live with me right now."

I did not want to be let down by the one person I loved most in the world. I knew he had his family in Boston. I knew he was busy, and I didn't want to feel like I didn't matter and be turned down again. What if I did tell him and the response I got was exactly what I thought it would be, and Colleen found out? I was scared of what would have happened next, so to keep that from happening, I just never said anything.

"I don't know," I said.

He stared at me for a long moment and continued to eat. What was there to say, really? We finished up, got back into the car, and continued to drive home. I fell asleep again not long after we had dinner and woke up at my new home in Medford, Massachusetts.

We left my things in the car and went inside. The house was dark, and no one was up. Jeannie had the couch made up for me with a note on the pillow. I'll never forget the words on her note to me. It said, "Steven, welcome home. I'm glad you're here. Love, Jeannie."

(Just so you all don't get confused, the woman my Dad married, Jeannie, is obviously my stepmother, but I refer to her as my mother. I have for over thirty years. My biological mother, I refer to as just Colleen. It's not to be disrespectful; it's just the way it is. It's what I feel inside. Jeannie is my mother. She has treated me like her own. She is the only loving mother figure I've ever had in my life.)

My Dad went to bed as I lay on the couch for what seemed like forever. This really is for real, I remember thinking. I thought about pushing everything that ever happened in my life up until this point completely out of my mind forever. Things happen, I told myself, and I'm no different than anyone else. As I lay there thinking, the feeling of peace I had disappeared. I began to wonder and worry about what this new life would entail. Everything up to this point in my life was rotten.

Would I make friends?

Would I continue to get picked on?

Would I be accepted?

Would my life change?

Would everything remain the same?

-Haggai 1:9-
"You looked for much, but indeed it came to little; and when you brought
it home, I blew it away. Why?" says the LORD of hosts.
"Because of
My house that is in ruins, while every one of you runs to his
own house.
(NKJV)

I'm trying to rebuild this temple that I live in called my life and body. I have actually been trying to build it for the last seven years, and I'm just starting to understand what the problem has been all this time. My mind, body, and soul all need a fresh start, but sometimes it's so easy for me to just sit there and dwell on the negative things, and when I do that, my mind will start to run wild. I do not think that everything in my life was entirely my fault, but the second I start to point out what's not my fault, it starts to become me just not taking responsibility for the things I've done. It's not that I can't think about the hurt I have inside; I just need to focus on what it is I need to change in me before I move on to the next situation that needs to be dealt with.

The enemy wants to steal my testimony away. Sabrina said that to me years ago. He doesn't want me to tell you what Jesus has done for me or how He has changed certain parts of my life. He is working in me now and trying to change things, and the enemy will stop at nothing to prevent this.

What I need to do is build this temple up that God has given me. I do that by living my life in a way that will allow God to build it back up Himself! That's how I build it, by letting Him do it.

The Christian band, Casting Crowns, has this song, "Courageous," and in the song they have a verse that goes like this, "The only way we'll ever stand, is on our knees with lifted hands. We were made to be courageous."

I absolutely love that line, and it's so true. Even in times like this right now in my life, I go through these periods where I'm so high on the LORD that I feel invincible. But this morning, as I sat down to write, I got into a fight with Sabrina on the phone about something stupid. I feel that God is just so far away from me. It feels like He doesn't even care about what I'm going through. That feeling like He doesn't care is just so strong. It feels real, and it sucks! I hate that feeling, and the enemy would just love for me to hold on to that.

I want to stand up for Christ, but the only way I'll ever stand is on my knees with lifted hands. I was made to be courageous.

Another thing that's tough to take sometimes is when it feels like everything I read in my Bible seems to be talking about destruction. What makes it worse is that I really feel like that's where God is taking me. It's just so hard to deal with sometimes.

If only I were stronger!

If only I were different!

If only I were smarter!

If only I was never born!

That's what I feel like sometimes, as if I were never born and didn't have to deal with this life, but that's negative thinking. I'm here, and I have to live this life, so I need to make the best of it, and for me to make the best of it, I need Jesus Christ.

"It ain't those parts of the Bible that I can't understand that bother me, it is the parts that I do understand."
(Mark Twain)

God loves me. He loves you, too! He wants me to always think of and remember all the love that's in the Bible. Included in His love for me in the Bible is all the destruction that happens to those who walk away from Him and dishonor Him. When all else fails, He wants me to remember that my Bible is His love letter to me. He wants me to believe it in my heart and hold onto it for dear life.

-Psalm 107:17-
"Fools, because of their transgression,
and because of their iniquities, were afflicted.
<u>*(NKJV)*</u>

This is where I began to beat up on my own life. Could it have been because this is what I had learned to do for so many years? You just cannot blame what has happened to you in the past and use that to justify why you act this way now.

I didn't know what real love was; it was foreign to me. I was a lot more comfortable in the pain I created for myself. It was familiar, and I knew what to expect. When you tried to love me, I just pushed you away. I didn't understand it. It just didn't seem normal to me.

-Luke 22:31-
"...Simon, Simon! Indeed, Satan has
asked for you, that he may sift you as wheat."
<u>*(NKJV)*</u>

I have wondered many times in the past, at what point did satan ask God to sift me like wheat. I believe God allowed satan to sift me as wheat for a season, then to leave me alone, to sift me again, then leave me alone again.

141

-2 Timothy 2:9-
for which I suffer trouble as an evildoer, even to the
point of chains; but the word of God is not chained.
<u>*(NKJV)*</u>

It matters not what I go through or how many times I fall. It matters only that I get back up, undefeated, unwilling to surrender to the enemy. His word will not fail, and no matter what, whatever He has decreed for my life, it will come to pass.

It felt good to be somewhere I wasn't hated or despised. I could tell that Jeannie was uncertain about me. I don't think it was because she didn't want me there; I believe it was because she didn't want me there under those circumstances. They had received plenty of phone calls in the past about my behavior. To say that she was apprehensive was an understatement. Nevertheless, she welcomed me into her home with open arms. I was not her biological child. It's tough to have the same kind of love for any child that you have for you own, but she still loved me.

We lived in the bottom apartment of a duplex that Jeannie's Grandmother owned. It was a two bedroom. My parents had one bedroom, and my sister Natasha and twin brothers, Jarred and Justin, slept in the second bedroom. I am six years older than Natasha and ten years older than Jarred and Justin. I slept in the dining room on a fold out bed. It wasn't the best arrangement, but it was home. It was comfortable. I'm not exactly sure how long we lived like that. My parents bought the house right next door, but my dad, being Mr. Carpenter in his free time, would make it a while before we could move in.

It was time to go get registered for school. I was a little nervous, so my dad let me relax for a couple of days. To make a long story short, he took me to get registered, and I was all set to start school and would be going to The Roberts Junior High. I was in the seventh grade. I didn't have any friends, so Jeannie set it up for me to walk to the bus stop and to school with another kid who lived across the street. His name was Mark, and boy oh boy, was I in for a messed up first day of school. He met me outside my house one morning, and right away I thought he was a dork. There was just something about him that I just didn't like. He seemed a little weird. Something was off with this kid. I walked to the bus stop with him as we made our way to school. We walked down this street to get to the school, and everyone was just looking at me. They were all giving me dirty looks. I could not for the life of me understand why. I was about to find out.

Mark failed to tell me that the street he took me down was the street that only the "eighth graders" were allowed to walk down. Really? I thought it was kind of pathetic, and come to find out, when you're in the "seventh grade," you can get beat up for walking down the wrong street. I didn't care though. I felt like it was starting all over again. But hang on, there's more fun to the story. The best part was about to happen. I went to my homeroom and was introduced as Steve, the new kid. Not all that bad I guess, but I continued to feel the looks from everyone.

I tried my hardest to mind my own business and make it through all my classes. Lunchtime came, and I didn't know where to sit, so I found a spot all by myself and tried to eat my lunch. The lunchroom cleared out and we went outside to recess. This is where the best part happened.

I'm standing all by myself, minding my own business, when I was invited to come and hang out with a bunch of other kids. Cool, or so I thought. Then it happened.

"You're the new kid, Steve, right?"

"Yeah, I just moved here."

"Yeah, we know. You're the new kid from down over on Fourth St., right? You just moved here, and you walked down the eighth grade street this morning with Mark. Are you gay, too?"

Here we go again!

"What? I'm not gay!" I said.

"Yes you are. You're a fag, and you better not walk down our street again, or you're going to get your butt kicked. You need to walk down the seventh grade street."

I looked around and walked away. That was my first day at my new school. I knew there was something funny about that kid Mark. It was also true: Mark was openly gay at school and grew up to be a very gay man indeed. When I got home from school that day, Jeannie asked me how my first day went.

"It was okay," I said. "Mark is gay, so everyone thinks I'm gay now too. And he took me down the eighth grade street, so a few of the other guys want to beat me up now."

"What are talking about? Mark isn't gay, Steven. I know his mother. And what do you mean, 'The eighth grade street?' "

I explained to her what the deal was. I'm not sure if she believed me or not, but it was the truth. I tried to tell her that Mark was indeed very gay, but that she just would not believe.

The next day, I did not want the company of Mark, so I left before he had a chance to meet me outside. I got off the bus near the school and decided to walk down the eighth grade street again by myself and did it with a rather large chip on my shoulder. I was trying to make a statement. I didn't want to get pushed around anymore. I wanted to make a point by standing up for myself and to show the other kids I was not scared and that I wasn't going to be messed with. I was going to show them I was not a punk.

Later, I would figure out it was a really stupid move on my part, but for now it made me a few friends in my class, and you guessed it, they were the wrong friends. There was Mike, Jeremy, Dave, and Doug, and they were just like me. We were all a year older than everyone else in the seventh grade, because we had all failed one grade or another. We were the rejects who didn't care about school. We tried to act as though we were cool and everyone else were the losers. So naturally, we bonded.

-John 11:54-
Therefore Jesus no longer walked openly among the Jews,
but went from there into the country near the wilderness, to a
city called Ephraim, and there remained with His disciples.
(NKJV)

God is a gentleman. He will not stay where He is not wanted. He cannot live amongst sin or dwell in the middle of it. He can tug at my heart and call out to me, but if I choose to reject Him, although He doesn't like it, He will respect it. Don't get me wrong, there are those times when He needs to do something drastic in our lives, and no matter how hard we may try to fight it, whether we like it or not, it's going to happen. For the most part, though, if we choose to ignore Him, He will retreat until we recognize we need Him and ask Him to come into our lives. He accepts our decision to walk away from Him. He doesn't want to control us. He doesn't want slaves. He wants us to choose Him freely. What fun would it really be for Him to make us love Him? Have you ever tried to make someone love you? Have you ever tried to make someone choose you? It doesn't work. He wants you to choose to love Him on your own.

"How could a good God allow so much evil, pain, and suffering – or does He simply not care?"

Mark Mittelberg
(The Questions Christians Hope No One Will Ask)

I'm in the middle of reading the above-named book right now for a ministry that my mentor, Pastor Jeff Chaves, is doing. I'm in his Bible study and ministry called The Gospel Strike Force. We're reading this book and are training to go out to try to win souls for Christ. At the very least, we are hoping to plant seeds. Pastor Jeff is trying to prep us for the questions that we might get asked when we actually go out to minister. We all have the choice to make decisions. It's in making these decisions that affect people's lives. I cannot explain, nor do I have an answer for:

the woman who gets raped.

the child who gets molested.

the kid who gets beat.

the child who is neglected.

the little one who gets force fed food that will make him puke.

the family that gets killed.

-Habakkuk 1:3-
Why do You show me iniquity, and cause me to see trouble? For plundering and violence are before me; there is strife, and contention arises.
(NKJV)

I did okay in my new school for a little while. I went to school every day and even did my homework. I tried to pay attention and do what was asked of me. I got a paper route delivering the

Boston Globe and had four streets to deliver to. It made me feel like I was worth something. I can honestly say that I tried really hard, but trouble was lurking its ugly head just around the corner. I was hanging out more and more with Mike, Jeremy, Dave, and Doug, who all lived in the Riverside Projects. There was always something going on there that I should not have been involved in. We would all just hang out, drink, smoke, and cause trouble.

I was at the bus stop one day and got into it with one of the other kids. I wasn't going to get punked out or pushed around any longer. It wasn't like I got picked on non-stop, but I did get messed with a little. I hung out with my four friends, and they never messed with us as a group.

I'm at the bus stop waiting for my bus, and this kid, Donald Skoog, and I had some words back and forth. He kept calling me a faggot, looser, and punk. He kept telling me that he was popular, that no one liked me, how he could get someone to kick the crap out of me, and that I had better be watching my back. There were a bunch of us at the bus stop, and all the other kids were laughing at me because of all the things he was saying. They all thought it was amusing. I'm sure it was to them, but inside, I had started to boil with rage. I remember thinking that I wasn't going to let this happen again. I'm not going to be the kid who is the focal point of ridicule and the one that gets messed with all the time because he never does anything about it. While everyone laughed at me, and Donald kept messing with me, a large evil smile crept into my soul. Donald didn't have all his friends at the bus stop with him either, and it was time to make my point. It was now time for me to stand up for myself while I was alone and by myself. I was scared, but there was also an excitement and a thrill. Donald was sitting on the curb, which I realized was a defenseless position. I simply walked over to him and said, "Oh yeah?" Bang! I punched him in his head.

"Hey man. What the hell?" he said.

Bang! I punched him in the face again.

"Get up Don!" I yelled.

He just looked at me through red eyes. He didn't cry, but I could tell he wanted to come after me, but he never got up. What he did say was, "That's okay. You're going to get your butt kicked tomorrow!"

Bang! I punched him a third time.

"You can't fight your own battles? Come on, Don! Get up!"

"You'll see. I'll get my friends, and tomorrow you're dead meat."

Bang! I punched him a fourth time. I looked around, and not one of the others came after me. They were all shocked that I just hit one of the more popular kids in school. Donald never got up from the curb. I knew he had friends, and his friends were willing to protect him, but I didn't care. I just walked away from him and waited on the bus to show up. I felt tough. I felt strong.

-Titus 1:15-
To the pure all things are pure, but to those who
are defiled and unbelieving nothing is pure;

but even their mind and conscience are defiled.
(NKJV)

That night, before I went to bed, I got out my folding knife and put it in my backpack to take to school the next day. I wasn't sure if anything was going to happen, but I wanted to be ready. The next morning at the bus stop, no one talked to me. I kept my hands in my pockets with my right hand wrapped securely around my knife, just in case. I got to school and right away; I knew there was going to be trouble. I was getting dirty looks from everyone. My friend Mike said, "Dude, I heard that you hit Donald yesterday at the bus stop. They said that it was a cheap shot. He said that Brandon and Mike are going to kill you after school."

"I can handle it." I didn't tell Mike I brought my knife.

Sure enough, word was all over school that I was going to catch a beating after school. Everyone said I was a loser and couldn't fight fair, because I was a punk. My stomach was in knots that day as I went from class to class. I was picked on, ridiculed, and laughed at.

One of Donald's bigger friends, Mike, caught up with me at my locker. He tried staring me down, but that was just not going to work. I held his stare, and he realized he wasn't going to intimidate me very easily, so he said in a loud voice, "You're a punk! You can't fight fair, can you?"

"No, I can't fight fair at all."

"I'm going to kick your butt after school. What do you think about that?"

"Cool. I haven't had my butt kicked in a while."

"You think this is funny?" Mike continued.

"Yes," I said smiling, but I was terrified inside.

"Go ahead; keep laughing, and I'll kick your butt right now."

"No you won't. We're in school."

His face was beet red while my hands were in my pockets. I was trying to look relaxed while my hand was around my knife.

"I'll see you after school," he said and walked away.

"Okay, fat boy," I replied.

He turned to look at me again but kept walking away. My friend Mike was there and came up to me smiling.

"Man, you sure were cocky with him. You sure you don't want us to help you out? I think he's serious."

"No, it's cool. I can handle it."

"Okay, but we're going to be there too in case anyone tries to jump in." Ah, Mike was always faithful. He liked trouble as much as I did and was willing to stand by and make sure no one else jumped in. Mike liked to fight. It was nice to have him as a friend. What more could a kid ask for? I still just wanted to do this on my own. I knew I couldn't be a wimp forever. I would at least make the effort to try.

The day finally ended, and it was time to go home. Without exaggerating, I'd have to say that there were at least fifty to sixty kids waiting for me to get my butt kicked. Donald was there, yelling like a little Chihuahua that barked his head off behind the bigger dogs, because he knew he was a punk and couldn't fight on his own. That little dog that nips at you when you're not looking, but when you turn around, it runs away and only seems to stand strong when the Pitbulls are in front of him.

"I told you that you were going to get your butt kicked!" Donald said.

"Okay."

Then Brandon chimed in, "You better watch yourself. Mike's here to kick your butt."

"Up yours, Brandon."

"You don't know who you're messing with. I'm going to kill you. What do you think about that?" Mike said.

I just smiled at him and said, "I don't know yet; let me think about it."

That did it, and he came after me. As he ran at me, all I did was take one step forward and kicked him in his stomach as hard as I could, and he wobbled back a few steps. I couldn't believe it!

"Kick his butt, Mike!" someone yelled.

He ran at me again, and I kicked him again as hard as I could, and he fell backwards again. He didn't fall down, but I could tell that he was actually hurt. Then Brandon started to come at me but then stopped. I turned around to see the few friends I had were standing there, ready to jump on Brandon or Donald if they decided to come at me. Brandon thought about it and stepped back. My friend Mike said, "What's the matter, Brandon? You can't let Mike fight his own battles?"

"Go ahead; come at me again, and I'm going friggin stab you right here," I said as I now had my knife out and pointed in their direction.

"You're a freaking psycho!" Mike said.

"No, I'm not. I'm just messed up in the head."

Not one word was spoken by anyone in the park.

-Job 19:10-12-
He breaks me on every side, and I am gone; my hope He has uprooted like a tree. He
has also kindled His wrath against me, and He counts me as one of His enemies. His
troops come together and build up their road against me; they encamp all around my tent.
(NKJV)

It sure feels like that sometimes, like the LORD Himself is against me. At times I feel like everywhere I turn, even when I'm trying to do well, He is there trying to break me down. Sometimes I feel like I am His enemy. I never know for sure when the LORD is getting ready to break me down again. I need to be ready. The enemy loves to tell me that I can only ever be an enemy to God. I have surely been that in the past, but I also know for certain that if I'm praying with an honest heart, diligently seeking His counsel through His word, trying my hardest to be led by Him, then I cannot be His enemy. Sometimes, for me, it's just good to be still as the Bible says, take a break from life and really try to listen to what God is telling me.

When I'm on fire for the Lord, I can get so caught up in doing "Godly" things that I get lost in the moment of trying to serve Him, because I'm too busy trying to serve the idea of serving Him. Right now, I'm loaded down in life and am extremely busy. I go to church on Sundays and play bass guitar on the worship team at The Las Vegas Rescue Mission for two services on Sunday nights. I also go to counseling. I am on an outreach team called The Gospel Strike Force that meets twice a week, and I have band practice two to three times a week. I am also in a Christian rock band, and we play five to six times a month at different locations. I get up at two in the morning to read my Bible, pray, and spend time with The Lord. I try to continue to write this book, spend time with my kids when Sabrina lets me, try to be involved in whatever outreach that my church may be doing, and looking for a job. And to top it all off, everywhere I go, I have to take a bus. When you live in a desert like Las Vegas, one hundred twenty degrees takes its toll on you. Right now, there is no way I would be able to do this much and have a job, and a job is something I need.

The Lord spoke to my heart and told me to quit my band. I was adding up the hours that I spent traveling to band practice, and it totals almost thirty-six hours a week. This does not include our actual playtime during gigs. When all is said and done, I spend about one hundred thirty hours a month with my band; now it's time to quit. We have three shows next week, and I am dropping out after the last one. Now add on top of all that everything I listed above plus the stress and arguing that comes with a divorce.

I believe that inside of every person, given the right circumstances, is an explosion for Christ. I get scared at times at what the cost may be in doing that. I'm tired of the enemy having a foothold in my life. Trying to write this book, in itself, has the enemy very involved in my life. I can only pray that the LORD gives me the strength and courage to press on no matter what.

My goal is to put this book into the hands of twenty-five million people. Then I want to make a DVD of my testimony at a large church. After that, I would like to go on a testimony tour across the United States to start, and then maybe tour abroad, touring churches and rehabs, testifying as to the work that Jesus has done in my life.

What kind of man would I be if I showed my kids I'm a failure, that I didn't trust in The LORD enough to persevere, that I didn't trust in Christ enough to trust Him with my life, that I didn't trust Him, period? It's time to break this generational curse that's been passed down in my family because no one ever trusted in Christ.

It's all about Jesus!

All the time!

I want all my children to trust in God with all their hearts and know that they can go to Him with anything, and know that He can and will move in their lives! If I have to sacrifice my own life in the process to get that point across to my kids, then that is exactly what I will do. My desire is to have my children, and everyone in the world, experience a loving relationship with Christ. That's the only thing that matters in life. That's the most important thing there is.

"I like your Christ, I do not like your Christians. Your Christians are so unlike your Christ."
(Gandhi)

That is a very strong statement. The sad part is that it's so very true also. That is exactly how I do not want to be perceived by anyone, much less my children. I want to grab hold of Christ and never let go. I do not want to be one of "those" Christians. You know, the one who claims to be a walking, talking Christian but doesn't have one ounce of Christ in him. I don't want to be the kind of person who people look at and say, "If that's what believing in Christ is about, then I want nothing to do with it."

-Job 20:16-
He will suck the poison of cobras;
the vipers tongue will slay him.
(NKJV)

I read this verse yesterday morning and was taken aback by it. I really sat and meditated on it for a while and let it sink into my heart. That's what I'm doing when I'm not listening to the LORD: sucking

156

the poison of cobras, enjoying the evil that's surrounding me.

The only thing the situation with pulling the knife at school did for me was give me a false sense of safety and security, along with a rotten attitude that was tough to match, a cockiness that grew by the day, and a chip on my shoulder that was so large I felt my life was bulletproof.

Things were becoming stressed in our house. There just wasn't enough room for all of us, and sleeping on a fold out bed was getting old. Jeannie's grandmother, Nonie, would spend the days downstairs with us and babysit us at night when Jeannie was working. My dad worked a lot and was usually in his room sleeping. Nonie was very old. She was in her eighties and had to not only babysit four kids but had to deal with me as well.

Well, it wasn't long until we moved into our new house next door. Believe it or not, this place was smaller than the other house, but my parents worked hard and made it work. It was only a two bedroom, so my dad had to build a wall to close off the living room, thus making the dining room their master bedroom. It was nifty, actually. My dad, as it turned out, is one heck of a carpenter. Even someone who makes their living doing carpentry would be impressed with my dad's work.

I always felt like Jeannie's family didn't like me very much. I really don't know how much of that was just my self-esteem issues, or if they just really didn't want me there. They were a real family. I was attracted to the love I saw them all give each other. I was always referred to only as Steve's son, and it began to hurt. To them, I became a headache that just wouldn't go away.

There were some kids at school who were upset I got the better of Mike S. and his friends at the park. What happened made me a little popular with the friends I hung around with and drew some revengeful looks and attitudes from those I was not friends with. I was told that this kid Russell was going to kick my butt now. He was in the eighth grade and voted most popular kid in school two years in a row. He had many friends and was what all the other kids considered cool. He had been in a few fights and always won. A deal was made that we would meet up with each other at the same park down the street around eight o'clock that Friday night. He agreed he would not allow any of his friends to jump in, no matter what the outcome was, as long as I agreed not to bring a knife. It sounded fair, so I agreed. I had zero intention of not bringing my knife, and I would use if I were to get my butt kicked.

We met up at the park that Friday night. My friends and I got there a little early, and to our surprise, Russell and his entourage were not there yet. I was scared, but I did a good job of hiding it. We were not there very long when Russell and his group of friends were walking up the street to meet us. There were a large number of people with him. What I remember the most about it was that fact that there were more girls with him than anything else. I remember thinking two things. One was that this is going to suck. I'm going to get the crap kicked out of me; then I'm going to have to stab him. The second thing was that I have to get the crap kicked out of me in front of all these girls. Well, everyone takes a beating sometimes. I'd been beat plenty of times before by Colleen and Dan so that getting a butt ripping by an eighth grader didn't faze me all that much.

We met up in a circle again, and as before, there was a crowd. I wore glasses and didn't want my eyes to get cut from my broken glasses, so I handed them over to my friend Mike. Then all the crap talking started from Russell's side. I was warned that if I took my knife out, then all bets were off and they could all jump in. I agreed.

Russell and I began to dance around a little bit. I didn't have my glasses on, but from what I could see, he looked pretty pissed. Then it happened. BANG! Right in the side of my face! I felt the blow but didn't feel any pain. I stumbled back a few steps and opened my eyes so I could see the next punch coming. To my own surprise, I didn't fall down.

"We told you you were going to get your butt kicked!"

"Ha, ha, ha!"

"You're a freaking loser!"

Russell did a very stupid thing. He waited a few moments before coming at me again. That gave me the second I needed to get my bearings straight. I was leaning back with my fists up. He came at me again, and I saw him starting to take a swing. I closed my eyes, took a step forward, and took the biggest swing I could possibly take. BANG! I connected, and connected HARD! I kept my eyes closed for a split second, because I didn't know if I was going to get hit too. When I opened my eyes, Russell was laying on the ground holding his face. I did not give him the chance he gave me at all. I leaned over him and punched two more times in the side of his head before I backed off. All his friends just looked at me in complete disbelief. He started to get back to his feet, so I went at him again with every intention of punching him another time or two, but he took off running. I took off running behind him as he ran across the Fellsway, which is a really busy street in Medford. Across the street there was a bus at the bus stop, and he tried to get on. I pulled him off the bus by his shirt and punched him a few more times, be he got loose and ran off. I was pumped with adrenaline and couldn't believe what just happened. I started to walk over to the park and saw my friends walking towards me with my friend Mike leading the way with a big smile on his face.

"Good job, psycho," Mike said to me.

"Where did everybody go?" I asked.

"They all left."

I started to feel the knot swell up on the side of my head from the punch I took. Not much else was said. We all just walked home, and that was the end of that. That was the last time I had to fight at school. No one messed with me anymore.

-Psalm 25:7-

> *Do not remember the sins of my youth, nor my*
> *transgressions; according to Your mercy*
> *remember me, for Your goodness' sake, O LORD.*
> *(NKJV)*

You know, it's crazy, because as I write this, I think of all that God has done for me. I think about His mercy. I think about His love for me. I think about His compassion. I think about His forgiveness, in which He is so faithful to daily give me. He never stops forgiving and loving, never. He is true and faithful, even when I'm not and don't deserve it.

I hung around with my friends at the Riverside Projects in Medford all the time. My parents didn't want me hanging out there. I tried to tell them the projects were just fine, that no trouble ever happened, but they knew better. There was all kinds of trouble to get into there, and my friends and I relished every opportunity.

It was around this time that I found out that my parents had a bunch of money hidden in their bedroom. The money wasn't theirs though. They ran a bowling league in Malden called The Rowdy Bowling League. They still do to this day. I stole a lot of money out of that bowling league, and I'm talking about thousands of dollars. At first, I would steal twenties and fifties. I always had at least a couple of hundred dollars on me at all times. I would go out all the time. I would go to the movies, travel to Boston, go out to eat, and even go bowling at the same bowling alley in Malden. It became a drug to me. I loved the thrill. I knew full well that I couldn't steal the amount I was stealing and not get caught. I was out to have as much fun as I could until I did get caught. I didn't really care who I hurt. I was addicted to the money and stealing so bad that I couldn't stop. At one point I stole exactly one thousand dollars, all in hundred dollar bills, because I wanted to buy a guitar. Mike played the piano, and his brother, Joe, played guitar. I remember showing the money to my friends at school the next day. They were amazed at the guts I had to be stealing that kind of money from my parents.

After school that day, Mike and I went to a music store in Medford and looked around for a guitar. I wound up buying a twelve string accoustical electric Washburn guitar along with a small Gorilla amplifier. The total cost was about seven hundred dollars. I paid for the guitar and walked back to Mike's house. I couldn't bring it to my house, so Joe said he would keep it for a while.

About a week later was when the crap hit the fan. I was babysitting my two cousins, Nichole and Marissa, for my Uncle Joe. He let me watch them a couple times a week for a few bucks. Well, I was starting to get nervous because I had not received the phone call yet from the music store telling me that my guitar case was in yet. While I was watching my cousins, I called the music store and asked the guy if my guitar case was in yet.

"Yes it is. We actually just called and left a message for you to come and pick it up."

"Who did you leave a message with?" I asked.

"I left a message with your dad, I think. He sounded a little surprised."

I must have paused for what seemed like an eternity.

"Okay, thanks" I said.

I didn't know what to do. I didn't want to go home, that's for sure.

Well, of course Joe came home and took me home. When he dropped me off at my house, I went up the stairs and acted as if I was going inside. I waited for Joe to pull away, then I took off. I never went into the house. I was too scared to go home, so I ran away. I went to the projects to see if I could stay at one of my friend's houses, but none of their parents said I could stay the night.

Mike's dad had a van that he parked next to one of the buildings, and he usually left it unlocked. When I got to the van, it was unlocked. Boy, was I was happy. I was scared that I might actually have to sleep outside in the rain, but I got to sleep in the van that night. I woke up to the sound of the van starting up the next morning. Mike had an older sister who drove the van in the mornings, and because it was cold outside, she had to start it up to let it run for a few minutes to warm it up. While it warmed up, she went back into the house. This was good, because it gave me the chance I needed to get out of the van. I hurried as fast as I could and got out of the van and went and waited for Mike and Dave where I usually met up with them before school. Like clockwork, he came out not long after. As we walked over to meet up with the others, he said to me, "Dude, you're in big trouble. Your dad called here last night and talked to my dad. He said that you never came home last night. He knows that you were here, asking if you could sleep over. He talked to my dad for a while. He knows about the guitar, and your dad is coming over here today to pick it up. What happened?"

I told him all about how he found out and about me running away after Joe dropped me off the night before.

"Where did you stay last night?"

"I couldn't find anywhere to sleep, so I slept in the back of your dad's van. It was unlocked, so I slept in the back of it. Is that okay?"

"Yeah, I guess so. Just don't get caught. My dad told me to tell you that I can't hang out with you anymore."

"Okay. Are you going to listen to him?"

"Not really. I'll hang out with you, but you can't come over my house anymore."

"Okay."

"What are you going to do?"

"I don't know."

We met up with the others and walked to school. In the middle of the day, I was called to the principal's office and was told that my dad was coming to pick me up. They wanted to know if anything was wrong. My dad told them that I ran away from home the night before and never came back. I didn't tell them anything. I just kept my head down. I wound up running away from the school while I was waiting on my dad.

When I got to a friend's house, I told him what was up and he told his mom the truth of what was happening. To my surprise, she said that I could stay there and asked me if I would like to take a shower and put on some clean clothes, to all of which I gratefully accepted. I was tired, dirty, and just wanted to relax. While I was in the shower, my friend knocked on the door and poked his head in.

"Dude, my mom called the cops. They're downstairs waiting for you to come down after you're done showering."

"Really?"

"Yeah. Sorry, Steve."

"That's okay," I said.

What else could I really say? They lived on the second floor, and the only way out was if I jumped out of a two-story window. Even I wasn't that stupid back than, yet. I finished up and went downstairs to find two cops waiting for me.

"Steven Gray?" they asked.

"Yes."

"Come on with us. We are going to take you home, okay?"

"Okay," I didn't know what else to say.

"Sorry, Steven. I know your parents must be worried about you. I had to call the cops," Dave's mother said.

"Yeah, thanks."

"It'll be okay. Just go home and hang in there. It can't be that bad."

165

They put me in the back of one of the cars and took me home. When we got there, my dad was waiting for me. He thanked the cops and told me to get upstairs. For the first time in my life, my dad looked like he wanted to hit me.

"Didn't Joe drop you off last night?" my dad asked.

"Yes."

"Why didn't you come in the house?"

"I don't know."

"Where did you go?"

"I don't know."

"Steven, why did you run away?" Jeannie asked.

"I don't know," I said again.

"Steven, we are going to sit here until you start talking to us. Do you understand me? I don't care if it takes all night. I want some answers," my dad said. He was adamant about it. There was no doubt in my mind that we would, in fact, sit there all night.

"Where did you get the money for the guitar?" he continued.

Silence.

"Where did you get the money for the guitar, Steven?" he asked again.

Silence.

"Steven! Where did you get the money for the guitar? Did you rob someone?"

"No."

"Then where did you get it from?"

"I don't know."

Then my dad got extremely upset and yelled, "Don't freaking lie to me! Where did you get the friggin money for the guitar?!"

I had never in my life been yelled at by my dad like that.

"From the bowling league money," I said.

"What?!" Jeannie said, looking horrified.

"I took it from the bowling league."

"How did you find the money from the bowling league?"

"I just found it."

"You were looking around in our room?" my dad continued.

"Yes."

"Why were you snooping around in our room?"

What could I say, really? Jeannie put her head down as my dad went into the room to start counting the money. I can't say for sure, but if I had to guess, I would say that I probably took somewhere in the range of three to five thousand dollars altogether.

"How much is missing?" Jeannie asked my dad.

"I don't know for sure, but it looks like a lot."

They were beyond upset. They were so far past the point of being angry that I truly do not think they even knew how to react. It wasn't just them I had stolen from, it was the bowling league that they were responsible for. I had stolen from a group of people I didn't even know. They were heart broken.

Jeannie had had enough of me by this point. A few years later, I found out that my dad had to cash out their life insurance policy to replace the money that I had stolen.

———————

Not long after my Christian band started playing a few gigs, I wrote a song about how I felt about my life. We never did get a chance to put music to it, but here it is:

Just As Job

Why wasn't she barren
My birth
No one shouted for joy

Never nursed
Was cursed
Kicked around & tossed like a toy

My morning star – was dark
My life – a still born child
The infant – no light of day

Living in ruins
Pardon my offense
Now You want me to pray?

Received me?
Not one knee!
Pushed aside
No one cared
Clouds settled over it!
Blackness overwhelmed it!
Darkness seized it!
I claimed it!

Why did I not perish at birth
And die as I came from the womb?
This life
My tomb

Why have you let me down?
Why have you pushed me down?
Why have you thrown me down?
It was cold
And all alone
Not a rock
And never a stone
But through me, God still let His glory be known!

My ingredients:
Bitterness
Shame
Self-will &
Deception

My life
My will
My image of God?
My perception

For it did not shut the doors
Of the womb on me
To hide trouble from my eyes

Why have You made me Your target?
Have I become a burden to You?
Please tell me why!

I'm double minded
Struggling
Rebelling
My intentions
What are they?

Hungry
Angry
Lonely
Tired

These waves are unstable
This is my portion?
Now I'm divided!

Why is my life dry from drought?
Why did you put me out?
Why was I filled with doubt?
It was cold
And all alone
Not a rock
And never a stone
But through me, God still let His glory be shown!

Submitting
Surrendering
Resisting the devil
Teach me not to stumble

Expecting less than what I think I deserve
Crawling To God
That's my definition of humble

Always my Rock
Never a stone
Crawling To God
Let Your Glory Be Shown!

-Joel 2:9-
They run to and fro in the city, they run
on the wall; they climb into the houses,
they enter at the windows like a thief.
(NKJV)

How my parents hung in as long as they did, I have no clue. It probably had something to do with Jeannie's prayers. My dad has never believed in Jesus Christ, at least not up to this point in my writing this book. Jeannie's a different story; she very much believes that Jesus died for her sins, and I know she prays, a lot.

I continued to do what I was doing. I was grounded, but that didn't stop me from hanging around with my friends and getting into trouble. When my parents weren't home, I wasn't allowed in the house. They bought a safe to keep all the bowling money in, and I was watched at all times.

One time, Jeannie took my twin brothers, Jarred and Justin, to the store for a slushy. As soon as she was out of sight, I kicked in the basement window and ran upstairs to try to find the money. I went to the filing cabinet and used a hammer to open it. BINGO! In one of the folders was one hundred dollars. I took it and ran out of the house. I walked as fast as I could down the street in the opposite direction and off to the projects.

It's really funny how the LORD works. Just before I was writing this last page, I came across a verse in the book Judges and couldn't understand why I was dwelling on it.

When I took the grocery money and split, as I was walking to the projects, I remember thinking,

"What am I going to do? I have nowhere to go." I actually said the next words out loud, "God, please help me."

-*Judges 10:14*-
"Go and cry out to the gods you have chosen;
let them deliver you in your time of distress."
<u>*(NKJV)*</u>

I wanted to follow satan and cause as much trouble as I could. Why not just let the god I was following try to deliver me? Instead of seeing the light and realizing how much trouble and out of control my life was becoming, I plunged deeper.

———————

When I got to the projects, my friends and I went out, and I bought two porn videos from a store as well as a gallon of vodka from some older kids in the parking lot. We took the videos to my friend's house to watch them and drank some vodka. We were a bunch of fourteen year old boys, drinking vodka, and watching porn. That's how the enemy decided to deliver me from my troubles that night, with porn and alcohol.

Later that night, I really needed a change of clothes and decided to break into my parents' house to get a bag of things I needed. I thought of the ladder that Paul, Jeannie's brother, was using to put the siding on our house. He lived next door to us, and the ladder was in his backyard. I had the bright idea to try to break into my house at one in the morning to get some clothes. I leaned the ladder up against the house to the window of the room I shared with Jarred and Justin. I tried to be as quiet as I could, because Jeannie was a very light sleeper.

I got up the ladder and into my room with no trouble at all. I even turned on the light and wound up waking my brothers in the process. I packed a small bag with a few things and threw it out the window. I told my brothers to go back to sleep and not to tell anyone that I had come home. I put the ladder back and headed back to the projects to sleep in the back of an empty trailer of an eighteen-wheeler. I was tired of everyone looking at me as if I was the problem. I wanted everyone to feel sorry for me. I wanted them to think I was the victim, not the perpetrator in all this.

What I think about most is how often I have written in here, "I don't care." That sucks. I don't know what else to say to that. It sucks to see I was such a lost child. When I was going through all this, I really thought that I had it all together. I thought that there was nothing wrong with me. My intentions were to make people think I needed help when I really didn't, but I needed a lot of help.

"Unless the Spirit of God is doing the work of conviction, is awakening the dead heart, and generating faith, nothing's going to happen, no matter what you do. And then only the true message of Jesus, connected

*with the work of the Spirit, will produce
salvation."*
John MacArthur
(Hard To Believe)

That is so true. Nothing will happen to change a life unless it's God motivated and Spirit induced. You have to really give into the LORD and allow Him to work in your life. You have to believe that He can make that difference in your life. It's not about me. It's all about Jesus Christ! It has to be, and what He can do to change us from the inside out. God needs to do the work. The Spirit needs to lead us. If we don't allow that to happen, then I believe I am just perverting the Gospel of Christ!

<u>Chapter Six</u>

My parents knew that I wanted out. I think they were just biding their time. Their only job was to protect Natasha, Jarred, and Justin. I say this because there really was no way that they could protect me. I was too out of control and going to do whatever it was I wanted, regardless. I was a loose cannon, and they would have only made things worse for themselves had they tried.

I ran away again for the umpteenth time. I did not want to be there anymore. I wasn't trusted. I had stolen their money, their alcohol, their sanity, and took their trust and flushed it down the toilet. I had broken things and lied so often that neither they, nor I, knew what the truth was anymore. I didn't even have the friends I used to have. We were all troublemakers, but even they thought I was too out of control. Nothing was taboo for me. I wanted to start trouble all the time and stay in trouble. It didn't matter to me. I never cared if we got caught.

One night I ran away and had nowhere to sleep. No one would let me stay at their house, so I slept on one of the front porches of someone's apartment. It was very cold and raining out. I tried to stay dry by scooting as far back against the wall as possible, but it was useless. Eventually I fell asleep. I woke up the next morning, very early, to a police officer.

"Hey buddy, are you ok?" the cop said. He was nice and didn't treat me like a punk.

"Huh?"

"What are you doing here? It's raining out."

"I was just sleeping," I said.

"Is your name Steven Gray?" he asked.

"Yeah."

"What's going on? Your parents are worried about you. They called us last night."

"I don't want to be there anymore."

"Do they hit you?" he asked.

"No. I just don't like it there."

"Okay then. Why don't you get up now. I need you to come with me, okay?"

"Okay."

What was I going to do, tell the cop I was cool right here? I got up, grabbed my bag, and followed the cop to his police car. He put me in the back seat and went to the police station. Once there, I was passed off to another cop who asked me all these questions about my home life. They asked me if I was okay and if I was abused at home at all. How I would have loved to be sitting in front of a cop asking me all those questions when I lived with Colleen. When he was done, he took me to a waiting area and told me to sit still until my dad came to pick me up. I thought about splitting again, but I was in a police station, and all the doors were locked. The cop came back out a few minutes later and told me that my dad was on his way to pick me up. He gave me a

176

piece of paper with a name and number on it. It was
the name of another police officer and his direct line.
He told me that he wanted me to take the night to
think about what I really wanted. If I felt like my
home life was that bad, then he instructed me to call
the police officer on the paper, and he would arrange
a ride for me to get to Social Services.

When my dad picked me up, I couldn't tell if
he was mad or what. He didn't talk at all on the
drive. When we got home, I went directly to my
room and stayed there all day and night. The
following morning, I called the officer, and he sent
another officer over to my house to pick me up and
take me to Social Services.

-Psalm 78:17-
But they sinned even more against Him by
rebelling against the Most High in the wilderness.
(NKJV)

I was under the age of eighteen, and that
meant the state had to take care of me. I knew that
and took full advantage of it. I couldn't keep pulling
the same crap I had been at home any longer. What
little trust there may have been was now long gone. I
wasn't exactly sure what that was, but I needed
something else. I needed somewhere else.

What is not true, however, is to think that
we can ever be totally independent from
God.

-

> *... in the end you are the one who decides*
> *what you will do.*
> **Dr. Charles F. Stanley**
> **(Winning On The Inside)**

The officer asked me if I was sure that I wanted to do this. I knew he didn't want to take me there, but the laws have changed over time, and he had to take me. When a kid says he doesn't want to stay at home anymore, all they have to do is go to Social Services or Child Protective Services and make up a story. At that point, the state is required to care for the child until they are eighteen or placed back with their parents.

I wasn't going to make up a story about my parents hitting or abusing me. I was a bad enough kid and could b.s. my way out of my house into state care without a fabricated story about my parents. Truth be told, I really did love them. I loved them a lot. I just did not know how to understand love. I didn't know how to act when people showed me they cared. Life's experiences had showed me something entirely different.

I got to Social Services, checked in with the front desk, and waited. I waited forever. My name was called and when I went back, I got to sit in another waiting room for another hour. This waiting room, however, was for one person to wait by themselves. It had a two-way mirror, and I was observed from the other side.

Eventually, a woman named Freya Courtney came in to meet with me. She tried to be nice, but it was that fake kind of nice, kind of like I was bothering her, or like I was another numbered file she had to deal with before she went home, or maybe I interrupted her lunch. Freya would be my caseworker for the next few years. She was the one that was in charge of placing me somewhere. I didn't like her. She was very calm, very cool, and very short. There wasn't much to it. It was a very short meeting. Like everyone else, she wanted to know if I was abused at home. When she determined that I was not, she tried to get me to go back home.

"If I have to go back home, I'm going to kill myself."

Off to a hospital I went. I had to wait in the same room, for safety reasons, until my dad came to pick me up and take me to the hospital, but I didn't have to wait for very long. My dad picked me up and took me to some emergency room to talk to a nurse about my suicidal tendencies. I was very timid and shy.

"Would you feel more comfortable talking to me by yourself without your dad sitting right there?" the nurse asked me.

"Yes."

My dad left the room and waited in the another waiting area. She went through all the same questions I had to answer for the cops and Social Services, but this time, I embellished my stories. Almost none of it was true except for the fact that I never lied and said that my parents were treating me bad.

"Did you ever attempt to kill yourself, Steven?" the nurse asked me.

"Yes."

"What happened? How did you try to kill yourself?"

"I tried to jump in front of the Orange Line at the Downtown Crossing."

"What happened?"

"I just don't want to hurt my parents no more." Then I started to cry.

"Well, we're going to try to get you the help you need, okay?"

I stayed silent.

The nurse let me use the bathroom to let me get myself together, and when I came back, she sat me down and told me that I was going to this hospital called Charles River Hospital. It was a psychiatric hospital for troubled kids.

I got there, checked in, and felt a big sigh of relief. Satisfaction filled me as I watched my dad leave and was taken to my room. The hospital was a lock-down unit. It was strange, because some of the others who were there were just like me in the sense we were just acting out, and no one could really tame us. Some of the others, however, were really messed up in the head. I mean that. They had serious mental issues.

There were kids who had flashbacks from when they were molested by their parents. Some of them had MPD; it was nuts. This one girl would flip out from time to time, screaming at the top of her lungs, remembering all the times her father had raped her.

"Daddy, no! Daddy, no! Please, daddy!"

This girl was having flashbacks from when her dad was sexually abusing her as a young girl. My heart went out to her. In her mind, she was taken back in time to when she was in the middle of being fondled and touched by her dad. In her mind, it was happening at that very moment, and there was nothing anyone could do. Another girl was so far out of her mind that some of us jerks would mess with her. Her mind was junk. We would tell her stuff, and she would believe it. I messed with her like this.

"Hey, Suzie, how old did you say you were?" I would start.

"I'm sixteen."

"Wow, really? You look like you're in your sixties. Your face is wrinkled. You're not sixteen. You're an old woman. Go look in the mirror."

"No, I'm not. I'm sixteen," she would say with tears in her eyes.

"No, you're not; you better go look. You're getting older right in front of me, huh guys?"

"Yeah. You're an old woman. What's wrong with you?" some of the other guys would chime in.

"Oh my gosh!" she would scream out, then run to the bathroom to look in the mirror. She would come running out, screaming, crying, and yelling for help for someone stop her from aging. In her mind, she saw herself getting older because we told her she was. Once we told her something bad, telling her the

181

truth wouldn't help. Usually, she would be put in restraints, because she would try to claw at her face. Once medicated, the staff could talk some sense into her, tell her the truth, and she would be okay.

This next part is a complete trip. Some kids had Multiple Personality Disorder, MPD. Now this was something not even I thought was funny. Some of these kids were so messed up from being abused that they had these altered personalities that came out from time to time. Let's say I was talking to someone named Jennifer. Well, in the middle of talking to her, this other "person" would come out. This person had a different name, and sometimes, a different way of talking. To look at her, it was still Jennifer, but the mind told her it was someone different. They were almost always violent, and when I say violent, I mean violent. Their personalities were either violent or sexual. It was crazy. Some had more than one personality that would come out at different times. There wasn't much anyone could do about it. This was my home now. I was happy to be around other kids who were just as bad as I was. I was comfortable here.

-Ephesians 2:3-
among whom also we all once conducted ourselves
in the lusts of our flesh, fulfilling the desires of the
flesh and of the mind, and were by nature children of
wrath, just as the others.
(NKJV)

Lust had come on me hard, and I loved it. I never looked at a girl without thinking about what she looked like naked, wondering what it would be like to have sex with her. When talking to any female, I never hesitated to look them up and down. I was going to look at whatever I wanted to look at, for as long as I wanted to look.

When I first got there, there was this girl, Robin, who liked me and would kiss me whenever staff wasn't around. Robin was the first girl who kissed me like an adult. She said she wanted to show me how to become a better kisser. It wasn't long before Robin got transferred to another hospital, and when she did, this other girl came in, and I noticed she kept looking at me. I was a boy, so I was just happy to be getting any kind of attention from anyone of the opposite sex. I was young and horny, simple as that.

One day she went off on the staff, and we were sent to our rooms while they tried to put her in restraints. She had taught me a thing or two, and just the sound of her voice while she yelled, screamed, and tried to fight the staff, set me off too. I came out of my room, grabbed a chair, and threw it at the staff member holding her down. They were surprised to see me and didn't see the chair coming until it was too late. They had two kids going off at the same time now. I hit one of them with the chair, and it bounced off him and hit a window. After the initial shock, two of them started to come after me to put me in restraints, so I threw more chairs, our food plates that had just come from the kitchen, and started yelling, "Leave her alone, you! Try coming after me!"

And they did. It didn't take very long for them to subdue me, put me in restraints, medicate me, and leave me in a padded room for a few hours. When I woke up, they told me my things were already packed. They were moving me to a different part of the hospital. I was bummed out, but only until I met this knockout, Heather.

Heather was gorgeous. I thought she looked like an angel. It worked out well, because she liked me also. She told me she wanted to marry me and have sex. All I heard was sex! Woo Hoo! Yeah for me! I was going to get laid soon, and that's all I cared about. How did I respond? I stole Jeannie's wedding ring, brought it back to the hospital, and asked Heather to marry me. We made our childish pledge of love and said that no matter what, we would get married when we turned eighteen. We told each other nothing could stop the love we had for each other. The next day, Heather was sent home. She gave me her number and said she couldn't wait to marry me.

My dad called and asked me if I knew where Jeannie's wedding ring was. I had never been happier that Heather was gone. Of course, we would still get married, but at least she wouldn't know I stole the ring. My dad asked me over and over if I knew where the ring was. I didn't think twice about taking the ring. I didn't even think about how Jeannie felt.

A little while later, I was in my room when a staff member came in and told me that my dad called them about the ring. They repeatedly asked me, "Did you take your mother's ring?"

"No," I lied.

"Are you sure? Because we are going to search your room, and if you took the ring, we are going to find it."

"You're not going to find anything in here because I didn't take her wedding ring. Go ahead; search my room jackoff."

Three staff members came into my room and searched everything. I'm glad I didn't have it, because if I did, they would have found it. They looked in places I had no idea I could have hidden something.

"I told you I didn't take the ring! Are you happy now? Get the frig out of my room."

"Let's go; you're getting strip searched," they said.

I'm not entirely sure, but I thought strip searching a fourteen year old boy would have been against the law. So I said, "No you're not."

"Yes, we are. You're getting striped searched, or you're getting put in restraints until you let us strip search you."

Wow, I could not believe it. This was just so wrong.

(Side note: If this book ever comes out, I'm going to look into the situation of when I was forcibly strip searched by three male staff members, at the age of fourteen, at Charles River Hospital.)

A man really believes not what he recites in his creed, but only the things he is ready to die for.
Reverend Richard Wurmbrand
(Tortured For Christ)

It never mattered what came out of my mouth. My actions tell the kind of person I am. It was true then, and it's true now. Back then, I was ready to die for the enemy. These days, I'd like to think I could stand up for Christ, the way He has continually stood up for me.

It did not take long for me to go after another girl the second one batted her eyes at me. I kept in contact with Heather as much as I could. I wrote her letters, and she wrote me back, but I wound up meeting another girl named Robin, not the same Robin as before. She was trouble from the start, and I liked that about her. She told me that if I could help her break out of the hospital, we could stay with her boyfriend in Boston, do drugs, and hang out.

"Sure!" I said with a smile.

One night, we went downstairs through a door the staff left unlocked. I kicked one of the doors open that led to the kitchen. Once through that, there was another door that went outside which the kitchen workers came and went through. I kicked that one too, but it didn't open. It took two more kicks before it opened up, and Robin and I split.

We ran, jogged, and walked through Wesley, Massachusetts to go meet up with her boyfriend who was waiting for us. As promised, we headed into Boston to stay at her boyfriend's dad's house who was away on business for a while. For a week and a half we did drugs, drank, and caused all kinds of trouble.

They had a housekeeper who lived in the basement who was never home, so I went down a lot to snoop around. I found some money and stole it. I looked through her personal things and found some sex toys. I searched the entire house while Robin and Justin had sex in his room. I found a little money in their parents' room and took that also.

One day, while loaded, I bought some India ink, got drunk, and put five homemade tattoos on my left arm and one on my chest. I always thought tattoos were cool and wanted some. I was fourteen and just partied hard for over a week straight, and this little fourteen- year-old body needed a break. I left Justin and Robin behind, went and found a cab, got in, and asked him to take me back to Charles River Hospital. I was done. I got back to the hospital, and to my surprise, they paid for the cab. They brought me back to the same unit and put me in the restraint room where I slept for two days straight. The only time I got up was when the nurses came in to check on me to see if I was alive.

My time at Charles River Hospital was just about done. About a week later, my case manager, Freya Courtney, came to pick me up and took me to a foster home in Woburn, Massachusetts.

-Jonah 4:3-
"Therefore now, O LORD, please take my life
from me, for it is better for me to die than to live!"
(NKJV)

That's how I felt, like nothing was ever going to pan out the way I wanted it to. I didn't want to leave the hospital. I liked it there. It felt safe. There was trouble to get into, and I felt as if I connected with the others.

I didn't like the foster home I was sent to, and I didn't like the guy that ran it. His name was John and felt like he was just a mean old man. I couldn't do this, and I couldn't do that. I felt like I had to walk on eggshells around him. I was afraid of farting too loud. It sucked, and I didn't want to be there.

I started to wonder what my future held. I was only fourteen, but I knew I would be kicked out of state care when I was eighteen. I began wondering if it was time to get my crap together. I really thought about it, but then thoughts of suicide entered my mind, and I wondered if I could really do it. Everyone thought I needed to be on medication.

One day, John told me to go do something outside for a change. He said that I had been in my room long enough. He said that he was going to the mall in about an hour to get some things, and if I wanted, I could go with him. He eventually came out of the house and asked me if I was ready.

"Yes," I said.

We drove to the mall, and I wondered what kind of pills I could buy to take that night so I would not wake up in the morning. I chose pills, because I heard that you just fall asleep and never wake up again. I was a wimp and couldn't stand pain.

When we got there, he told me to meet him at CVS in a half hour. I agreed and went on my way. I went directly to CVS and bought a Circus Magazine, so I could check up on all my favorite hair metal bands before I killed myself that night. I also got a bottle five hundred count aspirin. I didn't have a lot of money, so I tried to be economical. I found I couldn't afford a whole lot of pills, and what I needed was a large quantity. I got to the register to pay for my items and wondered if that much aspirin could actually kill a person. I didn't want to ask before I paid in case they wouldn't sell it to me afterwards. After I paid, I asked the cashier, "Can this much aspirin kill you if you take it all at once?"

She looked mortified. I really wanted to know.

"Well, can it kill you if you take it all?" I asked again.

"Well, I suppose so dear. Why do you ask?"

"I just wanted to know, thanks." Then I walked out.

"Wait a second, young man. Why don't we go together and ask the pharmacist?" she said.

Yeah, right. I just kept walking. Was she crazy or something? I just wanted to make sure it could. I met up with John at his car a little while later.

"I thought I told you to meet me at CVS? I was looking for you." John said.

"I couldn't find it. Sorry."

"What? It's right there," he turned to show me the gigantic red and white CVS sign not twenty yards behind him.

"Oh wow!" I said.

He gave me a dirty look and told me to get in the car. On the way home, he asked me what I got and I showed him my magazine. He gave a dirty look and I smiled. I didn't care. I was going to die tonight.

Before I went to bed that night, he told me to go take a shower. When I was done, I tried to choke down as much of the aspirin as I could. It was easy at first, but the more I tried to take, the harder it got. I thought it would be funny if I lived and was sent back to Charles River Hospital. I got down as much as I could. I started to feel a little weird, so I rushed off to bed. I didn't want to die on his floor. Out of the five hundred pills, I probably took about four hundred or so before I thought I was going to puke them all up. I went and laid down and waited to die, but I couldn't fall asleep. I was wide awake, and my stomach was starting to hurt. I lay there for a couple hours before I went downstairs to see John.

"How come you're still up?" he said with an attitude.

"I can't sleep. My stomach hurts," I was in real pain, and he started to see that.

"What's wrong?" he asked.

I handed him the almost empty bottle of aspirin.

"Did you take these, or do you need a few for your stomach ache?" I think he knew the truth though.

"I took them," I said.

"How many?"

"I bought it today at CVS. It was brand new. I just opened it."

"And everything that's missing, you just took?"

"No. I didn't just take it." He seemed to relax a bit. "I took them a couple hours ago.

"Damn! Let's go! NOW!"

He grabbed me and threw me in the car. He had to call Freya and my other case manager, Maureen Green. Maureen was a case manager for foster homes. After he called, leaving two quick messages, we were out the door, in the car, racing to the hospital. Everything happened so quick. The nurse in the emergency room was shown the almost empty bottle. I was grabbed, thrown down, strapped to a gurney, and a tube was stuck up my nose that went down into my stomach to start the slow and agonizing process of pumping me full of liquid black charcoal to cleanse my body of all the toxins that shouldn't be there. I was in the ICU unit and stayed there for about three days before I was moved to a private room where a nurse had to sit with me one hundred percent of the time to make sure I drank my liquid charcoal and didn't try to kill myself again.

My worst fear at the time became a reality. I tried to commit suicide but didn't die. On my last day in the hospital, a nurse came in to ask how I was doing.

"Fine," I said.

"Are you going to try to kill yourself again?"

"Not anytime soon. Next time, I'll do it right."

"Steven, why do you want to die?" she asked me.

"Why do you want to live?" I asked her back.

Of course, there were plenty of reasons she could have given me, but she didn't. She looked sad. It was as if she really cared or something. Strange.

"Well, we're going to try to get you some help. You're being released from Mass General this afternoon, and you're going to another hospital. It's not like this one though. It's a psychiatric hospital for younger people. It's called Charles River Hospital. Have you ever heard of that place? It's a nice hospital. You'll get the help you need there."

"Yeah, I just got out of their a couple weeks ago."

"Oh! I see."

-Jude 1:13-
***raging waves of the sea, foaming up their
own shame; wandering stars for whom is
reserved the blackness of darkness forever.***
(NKJV)

And for almost the next two years, I bounced around from hospital to hospital. I would start some crap, get into trouble, and wind up getting moved to another hospital. I never found a real home. After a while, I was sent to a foster home in Amesbury, Massachusetts. I was only there for a couple of months, but I met this girl, Tammy. We hung out a lot and spent a lot of time getting hot and heavy. It was a weird feeling because she really liked me a lot. Her dad really liked me also. I was not used to that sort of thing. Her dad loved it when I came over and hung out with Tammy. He would always say to me, "You're number one!"

Just like I always did, I found the wrong crowd and started drinking and smoke pot. I loved not feeling things. With the weed and alcohol, it just felt like a party all the time. I never had any worries. Something didn't feel right, though. Things were going well, as well as I could expect anyway. I could come and go as I pleased. I drank when I wanted to drink. I got high when I wanted to get high. I even had a girlfriend who actually liked me and wanted to be with me, but something just wasn't right.

Then it hit me, I didn't have to change the person I was. I didn't have to lie about where I came from or what I had done. People just accepted me for who I was. I was so used to playing the part that I became uncomfortable in my own skin. I needed trouble. That's what felt right.

_____

I'm not sure if this makes any sense to you. I get confused seeing how I was back then. It's just how I was. I'm not that person now, far from it actually. I was just so lost. I can see the enemy really working in and around my life. I didn't even know it was happening. I couldn't see it then. Even if I could have, I wouldn't have cared. I was a very disrupted and disturbed child. The year was 1991, and I was fifteen years old. I drank. I did drugs. I stole. I lied. I cheated. I had already spent a total of four and a half years in state run institutions for troubled kids.

———————————

My time in Amesbury was about to end. I was accepted and loved by a girl. I wanted to leave. If I had stayed in Amesbury, I would have married Tammy Quimby. I wanted new territory. I needed new surroundings. I had to tell Tammy that I was leaving.

"I'm going to go to the emergency room and tell them that I want to commit suicide. I don't want to be here anymore," I told her one night.

"What?!"

"I just don't want to stay in Amesbury anymore."

"Steve, why? Please don't," she begged.

"I'm going to. It's the only way I can't get out of here."

"Please don't. I love you."

"I love you too. I'm not really going to kill myself. I just want to leave for a little while; that's all. I'll be back. I promise."

And that's how it happened. I just wanted out. The hospital had asked me why this and why that. In the end, I held firm to the fact that I was suicidal and was going to kill myself.

I was sent to a psychiatric ward in Somerville, Massachusetts, one town over from my hometown of Medford. It was like any other psychiatric hospital I had been in before. People came and people went. There were those who went off and became violent, and there were those who stayed quiet and talked to themselves. Some broke out. Others never wanted to leave.

While I was there, two very unbelievable things happened. The first thing was that for the first time, I had actually taken a step back and looked at all that was going on and realized I didn't want this any longer. I didn't want to be in anymore hospitals. This was beat. It sucked being here, and I thought about all I had done in the last few years.

I thought a lot about Tammy. Why had I walked away from her? I missed her and wanted to be back in Amesbury. I was stuck here and needed to get out. The only way to do that was to behave myself and show the staff and my social worker that I could get my crap together. I didn't want to go home; I just wanted out of the hospital.

I met this girl, Shauna, who wanted the same thing. We hung out a lot and talked about what we would do with our lives when we got out. We liked each other, and it was nice to have a real friend. Shauna was due to be released soon, and we talked about keeping in touch. This was something different. We enjoyed each other's company and conversation. I could tell that we would be friends for a long time to come. We both knew that we would hang out in the future. It was as simple as that.

She left, gave me her number and address, and we both promised to stay in touch. My relationship with Shauna was different from anything I had ever experienced. We could either talk or sit with each other and not say a thing and still feel comfortable. We never kissed. We never held hands. She would rub my back when I cried. I would hold her shoulder when she cried. Shauna would hug me out of the blue and just start crying. She once cried for so long and nestled her face in the crook of my neck, and I could feel her breathing on my neck. It felt nice. I went to pull away after a while and she just said, "Please don't."

I could not wait to see Shauna again in the future. We gave each other a very long hug that seemed to linger. She whispered in my ear, "I love you, Steve. Thank you."

I couldn't speak. I just looked at her. My eyes were filled with tears, but I never cried. She kissed me on the cheek, then left. A part of me loved Shauna for all the right reasons. I had never experienced this kind of love before. Yes, I believe I fell in love with her then. I never knew it though until I wrote this book. I couldn't wait to see her again.

Shauna committed suicide not long after leaving the hospital. It was here I first realized that life is indeed precious. For the past twenty-eight years, I have thought about Shauna on and off, always remembering her smile, her tenderness towards me, the words she whispered in my ear. Her death affected me. I swore to myself then that I

196

would never let the death of anyone ever affect me again.

-1 Corinthians 15:55-
"O Death, where is your sting?
O Hades, where is your victory?"
(NKJV)

Shauna was diabetic. She bought a pound of sugar, ate the entire bag, went into diabetic shock, then a coma, then she was dead. A life was gone just like that. I never knew Shauna's full story. She was a very quiet girl. I do know she was abused, but to what extent, I don't know, nor will I ever. She never talked to anyone except for me and kept to herself. (I miss you Shauna!)

The second thing that happened was this: I got a letter one day in the mail. I looked at the return address, but there was no name, just a return address from Marshfield, Massachusetts. I opened the letter and a ring fell out of it. It was Jeannie's wedding ring! It had been almost two years since I gave that ring to Heather.

Inside the envelope was a letter from her explaining that she called around to see where I was so that she could return the ring. She said that we had grown apart and that she was in love with someone else. She wished me well and said goodbye.

The thought of returning the ring to Jeannie came and went. I wanted to give it back to her, but then she would know that I really stole it. I put the ring in my pocket and waited to decide what I would do with it some other time. I was released from Somerville Hospital soon after that. My social worker, Freya, came to pick me up and brought me to my new home, another residential home for troubled kids, except this place was for teenagers. The home was called, I.F.F.L.L., which stood for The Institute For Family Life and Learning, located on Liberty St. in Danvers, Massachusetts.

When she dropped me off, she told me it was a good place, and that if I behaved myself for a year, she could place me in a foster home again. I really had to prove I could be trusted, she explained, before she could move me. I told her I would behave myself just fine here. She brought me inside, checked in with the front office, told them I was sitting there, and went to leave. Before she got to the door, she turned around and said, "Steven, please behave yourself. Please? Can you do that for me?"

"Yeah, sure!" I said with a smile.

She looked at me for a long moment, then turned around to leave. It was April of 1992, and I was fifteen. I was going to be sixteen the following month.

-Malachi 3:15-
"So now we call the proud blessed, for those who do wickedness are raised up; they even tempt God and go free."
(NKJV)

Well, here I was in my new home. It was okay. Everything was on property. There were three houses numbered One, Two, and Three. Each house had its own specific use, its own set of rules, and catered to our individual needs, so they said.

House Three was for those of us doing well and were about to be placed either in foster care or on our way home. House Two was co-ed, and there was no way they were going to allow me in that house. They told me that upon arrival. There were about ten or fifteen girls in that house, and most of them were nice to look at. They were all troublemakers of course, and that alone turned me on. House One was for troublemakers, that's where I was placed. They also kept more staff on hand to keep a closer eye on us. The chores were tougher, and the staff rode us more than the other two houses. The school was also on property, as well as all our counseling sessions and whatever else. We did everything on location. On weekends, depending on where you were in the program, you got to go home for visits. If you weren't in any trouble, they took a group of us to see a movie. It was cool when there were girls that went with us. We would act like fools of course.

My first day was okay. I found out this place did not keep you much longer than a year. If you were not going back home to live, you went on a waiting list to be placed in a foster home. So much for what Freya had said to me then. I knew she was trying to keep me on my toes. With finding this out, it gave me the freedom to act as I so wished, within reason of course. In a year, I would be going to another foster home.

There were sixty teenage males in House One. There were another forty or so in House Two, along with the fifteen girls. House Three was in a league of its own. There were ten people altogether in that house. They acted as if they were so much better than the rest of us.

They took me to the house to get settled in and meet the staff. As I walked in, I saw an old friend, Josh, whom I had met in one of the psych hospitals. He was sitting in a chair outside the staff office. Josh and I had started a lot of trouble together, so I walked over to him right away.

"Hey Josh, what's up man?" I said.

"HEY! You can't talk to him!" said Steve, the guy showing me around.

"What? Why not?" I asked him.

"He's in trouble. He ran away a few weeks ago and the cops just brought him back. He has to sit there for a week and then the house gets to deal with him during the house meeting."

"What do you mean, 'Deal with him?'"

"He has to sit in a chair in the middle of the room while everyone gets a turn to yell at him for acting out and running away."

"That's retarded," I said.

"You don't know anything about this place yet. That's how we deal with things here. I messed up once too and had to get dealt with."

"You're not a staff member?" I was confused.

"No. I'll be going up to House Three in a couple weeks," he said in a cocky tone.

"Wow dude. I thought you were a staff member. We're all here because we're foul ups, did you forget that?"

"I'm going to let the staff know you're here and let them know that you have an attitude problem. You better get your crap right if you're gonna make here." He walked into the staff room and shut the door.

"What's up, Josh?" I said smiling.

"Not much. How are you doing?"

"I'm okay. I just got here. What's his problem?"

"He doesn't like it when people talk back to him. He's the overseer of this house. He thinks he's staff. He keeps an eye on things and lets the staff know if anything happens, and they listen to him too."

"That's crazy, man!"

"Yeah, but don't worry about it. You won't get into any trouble; you're new. Everyone comes in here with an attitude. They're going to talk to you about it though, so just be cool."

"Steven Gray! Get in this office, NOW!" came a voice from inside the office.

Here we go again. I walked in the office with an attitude.

"Sit down," Steve said.

"No, you sit down," I said back.

"SIT! DOWN!" said a staff member named Paul. "What's your problem?" he asked. "You don't like to listen?"

"What's your name?" I asked him.

"My name is Paul. I'm the House One manager, got it? Now answer my question."

"Well, Paul, I don't like being talked to like I'm a piece of crap. When you ask nicely, I'll answer you. Got it?"

He glared at me for what seemed like an eternity.

"Are we going to have a problem here, Steve?" he said in an even tone.

"I hope not, Paul. How are you doing today?" I said with a smile.

"What is your problem, Steve?"

"I don't answer to other guys in the house. I only listen to staff members. I will not do anything another resident tells me to do."

"We have a way of doing things around here. This program works. Steve told me that you have a problem with how we deal with the guys when they mess up. He also said you got rude with him out in the hallway. Is that true?"

"Yup."

"Why?"

"I think the way you deal with us here is retarded. You have a bunch of guys who have been arrested and caused a lot of trouble. You make them sit in the middle of the room to get yelled at? That's just stupid. You can't do your job yourself?"

"Steve, step out of the office for a minute, okay?" Paul said to the Steve that was showing me around.

"Listen to me, Steve. This place isn't too bad. Do what you're told, make some progress, and in a year you can get out of here, okay?"

"Sure."

"Am I going to have any more problems with you?"

"Maybe."

"You're a smartass too, huh?"

"I try."

"Listen to me very closely, tough guy. This place is what you make of it. You can make it easy, or you can make it hard." Then he leaned in real close. He was so close that I could feel his breath in my face. He towered over me. Sitting down, I looked like a two year old next to him. "Do not f-around in this house, and do not mess with me. Got it?"

He got the response he was looking for.

"Yeah, I got it," I said with as much humility as I could. He definitely got my attention, and he knew he did. After that, I was shown to my room and began to unpack my things.

-Zechariah 7:11-
"But they refused to heed, shrugged their shoulders, and stopped their ears so that they could not hear."
(NKJV)

God has tried so many times to get my attention in so many ways. I have a clear choice to either listen to Him or not. What happens when I choose not to listen to Him? My life always seems to get tougher. God has done so much for me in my life. There are times when I can really hear and feel what He is speaking into my heart, and in those times when I listen to Him, my faith grows stronger.

Something that just popped into my head is this: I have seen the LORD do so much for me. He has taken me out of jail when I should have gotten more time. He cleared up warrants for me when I was wanted. He fed me when I was hungry. He has answered specific prayers. He picked me up as a drug addict and delivered me from different addictions. He gave me back a relationship with my first son, Sebastian, after I walked out of his life. He has given me good jobs when I didn't deserve them. He protected me from being murdered when drug dealers were chasing me. He has taken me out of areas of this country and brought me elsewhere to protect my life. Yet, there are still times when I refuse to listen to Him. I will even tune Him out, trying to convince myself that I'm not really hearing Him.

He tries to get my attention in so many ways. We all need to do our best to heed His calling before He stops for a season. He isn't going to push Himself on us. If I refuse to listen to Him time after time, He is going to stop for a while until I realize I need Him back. Would you continue trying to get someone to listen to you when all they do is ignore you? I know I wouldn't try for very long. I know in my life God will eventually sit back and let me be thick-headed until I realize I need Him. I'm not saying He's going to stop working in my life. I truly believe He won't stop. It's just that He will stop speaking to me at times. Sometimes it's for a long season. I'm also not saying that this is how it is for all of you, but in my life this is how He works. The bottom line is this: He is trying to get your attention right now. Why do I still not trust that what He has for me is the best?

-Isaiah 57:4-
Whom do you ridicule? Against whom do you make a wide mouth and stick out the tongue? Are you not children of transgression, offspring of falsehood,
(NKJV)

That night, we had the house meeting I kept hearing so much about. The first topic was about me and introducing me as the newest resident. Paul was even nice enough to let them all know a few of the things that I had gotten in trouble for. He explained the situation earlier I had with Steve and how I thought the way the house "dealt" with us was retarded. He told everyone to introduce themselves. Then Paul asked me if I would like to add anything.

"I think you covered most of it Paul, thanks. You did leave out the part where you told Steve to leave the office and then threatened me. You know, the part where you leaned real close to my face and told me not to "f" with you. Do you remember that part, Paul? I could quote it for you if you like."

This comment drew mixed reactions from everyone, mostly shock though. A few snickers, a few laughs, and a few dirty looks from some of the others. I thought the best reaction came from the other staff. They had this look of worry. Maybe like they knew exactly what I was talking about because he had done it before. I can't be sure though.

"Hey Paul, does Social Services know that you threaten us here to try to get our attention?" I asked him.

"Okay, okay, let's move on now," Gary, another staff member, said.

This house grouped us in two different groups: Younger Peer and Older Peer. The Younger Peer were us guys who were relatively new. We did most of the work and had fewer privileges. When something went wrong, it was usually the Younger Peer that took the heat. The Older Peer made some of the decisions for us Younger Peer. They had the authority to pull someone's weekend pass for messing up.

"Because of what happened, we feel the best punishment is to pull your weekend pass and restrict you to property," said the leader of the Older Peer.

"Does anyone have anything to say?" Gary asked.

I raised my hand. Gary looked at me for a minute and said, "Really?"

"Yes. I have something to say about this," I said.

Paul and Gary glanced at each other for a second, then Gary said, "You just got here. You don't even know what's going on."

"Yeah, but I still have something I want to say."

Gary took a deep breath and told me to go ahead.

"I don't like the fact that other guys who are here for causing trouble get to make the decision on whether or not someone gets to go home for the weekend. That's not right. Why can't you do your job yourself? Isn't that what you get paid for?" I said.

"Listen, Steve, the Older Peer have been here for a while and have all proved themselves. They have shown that they can be trusted to make some small decisions. They wouldn't be Older Peer if they haven't," Gary explained.

"I don't really care, Gary. It's wrong. Does Social Services know that you do that here? Do they know you don't do your jobs yourselves? That you let residents make decisions for other residents? You need to do your job yourself. I'm gonna let my social worker know that's how you do things around here." Paul glared at me as if he wanted to rip my throat out.

"What's the matter, Paul? Are you gonna threaten me again?"

No one responded to what I had said, and the meeting soon ended. The kid who messed up was allowed to go home to see his family that weekend, and the Older Peer were not allowed to pull anybody's weekend family passes for any reason, ever again.

Just so you know, I'm not trying to sound tough writing this. That's just how I was. I was a very cocky kid who didn't care about much. I loved to stir the pot when I could. When I was in a controlled environment, there was no telling how I would react or what might come out of my mouth. I didn't have any boundaries. It was best I never found a weakness in you. If I did, I would pounce on it and do what I could to try to hurt you. I loved it. Take me out of the controlled environment and things changed. I became quiet and shy.

———————

I was loud and obnoxious most of the time. I tried to make some friends, but it was different here. These kids were the bad ones that no one could deal with, and things caught up to me quickly. I lied about everything. Whatever you had done, I had done it better. Wherever you had been, I had been there too, but gone farther. I made stuff up to try to look and sound cool. I became an outcast. I didn't care though; there were other outcasts as well. I was usually in trouble for one thing or another pretty much every day.

Life became even more difficult. I didn't know how to deal with certain things. I sure didn't know how to deal with my hatred for women. I was filled with rage all the time.

"Life is difficult. This is a great truth, one of the greatest truths. It is a great truth because once we truly see this truth, we transcend it. Once we truly know that life is difficult – once we truly understand and

accept it – then life is no longer difficult.
Because once it is accepted, the fact that life
is difficult no longer matters."
M. Scott Peck
(The Road Less Traveled)

I never saw the fact that it was me who was causing myself all this trouble. In my mind, it was everyone else. A couple of weeks later, I ran away. I ran away a few times, but always came back a few days to a week later. I would sleep under bridges and try to steal food so I could eat, but the cops always brought me right back. I got the usual every time: a chair for a week in front of the office, then a chair during the house meeting to be dealt with and yelled at.

-Habakkuk 2:10-
You give shameful counsel to your house, cutting
off many peoples, and sin against your soul.
(NKJV)

After a while, I was allowed to go home on weekends. I was surprised that my parents even allowed me to come home to visit. I was just happy to get out of the residential home on somewhat of a regular basis.

On Fridays, whoever was going home for the weekend was provided transportation via Social Services. I thought my transportation people were the best. They were cool and allowed me to swear and talk crap. A few weeks into my transportation deal, the guy driving asked me if I wanted a beer.

"Sure," I said.

His wife was usually in the passenger seat drinking also. I thought I was in heaven. It never occurred to me that this guy was a complete idiot for letting me drink alcohol in a moving car at the age of sixteen while I was on my way back to a residential home for being a foul up. He and his wife were not only breaking the law, but they were also jeopardizing my life and theirs by drinking and driving.

-Micah 3:2 & 4-
You who hate good and live evil; who strip the skin from my people,
and the flesh from their bones; - Then they will cry to the LORD,
but He will not hear them; He will even hide His face from them at
that time, because they have been evil in their deeds.
(NKJV)

On one of my weekend visits home, I was thinking about how bad my life sucked. I hated Colleen for what she did to me. I hated her for allowing her many men to use me as a punching bag. I went for a walk one night and decided to cut myself. I took a razor blade from my dad's work area and sliced my arm and leg until blood was pouring out. I was shocked at the amount of blood coming out and was starting to get light headed, like I was going to pass out. I remembered that Joe and Pearl, Jeannie's cousins, lived a block away, so I ran to their house. All I remember is Joe saying, "Oh my gosh, Steven, what happened?!"

Through all my tears and screams I yelled out, "I got stabbed!" I was a very sick and twisted child.

They took me into their house and called the cops and Jeannie. My dad was working. I remember them trying to calm me down. The cops showed up along with an ambulance, and I was taken to the hospital. I remember Jeannie climbing into the back with a look of horror on her face. The next thing I remember was being in the emergency room, getting stitched up, with both my parents there. Not a word was spoken, either at the hospital, or on the way home. I knew that they knew I just lied about getting jumped and stabbed. They knew I had just cut myself. I was starting to look like the lost cause they thought I was.

Everyone was tired of my crap. Even the other guys who no one wanted to talk to or deal with wanted anything to do with me. I was truly alone now. With no one to talk to, I did the only thing I knew how to do. I ran away. This time, I ran to a hospital and told the emergency room that I was suicidal. I gave them a razor blade I had in my pocket and was sent to a psychiatric hospital for another thirty day evaluation. At the end of my stay, my counselor from the residential home came to pick me up and drove me back to the program.

I wanted to do something right for a change. I still had Jeannie's wedding ring and decided it was time to give it back. My counselor had been talking to me about the ring for a while now, but I always denied taking it. No one knew I still had it. All my counselor wanted me to do was admit to my parents I stole the ring. My dad came weekly for counseling sessions with me.

"So, Steven, I'd like to talk about your stepmother's wedding ring," she said while looking at me. "Did you take her ring, Steven?" I was so scared. "Steven, we know you took the ring; we just want you to admit it. We know the ring is long gone. Did you take the ring?"

"Yes," I said as softly.

They looked at each other and then looked over at me.

"Why?" my dad asked me.

"What did you do with it?" my counselor asked.

I reached into my pocket, pulled out the wedding ring, and tossed it to my father. The look on their faces was complete and total astonishment. My dad picked up the ring and looked at it for a minute.

"Is that really your wife's ring, Steve?" my counselor asked my dad.

"Yes it is." He was amazed.

My counselor could not believe that I had just tossed my dad the wedding ring I stole from Jeannie more than three years earlier.

"Where did it just come from?" she asked me.

"My pocket."

"I mean where did you get it?"

"I've had it mostly the whole time."

"You what?" she said.

"I've had it in my pocket almost the whole time."

"What do you mean you've had it the whole time?" She just could not understand. "Why did you take it to begin with?"

"I asked this girl to marry me at one of the hospitals that I was in," I said.

"I see; and then what happened?"

"She sent it back to me almost a year later when I was in a different hospital. She said that she didn't want to marry me anymore, so I kept it in my pocket."

"You've kept that ring in your pocket for over two years?" she asked me in disbelief.

"Yes."

"Steve, are you sure that's the ring?" she asked my dad again.

"Oh yeah, I'm positive this is the ring."

My dad looked at me for a minute, "Thank you, Steven."

"I'm sorry. Tell Jeannie I'm sorry." More work had been done in that little ten minute session than in four years of counseling.

-Hosea 10:4-
They have spoken words, swearing falsely in
making a covenant. Thus judgment springs
up like hemlock in the furrows of the field.
(NKJV)

Nothing changed on the outside. The thought I had about maybe changing was as fleeting as the thought of hoping a politician would do everything he promised.

On another weekend visit home, I had the great idea of stealing my dad's car and taking it for a drive. He and Jeannie both kept their keys on the kitchen table. While the entire house was sleeping one night, I crawled out of bed and tried to grab the keys to the car as quietly as I could. I got the keys, climbed out of a window, left the house, and drove to Malden to see some friends. Between never driving a car in my life and the adrenaline that was pumping in my veins from stealing my dad's car, I almost hit two parked cars on the side of the street before I even got one block away.

While I was out driving, I backed into a wall and put a good-sized dent in the rear end. I was scared but was able to get the car back home quietly, park it, sneak back in the house, return the keys, and go to bed without anyone waking up. It was years before I found out that my dad knew I stole his car and wrecked the bumper.

One day, I was called into the office because they said they needed to speak with me. I walked in the office and saw Freya Courtney, my case manager from Social Services. I hadn't seen her in over a year.

"Hello, Steven" Freya said with a smile. "I have good news for you."

"What?" I asked.

"We found a foster home for you. You're leaving here Monday afternoon, and I'll be taking you to your new home. It took us some time to find someone who would take you because of all the stuff you've pulled, but we got someone to take you in. That's great, huh?"

"Where is it?"

"It's in Woburn. You might actually remember, because you were there before. Do you remember John's house? You took a bottle of aspirin there and had to have your stomach pumped."

"Yeah, I remember."

"Well, that's where you're going. Aren't you excited?" Freya seemed a little too excited.

"Yeah, sure," I said blandly.

"Maureen from Evergreen Services is coming down here on Friday to meet with you, and she's bringing John with her. They both want to see how you're doing. I told them that you've changed a lot and are ready to move on with your life in a positive way," which was code talk for, "I lied my butt off because I can't find anywhere else for you to go. Will you please just roll with it and at least act like you've changed?"

"Okay," I said.

"Okay good. I'll see you Friday at noon, okay?"

"If they're coming on Friday, how come I have to wait till Monday to leave?"

"Because, Steven, John would like to meet with you first."

"That means they want to meet with me first and then think about it, right?"

"Steven, will you please just do the right thing and act like you've grown up a little?" There was the honesty I was hoping for.

"Sure."

"Okay, I'll see you Friday."

Friday came, and we all met in the living room. Even I had to say it went well. We talked about a lot and even brought up my suicide attempt at John's house. I tried as hard as I could to say that I had changed and was looking forward to moving on with my life. John looked at me hard, like he was trying to see if I would kill myself in his house. Anyway, they said everything was fine and that they would both be there on Monday afternoon to pick me up.

-Romans 7:14-15-
For we know that the law is spiritual, but I am carnal, sold under
sin. For what I am doing, I do not understand. For what I will to do, that I do not practice; but what I hate, that I do
(NKJV)

The devil made me do it!

The truth is that there's a great war going on inside of me. A war between the enemy and me, and I'm trying to grab ahold of the good and choose to do the right thing. With the way that I have lived my life, I am easy prey for the enemy. It takes a lot for me to fight him off. It's not easy. I don't always win.

I got to John's house, and it didn't take long to get settled in. The date was Monday, May 10th, 1993. When we arrived, the three of us had another short meeting. Maureen told me that the following morning she and John were going to take me to Woburn High School to be enrolled. She also told me that she had talked to John about me being able to live there until I finished high school. I was a year behind and wouldn't graduate until I was nineteen. She said John was just fine with that as long as I followed the rules. They told me that I could get a job if I wanted to and that it was actually encouraged. When I did find a job, Maureen would take me to the bank to open up a savings account and that the account was to be verified weekly by showing John my paycheck stub and savings account book. At least fifty percent of my take home pay was to be deposited each week, without exception, and no withdrawals without the approval of either John or Maureen. So far, so good, I thought. My curfew was 11:00pm. When we got done with everything, Maureen and Freya left, and I went to lie down to take a nap. When I woke up, John was making dinner. He seemed like he cared and was much nicer this time around. He told me that he gave the guys that lived with him long term a little more freedom and a lot less crap.

"We have to get up early tomorrow to go get you enrolled at Woburn High School," he said.

"Okay," I said.

I lay in bed that night but couldn't sleep much. It was different being here this time knowing that I would be here for a while. I thought about the last time I was here and how I just wanted things to be different. Then my mind switched gears. I thought about getting a job and meeting some chicks. I was going to be seventeen in two days and I had two years to live here to try to be a different person.

The next day, Maureen picked up John and I and headed to the school where the principal, assistant principal, and the school counselor were all waiting for us to show up. The school had already been brought up to speed with everything I had done in the last four years. They knew about the hospitals, the foster homes, the stealing, lying, running away, drugs, drinking, and that I was now in another foster home.

I was given a schedule that even I thought was awesome. It was May, and I only had to go to three classes a day until the end of June. I would be allowed to go home after my third class ended at 10:30 a.m. In September I would be placed in eleventh grade and have only two classes a day for my eleventh and twelfth grade years. I had never been so happy to be classified a Special Needs child.

"Are you sure? I'm already behind, and my grades aren't that good anyway. I haven't gone to school steadily in four years." Then he said some words that I will never forget.

"Don't worry about that. You just make sure that you show up for school every day. If you do that, then we will make sure you graduate and get your high school diploma in two years." Even I knew that was wrong, but I wasn't going to complain with a deal so sweet.

"Can I stay home from school tomorrow? It's my birthday," I asked.

They just looked at me. I was dead serious but didn't push it.

"Okay, never mind. I was just kidding anyway."

They knew I was serious. Instead, I asked John, "Can I go to the mall and fill out some applications? I want to try to get a job."

This question drew smiles from them both.

"Sure thing!" John said. "I'll even take you there. I have to pick up some prescriptions anyway." After that, Maureen said goodbye and left.

While John and I were at the mall, I picked up ten applications and a Circus magazine so I could catch up on my favorite rock bands. It was important for me to know what Skid Row was doing. When we were getting ready to leave, John asked me if I needed anything else.

"Yeah, I just need to get a bottle of aspirin real quick. Is that okay?" I said jokingly.

It was a very sick try at humor and didn't go over very well. I really was kidding, but John didn't think so. That night, I filled out all ten applications and planned on going to the mall the next day after school to drop them off. I was going to get a job!

My first day of school went without a hitch. Nothing went wrong. I checked in at the principal's office, and he gave me a lock for my locker and all three of my books. There really wasn't much to it.

Only someone like myself could have made it difficult, and even I didn't have any problems with any of this.

I had three classes: Math, English, and Social Studies, and before long, my third class was over. It was 10:30 a.m., and I was on my way to the mall to put in my applications. The mall wasn't that far away, and with some luck, I could probably put a few applications in before the lunch rush hit. I walked as fast as I could, and I got there before eleven. The first place I hit was a pizza place called Papa Gino's, asked for the manager, and handed him my application. He looked at it quickly, looked back at me and said, "Do you know how to work a grill?"

"I never worked on a grill before, but I'm a quick learner, sir."

He smiled at me and said, "Do you have your social security card on you and working papers from your school?"

"Yes sir, I do."

"Okay, come on back. You're going to work the grill. My lunchtime grill man is an alcoholic who comes to work when he feels like it. We'll do your paperwork after the lunch rush."

And that was it. I had a job and was happy to tell John when I got home. At first, he was pissed because I didn't get home until about seven or eight that night. I never called him and had gotten out of school that morning. He had called Maureen and Freya, and they told him to call the cops if I didn't come home by curfew. I showed him the paperwork from Papa Gino's, and he was somewhat okay with that. Plus, I had my Papa Gino's work shirt on and a name tag.

"Why didn't you call?"

"You never gave me your number, John. I didn't think that they were going to have me start working right away."

What could he say? I was right. I was a go-getter, got a job, and started working right away. Even he knew he couldn't blame me for that.

"Congratulations on your job. Good man, I'm proud of you. I'll tell Maureen and Freya about it. Freya really thought that we were going to have to call the police tonight about you. Maureen was little more optimistic. How was school?"

-Ezekiel 22:4-
You have become guilty by the blood which you have shed, and have defiled yourself with the idols which you have made. You have caused your days to draw near, and have come to an
end of your years; therefore I have made you a reproach to the nations, and a mockery to all countries.
(NKJV)

I quit school the following week so I could work full time. I walked into the principal's office and told him I was quitting and gave him my books. It was literally that easy. He said okay and let me walk away. I didn't even need anyone to sign any paperwork, and I was underage. That was it. Just like that I had quit school. No questions, comments, or concerns. No paperwork. No phone calls to my foster home or caseworker. He didn't even ask me if I talked to them about it or how they felt. I was able to walk into my school, at seventeen years old, and quit just like that. I left the school feeling cool. I felt like I controlled my own life. No one could tell me what to do. I walked to a department store called Bradley's that morning and got a full time job, then walked to Papa Gino's and quit. I didn't even tell John when I got home that I quit. It was a week before he noticed I wasn't going to school.

"What's going on with you? How come you're not in school?" he asked.

"I quit," I said.

"What?!"

"I quit."

"What do you mean you quit? What did you quit?"

"I quit school."

"When?"

"Last week."

"What?!"

I didn't know what else to say. I looked at him and waited for him to say something else.

"How did you quit school? You need a parent or guardian with you."

"No, I didn't. I told the principal I wanted to quit. He told me to turn my books in to my teachers and then I could leave."

"What?!"

I was starting to get tired of all the "Whats'."

"You quit school just like that?"

"Yeah."

"Just like that?"

"Yes, John, just like that."

"You're going back to school. I'm calling Maureen, and we'll get this all squared away."

"No, I'm not," I said.

"Yes, you are."

"No, John, I'm not going back to school."

He looked at me for a minute, bewildered. I know he was shocked at the way I just talked to him.

"I'm going to call Maureen and see what we have to do; at the very least you're going to have to get a full time job."

"I already did."

"What?!"

"I said I already got a full time job."

"Are you working full time at Papa Gino's now?"

"No, I quit that job. I got a full time job at Bradley's."

"Well, you just have it all figured out then, huh?"

"Not really."

"You're making a mistake, Steven. You're making a seriously huge mistake. You do know that you have to be gone when you turn eighteen, now right?"

"That was kind of the point, John."

Now I was just being cocky, and he didn't deserve that.

"Okay. Well, I need to call Maureen now."

"Okay," I said, and left to go to work.

John was annoyed. For the next year all I did was hang out with the wrong people, smoke pot, drink, dabble in other drugs, and work. I was biding my time until I was eighteen.

"Maybe God is being gracious despite our stupidity. Maybe He's going to give us another day, another chance."
Todd Burpo
(Heaven is for Real)

-Jeremiah 30:14-
All your lovers have forgotten you; they do not seek you; for I have
wounded you with the wound of an enemy, with the chastisement of a cruel
one, for the multitude of your iniquities, because your sins have increased.
(NKJV)

On May 12th, 1994, my eighteenth birthday, I moved back home to my dad's house. Neither one of my parents wanted me there, but they weren't going to throw me on the streets either, at least not until I did something that warranted it. It was my birthday, so my dad gave me all of my savings bonds that he had saved for me. I bought a quarter ounce of weed and headed to New Hampshire to get the first of many tattoos. I got the Grim Reaper on my upper right bicep. This did not go over very well at home. I was eighteen and tired of feeling as if I wasn't wanted. I wasn't even treated like a family member. I thought long and hard, then finally made a phone call.

"Hello?"
"Hey, it's me," I said.

"Hey! How are you?"

"I'm okay. What are you doing?" I asked.

"Nothing, what's up with you? How've you been?"

"I'm okay."

"What's going on?"

"Nothing," I said.

I didn't know what to say next. There was a very long pause.

"Go ahead; ask me." I waited a very long minute, then I asked.

"Can I move back?"

"You know, I thought you were going to call and ask me that. I just had a feeling."

"Yeah, well, can I?"

"I'll call the Greyhound Bus Station right now in Boston and get you a ticket. You can take a bus here tonight. Okay?"

"Can I take a bus in the morning? I want to go hang out with my friends tonight and say goodbye."

"Yeah, that's fine. Your ticket will be waiting for you at the bus station. Call me when you get on the bus, and I'll go pick you up when you get here."

"Okay. Thank you. I'll call you in the morning?"

"Okay. I'll talk to you then."

"Okay. Goodbye," I said.

"Goodbye, Steven."

That night, I went out with my friends and got extremely loaded. I had partied before, but I really tied one on that night and never went home. I wound up passing out and woke up in the morning. When I woke up, I thought I was going to miss my bus. I called my dad and he said that if I got home within a couple hours, he could still take me to the bus station in downtown Boston.

"Cool. Thanks dad. I'll be home as soon as I can."

"We knew you wouldn't be home last night anyway," he said.

We got to the bus station, and my dad walked me into the sitting area. He made sure that my ticket was waiting for me. I could see in his eyes that he was relieved I would be gone. I also saw a father's sadness. I knew my dad wondered how long it would take me to grow up. He hugged me and said goodbye.

"I love you, Steven."

"I love you too, dad."

"Take care of yourself."

"I will."

With that, he left. I watched him go and wished I had been a better son. It sucked seeing people relieved to see you go so you don't cause them anymore trouble.

I waited for an hour before my bus was ready to load. I shook my head and wondered if I was making the right choice. Right then, I just knew that this was going to go very badly for me. At that very second, I regretted the phone call I had made and knew that I was going to regret getting on that bus. I wanted to call my dad and tell him that I changed my mind. The only reason I didn't run after him to tell him was the fear of him saying I couldn't come back home. I looked at the bus for a very long time. I finally got on the Greyhound and headed back to go live with Colleen again.

Chapter Seven

-Romans 9:17-
For the Scripture says to Pharaoh, "For this very purpose
I have raised you up, that I may show My power in
you, and that My name may be declared in all the earth."
(NKJV)

While I was in rehab this last time, I kept a journal. When you're in rehab, it can be one of the loneliest times of your life, and that gives The Lord the best opportunity to work on you. My heart was broken. My mind was broken. My life was broken. But my spirit was open to Jesus Christ. Some of the closest moments I've had with God came when I was in rehab. I was at my weakest. No one cared about me. No one trusted me. When I was unlovable, God was there to love me!

The following is a journal entry from December 2011:

12/17/11   1:45am

I'm sitting in the laundry getting the sheets and towels done and thinking about yesterday. I already read my devotional from Martin. I started to read Revelation yesterday and I'm blown away as to how God is speaking to me through it. I have highlighted and underlined so much of it already. I only have like two chapters left. It's written by John, so that figures. I have fell in-love with everything that John has written. God is showing me and really opening my eyes to what is to come. And if I reject His love it will not be good. So much terror, pain, and sorrow is coming in the end of days. I am actually starting to feel sorrow for those who don't believe. None of us can truly know what is coming, or how bad it really will be, but it's no joke. We all need to wake up and realize that the love of God is for all of us. And that the only way we can escape death is our belief in Christ as our Savior!! I really want to tell people about Christ and His love and what He has done for me! I want eternal peace! People need to know that Christ is the only way to life and freedom and that, also just as important, the terror and torture that awaits them if they reject His love.

It's in moments like this I know I can look back and see that God is still real. He keeps me alive!

-Ezekiel 20:16-17-
because they despised My judgments and did not walk in
My statutes, but profaned My Sabbaths; for their heart
went after their idols. Nevertheless My eyes spared them from
destruction. I did not make an end of them in the wilderness.
(NKJV)

My divorce from Sabrina is official now. It sucks, and I'm hurting. I am not sure what to think. I am currently paying almost $1100 a month in child support to two ex-wives, and I can barely afford it. It's Christmas time, and I leave for Boston to visit my son Sebastian this Saturday. To say that things are a little tight is an understatement. I just cannot do for my children as I would like to this year.

I wish I had a better story for you to read, but this is just how my life has turned out. This is my walk to find Christ. This is my crawl to God. These are my struggles to find His will. He hasn't destroyed me yet. He loves me. He's waiting for me to give up one hundred percent of myself. It's not that easy for me. I keep trying to hold on to certain things here and there, and I wind up failing every time. He is waiting for me, patiently.

-2 Peter 2:22-
But it has happened to them according to the true
proverb: "A dog returns to his own vomit," and,
"a sow, having washed, to her wallowing in the mire."
(NKJV)

Well, I got off the bus and there was Colleen to meet me. She picked me up as promised, and we headed back to Cairo, NY. On the drive back, she told me that she was going through a divorce with Dan and was dating this guy Ken. I was so uneasy on the ride back to her house. I didn't want to be here. I knew if I stayed with my parents in Boston, it would only be a matter of time before I was kicked out, and I didn't want that to happen. So now, I was in a situation I didn't want to be in.

Things were somewhat okay for a little while. I got a job up the street at a golf course doing landscaping. I busted my butt and was paid little. Colleen knew that I was putting up with a bunch of crap at work and offered to get me a job at the convenience store she worked at. She worked there during the summer, because she drove a school bus and there was no school for two months for summer vacation. I could not stand my job, so I took her up on her offer. I was only out of work for a couple of weeks before I got the job at the store. In the meantime, she told me that I would need a vehicle to get back and forth, so she offered to buy me a car. The car was a 1984 Oldsmobile Regency 98 and only cost four hundred dollars. It was one of the biggest cars I'd ever seen, and I swear, there was a face on the gas gauge just daring me to step on the gas. I agreed to pay her back for the car at fifty dollars a month. I was also paying her fifty dollars a week for rent.

The job at the store sucked. It was minimum wage, but was forty hours a week. I was on time for work when my car didn't break down, which was almost never. It wasn't long before I really started wishing I hadn't come here to live. I was in a town I could not stand, working a job I did not like. The only part of this I thought was cool was that I was old enough to smoke weed in the house, and even though I wasn't yet twenty-one, I was allowed to also drink. This was the only thing that made this situation bearable. To deal with living in Colleen's house again, I stayed stoned and drunk all the time.

Things soon became as stressful as always, just as I knew they would. I had to walk around on eggshells. Colleen was always drunk, and she made sure we all knew that this was her house and her rules.

My sister Belinda lived there when I first moved back, but moved out soon after. It wasn't because of me. Colleen and Belinda were always fighting, always abusive to each other. Colleen kicked her out, throwing her things outside on the driveway. I felt bad for my sister Rhonda. She was still in high school and had no choice but to put up with all the crap. Rhonda was a trooper. To this day, I have no clue how Rhonda came out of that house with a level head. She is a good girl with a nice job and knows what she wants in life and how to get it.

Ken, Colleen's boyfriend, started spending more and more time at the house. They would have sex all over the place. We could hear them all the time. It was gross and aggravating. I said something at one point about how disrespectful it was. The response I got was, "This is my house. You chose to come live with me. If you don't like it, then you can get the frig out." But I had nowhere to go.

I wound up hooking back up with my old friend James, the one who was paralyzed from the neck down. I had a car now, so I started to spend a lot of time at his house. Both he and his mother were happy to see me back, but neither of them could believe I actually asked to move back with Colleen. His mother knew it would only be a matter of time before things went south again.

James and I had a good time together. It was nice having a true friend again. He couldn't do much, but we didn't need a lot to do. It was just hanging out with him that gave me a little peace. We didn't pull the crap we used to. James knew I needed to get away from Colleen's house. As always, Joanne was nice enough to open her home to me.

> *"The life we live, not the words we speak, reveals weather our faith is authentic."*
> **John MacAurther**
> **(Hard To Believe)**

I didn't believe in God at this point in my life yet. I was pissed off at everything I went through as a kid. Being back at Colleen's house, the crap of having to put up with her again, and being micro-managed by her had me wanting to leave.

It was around this time I met this girl, Robin, who also worked at the convenience store. She was about my age and married, but that didn't stop me from getting with her. We would flirt and mess around from time to time. She smoked pot and told me that her husband had a garbage bag full of weed stashed in their house that he forgot about and was willing to give it to me.

"Free?" I asked.

"Yeah, he's got like a lot of weed in the garage that he forgot about. He sells pot on the side. If you want, I can get some for you." she said.

"Sure."

I really thought she was bluffing, so I tried calling her on it.

"Here, take the keys to my car and get it."

"Okay. I'll be right back," she said.

She wasn't gone long. Twenty minutes later she came back and gave me back the keys to my car.

"Did you get it?" I asked.

"Yeah, it's in the trunk of your car."

"You're lying."

She just smiled at me and said, "No I'm not. Go look."

I walked out, popped my trunk, and there sat a garbage bag. I looked back at her in the store and she just smiled. I opened the bag and could not believe what I saw. Sure as her word, it was a garbage bag full of about four or five pounds of pot. My heart sank in my chest. I could not have been happier. I walked back into the store and she said, "Well? What do I get now? Are you going to finally do me?"

"I sure am," I replied.

I was eighteen years old, given a garbage bag full of weed, and all she wanted back from me was sex. I felt on top of the world. Because of all the pot I had now, I started to sell some of it. I met a guy who wanted to trade some acid for my weed. I had no problem with that, so we traded up and I started to drop a lot of acid.

I didn't see it then, but I didn't need that in my life. I'm not just talking about the acid. I'm talking about the weed, how much acid I was taking, having sex with a married woman, and trying to control it all. I couldn't. I even drove around one night, smoking a blunt, tripping on two hits of acid, listening to music, and looking for hookers. I was out of control.

-Psalm 10:8-
He sits in the lurking places of the villages;
In the secret places he murders the innocent;
His eyes are secretly fixed on the helpless.
(NKJV)

Here is a story I often think about:

I was working at the store one night and had dropped a couple tabs of acid. At shift change that night, my relief did not show up for their shift, so I had to work a double. My car insurance was due the next day. I planned on going home to sleep a few hours, then drive to Albany the next morning to pay it. I had to work the overnight shift now, so I dropped a couple more tabs of acid and decided to have a couple beers, courtesy of the store for my troubles. The next day, the manager came in and said, "Steve, you really don't look good at all."

"Yeah, I haven't felt good all night," I said.

"Well, let me get the paperwork together and you can go. Thanks for staying."

"Yeah."

I really wasn't feeling well either. I was crashing and needed to go home, but I had to drive over an hour to get to my insurance company on time. As soon as he came out of the office, I hit the road and started driving to Albany. It was cold and raining, and I was trying hard to stay awake. I felt my head nodding, so I cracked the window so I could feel the cold air on my face. I started swerving left to right and tried shaking it off. Then I fell asleep at the wheel on the New York State Thruway doing sixty miles an hour in the freezing rain.

-Genesis 28:12-
Then he dreamed, and behold, a ladder was set up
on the earth, and its top reached to heaven; and the
angels of God were ascending and descending on it.
(NKJV)

Nothing in the world can shake or change what I believe about this. I know in my heart that God shot down an angel to keep me from killing myself and others. He did not block the accident, but He did block death.

I woke up to the sound of metal on metal. I had just rear-ended a white van that was in front of me. My car almost went sideways, but I caught it and straightened it out. In my rearview mirror, I saw the van do a couple 360s while a Greyhound bus just missed smashing into it. I was so scared that I didn't stop and just kept driving. I noticed a truck following me, so I pulled over after a couple miles. The driver from the truck came up to my window.

"Are you drunk?" he asked me.

"No."

"I was following you for a few miles before you hit that van, and you were all over the road. Why the hell didn't you stop when you hit that van?"

"I was scared."

I went on to tell him that I worked a double shift that night and was tired. Whatever effects I had been feeling from the acid, beer, and pot were long gone now due to how scared I was at that moment. Then the van pulled up behind us, and the driver came up to me.

"Are you okay kid?" he asked.

I looked at him as if he was crazy. I didn't know what to say.

"Are you okay?" he said again.

"Uh, yeah. Are you okay? I'm really sorry. I fell asleep."

"That's okay, don't worry about it kid; accidents happen. That's why they call them accidents. Let's drive up to the next exit and get off so we can exchange insurance information, okay?"

"Okay," I said.

I could not understand why this guy was being so cool.

"Are you sure you're okay, son?"

"Yeah, I'm just a little scared right now. I was on my way to pay my car insurance. I can't believe I fell asleep while I was driving."

"Well, everyone's okay. Don't worry about it too much."

He shook my hand, got back into his van, and pulled off and left. I stood there for about fifteen or twenty minutes wondering what the hell just happened.

God saved my life that day.

I turned around and went home. A couple weeks later, I got some paperwork from the insurance company about the accident and Colleen freaked. She got in my face, yelling and screaming at the top of her lungs. She was pissed off because I had used her insurance company. She got a discount as long as I did not get into any accidents. She went on to say I was fouling up her house, her life, and now her insurance company. What else was new? I knew I wouldn't be here much longer.

Another journal entry from January 2012:

1-10-12   1:20am

I'm still in the laundry-room finishing up all the I.P. laundry. I finished up some homework and have been just flipping through my bible reading different scriptures. I read two things so far in my reading that really hit my heart hard! One was in my daily reading that Martin gives me weekly. It said, "Who am I to say that God is not attentive?" I really don't know what else to say. To be honest, I feel like it's God saying to me, 'Who do you think you are, thinking and saying that I am not attentive to you'? I feel like I was just slapped by God. I'm not trying to make Him mad, but I feel like He's not being attentive to what I want Him to be attentive to. And that is selfish, I know.

The other thing I read that hit me was, Psalm 10:22 = The blessing of The Lord brings wealth, without painful toil for it. It's weird because I have absolutely ZERO clue what that is supposed to mean to me right now. But it hit me so hard that I know one day it will. One day I will understand it.

And I keep fantasizing that one day I just want to marry Reese Witherspoon.

10:02pm

Another day gone. I did not go to any of my classes today and I skipped chapel tonight. I slept and read. I don't know what to do. I keep fighting with my wife. She tells me that I am bitter and rude. I'm only bitter and rude to her. I'm honestly just trying to not talk to her so that we don't argue, but she keeps being rude. I don't get it. I am lost. I'm lost in this life, my mind, and spiritually. Why doesn't God just take me out of this life. What's the point? I really don't understand. Why keep me around? Is this a joke? I feel like I can start to get close to Him and then CRAP happens. ALL THE TIME! Back in the day, God used to send Angels to people. Why can't He send me one in a dream? I've asked with a pure heart! I even dared the spiritual realm to take my family away in a major accident. How messed up is that. This is not good. This life sucks big-time. HE wants me to be positive and press on but where are the rewards?

240

Today I moved to a bottom bunk. THAT'S the highlight of my fucking year!

God is attentive in our lives, even when we don't see Him. He was there all right. I just wasn't looking for Him in certain areas, because I didn't think He needed to be there. I felt like there were other areas that could use attention from Him. Why did I go back to live with Colleen? Why was I in rehab again? Why does my ex-wife look like such an angel?

"Few things sap the human spirit like lack of hope."
Don Piper
(90 Minutes In Heaven)

Hope. Now that's something I do not have much of. What is hope? What is faith? I find myself wondering if I even truly know and understand what having "hope" is like. I "hope" that I can be a better dad to my kids. I "hope" that I can be a good husband again. I "hope" that this book reaches people in a real way. I "hope" that God still believes in me, even after all the lies, hurts, wrongs, and pain I've caused other people in my life.

This is not easy for me. I don't mean just writing this, I mean trying to stay on the level, trying to stay clean and sober, trying to keep holding on to Christ, and sometimes, just trying to keep on living. I wish I had it all figured out. I wish I knew what to do when my world is caving in on me. I wish I knew how to handle the trying times the "right way." I continue to make mistakes and fail, but I will tell you this, I keep getting back up. Sometimes I don't even know why I get back up, but I do. Maybe that's what "hope" is to me, just getting back up again for another round, even when I know I'm going to get knocked down again.

People read books, magazines, and whatever else they can find about other people's lives, how they might have turned some things around, and they almost always say, "Wow, that's great!"

"Now that's a real man/woman."

"Oh, how wonderful is that!"

And even sometimes, "Now that is what I would like (insert the name of someone you know who is struggling here) to do."

Try to replace the person you just read about with someone you know who has gone, or is going through, some of the same things. You are amazed at the person you just read about, and would even like to one day meet them, shake their hand, and say, "You are an inspiration to so many." Why can't you treat the person you know the same way? The real person in the story has caused as much hurt as the person you know. But yet, the person you know who has caused that hurt to you, you can't give the same respect to them as you would the person you just read about? You want to congratulate the person in the story, but even though the person you know has changed his or her life as well, you just can't, won't, or don't give them the same respect. Why?

There may be many people who read this and feel the same way, but I can't help that. Does it mean that I don't care? No. It just means that I can only do so much. I can't force you to treat me the same way as you would someone else you know or read about who's done some of the same things I have. I can only tell you that I'm truly sorry and move on, because honestly, if you still harbor hate towards me, then I just don't have the time for you, nor will I waste my breath on you. Get over it. Christ did.

-1 John 2:22-
Who is a liar but he who denies that Jesus is the Christ?
He is antichrist who denies the Father and the Son.
(NKJV)

Any time I am not living for Christ, I am living for satan. If I do not love God, then I love the enemy. If I am not recognizing that Jesus is Lord, doing nothing for Him, then I am against Him. I want to be used by Christ. I want to wake up in the morning ready to fight for Him. It sucks to wake up and have the enemy happy because he knows that I will do nothing but hurt people. I do not want that anymore.

"We need to suffer some of the cussed wrongness of life in order to find its deep rightness. We have to feel pain we do not want to feel, carry burdens we do not want to carry, put up with misery we do not want to put up with, cry tears we do not want to

shed. If we feel no hurt now, we will, when it's all done, be the most miserable of all people."
<u>*(Lewis Smedes)*</u>

Around this time, Colleen started dating this guy Jimmy. It's fair to say that I didn't like this guy very much. He was an extreme alcoholic. There was some added aggravation for me with him, since he was the father of my best friend James. He used to beat James' mother Joanne, never paid child support, and never visited his kids. He lived one town over from his son, and my friend had not seen his father since he was a little boy. Colleen didn't seem to care. I guess I should not have been so upset. To look at the two of them, they seemed like a match made in heaven. They both liked to drink hard, smoke pot, and do as they pleased. When I met Jimmy, I told him, "I'm best friends with your son. How long has it been since you've seen him? Why don't you ever call him?"

He looked at me and took a pull from his beer bottle. I really wanted to smack this dude in the mouth.

I don't remember the exact circumstances of what happened, but very soon after Colleen and Jimmy started dating, I got kicked out of the house for whatever reason. I wasn't surprised. I did not care about Colleen, her attitude, her easy way with many men, or her well-being. The time had finally come.

I bought my sister Belinda's car, a 1984 Ford Escort, and still owed her four hundred dollars for the car. She had signed the title over to me with just my word that I would pay her, but I never did. I didn't have anywhere to go after Colleen kicked me out, so this is the car I lived in for a few days until I got my paycheck. When I did get paid, I moved into a bed & breakfast for $50 a week. It was the only thing I could afford.

I went to work at the convenience store and came home every day to an empty room by myself. I ran out of drugs and didn't have any friends. What little money I did have, I spent on rent, alcohol, and weed. I was back in a town I did not want to be in. At work, I took what I wanted, when I wanted, and thought I was the slickest person alive.

One day, while I was driving to the Laundromat to do my laundry, I rear ended a car that was stopped at a red light. I wound up crunching her car just enough so that her rear doors wouldn't open up. I caved in my front bumper and bent my A-frame. Perfect! I lived in a town where everything was miles apart and just wrecked my car. I thank God that I had not been drinking or getting high. I found a mechanic who hammered my A-frame the best he could for fifty dollars and sent me on my way.

A week after that, I got fired for stealing and my cash drawer coming up short. I was handed my final paycheck and asked to leave. I was in trouble. Instead of paying a few weeks of rent while I looked for another job, I bought beer, weed, and rode it out until I had to move out of the bed and breakfast.

Now I was living in my car at a rest stop on the highway. I didn't know what to do. I had no money, nowhere to go, and almost no gas in my car. I lived like that for about a month or so before I remembered that the girl Robin I used to work with lived up the road. I went to see her and told her what was up and she took pity on me. She filled my car up with gas and let me stay at her house that day. I was able to shower and eat.

Her husband worked during the day and had to drive an hour each way. With this being the case, she told me that I could come over to her house during the week from morning until early evening. Saturdays and Sundays I was on my own. I was a leach and just needed somewhere to go. All she wanted in return was sex. Five days a week I had food, shelter, access to a shower, and sex. She would always give me a few bucks for gas for the weekends so I could at least drive around and not have to park at a rest stop.

I was a healthy kid and able to work, but decided to go on welfare instead. I was given food stamps and free room and board at a seedy motel. That's all it took for me to feel okay with life. I remembered going two weeks at one point with only one popcorn kernel to eat, so this felt pretty good. There was a convenience store and gas station right across the street from the motel, and I had no gas in my car. Even though they knew me, I still drove over, filled my car up with gas, and left without

246

paying. Back then, you could fill your car first before paying. I was nervous but needed the gas to get to the store to steal food.

As I was driving, I got pulled over and arrested for stealing eleven dollars in gas. I called my dad collect from jail. He wasn't surprised where I was. He knew the time was coming. I told him when I got out at the end of the week that I wanted to come and visit for a day. I got out of jail the following week, and to my surprise, my car was still in the parking lot. I had a full tank of gas and I headed back to the motel to shower and change my clothes. Then I headed for Boston early in the morning to see my dad. It didn't seem like he really wanted me there. I was trying to test the waters and see if there was any way he would let me move back, but it just did not feel right. He was standoffish and never offered, so I didn't ask. I spent the day, and when I left to go back home, he gave me twenty dollars for gas.

When I got back, I went job hunting. I got a job at a Burger King and rented another room. What I didn't spend on rent, I spent on alcohol and cocaine. Smoking weed just did not do it for me anymore. I needed something heavier.

My car was not in good shape, and I was driving on suspended registration and no insurance. My tires were bald, my breaks were metal on metal, both my tail lights were cracked, only one headlight worked that was barely dim, and the entire car rattled. It was only a matter of time before I would be pulled over, ticketed, arrested, and lose my car.

While driving around one night, I saw the exact same make and model car as mine. In the middle of the night, I went back and stole everything my car needed. I stole all four tires, the brake pads, rotors, taillights, the caps to the taillights, the headlights and bulbs, and even took the spare tire. It took a couple days to replace everything on my car, but when I did, it drove like new. Then I quit my job, waited for my final check, packed what little I had, and started driving. I had nowhere to go, so, I drove to the only home I ever had: Boston, Massachusetts.

Chapter Eight

-Philippians 1:17-
but the latter out of love, knowing that I
am appointed for the defense of the gospel.
(NKJV)

On the drive to Boston, I thought about what I was going to do. I didn't have a clue. I didn't know if my dad would let me stay there or not and wondered what I would do if he said no. I was not very street smart at the time, so I was worried. I always acted first and thought second, not a good order. I only ever thought about myself. I had selfish motives with selfish ambitions.

About sixteen years ago, I attended a church called Valley Bible Fellowship of Las Vegas. The lead pastor, Pastor Jim Crews, did a sermon on needing Jesus. He pulled a four or five inch Jesus from his pocket, held it up, and yelled out, "HELP ME JESUS! HELP ME JESUS!"

Then put Him back into his pocket. He repeated this a few times and then placed the toy Jesus on the podium. His sermon was about pulling Jesus out only when we felt we needed Him to show up. This immediately struck a chord with me, because this is how my relationship with Jesus had become. I sat in that service nodding my head. He was right.

I never truly understood what God was saying to me through that service until a few weeks ago. I was pulling Jesus out, because I needed Him this way, at this time, to take care of this thing, my way. I should not have had to pull Him out. I should've never put Him away in the first place. I need Jesus more than ever now, and I can't find Him. I wonder if He'll even show up. There are very specific ways I need Him, ways in which, if they are not met, things will turn out extremely bad for me. He will take care of it in His own way and only how He sees fit. It's not until I'm all alone, people are gone, bridges are burned, and I'm on my knees begging because of a situation I got myself into, that I realize I never should have put Jesus away. Now I sit and wonder how bad the consequences will be.

———————

"God does not exist to make a big deal out of us. We exist to make a big deal out of Him. It's not about you. It's not about me. It's all about Him."
Max Lucado
(It's Not About Me)

Well, I got to Boston just fine and made sure to show up on a day that Jeannie was working. I did not want to ask to stay there if she was home. I was scared and I knew she didn't want me there.

"Hi Dad," I said as I walked through the door.

It had been about five or six months since I had even talked to him, and he didn't seem pleased to see me. He probably knew what I was going to ask.

"Dad, I don't have anywhere to go."

He looked at me for a few moments without saying anything.

"Can I stay here until I get a job and can find somewhere to live?"

He continued to look at me and then said, "How long do you need to stay here, Steven?"

Ouch! That hurt. That meant I would be given a time frame. I wasn't counting on that. I just wanted to live at home again. I couldn't make it on my own, but now I knew I had no other choice.

"I don't know, a month maybe."

He gazed at the ceiling of his bedroom for a minute and then said, "I don't know. I'm going to have to talk to Jeannie about it. I'll talk to her when she's on her break and see."

"Okay."

This sucks. I wasn't counting on no as a possible answer. I sure wasn't counting on a time frame if the answer was yes. I remember thinking that all my friends still lived at home, and here I was, unable to find a place to sleep. Why did I have to get Colleen as the woman who gave birth to me? Even then, though, I knew my parents had to protect Natasha, Jarred, and Justin. They had them to think about, and I was no role model.

"You can stay for one month, Steven. Then you have to be out, all right?" my dad said.

I was truly heartbroken. Neither one of my parents wanted me around. That's a hard pill to swallow. It still is.

"Okay." I said.

"You better start looking for a job, Steven. You only have thirty days."

"Okay."

I tried to be content that I didn't have to sleep in my car that night, or any of the next thirty nights that followed. I knew I had to start to change. I wanted to. I also knew it would be a long time before I would. My parents knew that as well. They gave me way more than I deserved back then.

-Amos 4:6-
"Also I gave you cleanness of teeth in all your cities,
and lack of bread in all your places; yet you
have not returned to Me," says the LORD.
(NKJV)

The next day I got my old job back at Papa Gino's at the Woburn Mall. I thought that maybe if my parents saw I was working and really trying, they would let me stay. I was proud and told my dad I got a job right away. Jeannie, on the other hand, reminded me I only had twenty-nine days left before I had to be out. I felt like I couldn't even be given the chance to prove I could do something different. I wasn't her biological child. Rent was expensive in the Boston area, and having only one part-time job was not going to cut it.

I began to dislike Jeannie. I started to think it was because I was not one of her real children. I felt like the stepchild again. I felt if I was her real son, I would have received more grace. I was just not one of her children; that's just the way it was. I was mad because I really, truly, and honestly did not have a family I could call my own. I had no one in my life that would help me as if they were helping one of their own children. I can understand why no one wanted me around, but I wasn't even given a chance, and it doesn't make it hurt any less. I was a bad seed. I was trouble. Was there any reason to believe otherwise? Nothing sucks worse than not having a caring and nurturing family of your own to be able to go home to when things are tough. At nineteen, the world can be a scary place when you're on your own. It can chew you up and spit you out, and indeed, it would. By the end of that week, I had a second job at McDonalds in the same mall. Between the two jobs, I was working about fifty hours a week. I figured I could maybe scrape by on that.

I started looking for a place to live, but it was tough. I couldn't afford most of what was out there. What little I could afford, no one wanted a nineteen-year-old kid living there. Meanwhile, I was reminded I only had a certain amount of time to move out. I wanted to say something sarcastic, but I didn't want to be kicked out sooner. I actually respected Jeannie. I may have not have liked her at the time, but I did in fact respect her. I did not want to cause her any more trouble.

A few days before I was supposed to be out, I still found myself with nowhere to go. I had a little bit of money saved, but it wasn't much. I came home from work one day and Jeannie asked me, "Have you found somewhere to live yet?"

Up to that point, she had never asked me how my apartment hunting was going. It was always that I only had "X" amount of time left.

"Not yet. I got this one place I'm looking at in Reading," I replied.

"I really hope you find something soon, Steven," she said.

Now I was stressing hard. I'd been turned down at every place I looked at. I had an appointment with the owner of a rooming house in Reading two days before I was supposed to be out. Originally, he said no because I was only nineteen, but I begged and pleaded with him, so he agreed to at least meet with me. When we met, he still didn't seem too sure. I clean up well and looked like I was ready to cry. I told him that I had two jobs that were verifiable. He took pity on me and said that as long as he was able to verify my jobs, he would rent me one of the rooms. The price was a hundred dollars a week. He said he usually only charged two weeks to move in, but since I was so young, he was going to charge me a four hundred dollar security deposit plus two weeks up front. The total move in was six hundred, but I only had four eighty. I asked my dad for help, and without question, he gave me what I needed.

So there I was, on my own, living in a rooming house filled with drug addicts. I didn't even feel good about it. I didn't like this place, but what could I do? At least it had a parking lot where I could park my car that had no insurance, registration, and expired plates.

I got a third job at a Dollar Store in the same mall. I wasn't going to be working at Papa Gino's much longer, because the manager kept pushing me for my car insurance information, since I now delivered pizzas. Soon after I got the job at the Dollar Store, I quit Papa Gino's so I wouldn't get fired. The Dollar Store was great, I thought. The manager and the assistant manager both got drunk on their lunch breaks and came back loaded. The Third Key, Matt, taught me how to steal money out of the register without getting caught, and we took whatever we wanted at the end of our shifts. I started dating the assistant manager and became carefree about what I was doing.

In the meantime, I got yet another job at the same mall at a shoe store that was full time, so I quit my job at McDonald's. Between my two jobs and what I was stealing from the Dollar Store, I felt like I was making good money. I had long since been spending most of what I made on hard alcohol and pot, but I had now developed a healthy cocaine habit as well.

Only four people worked at the shoe store. There was the manager, assistant manager, and two cashiers. The assistant manager was quitting soon, and the other cashier, Donna, did not want the promotion. To my surprise, I was asked if I wanted to train to be the assistant store manager.

"What?" That was my response.

It came with more money, so I accepted the position. All this did was allow me to buy more cocaine every week. In the meantime, though, my car had been towed three times for me not having insurance, and each time I had to spend a hundred bucks to get it back. Mind you, I had been getting drunk at both my jobs, smoking pot in the back room at night, and doing cocaine in the bathrooms. I was soon fired from the Dollar Store, so all I had left was the job at the shoe store. With my cocaine habit, on top of the alcohol and pot, my money situation was not good. I was running out of cash faster than it came in. I couldn't afford to lose this job.

Now, here's the kicker. On top of all that was happening, I left my house one day to go to work and my car was gone. I looked at the parking lot and wondered why someone stole my piece of crap. I was wondering how I was going to tell the cops that my car, which had no registration, no insurance, and expired out-of-state plates, was stolen. While wondering this, someone yelled out, "Hey man. Are you looking for your car?"

"Yeah! Did you see who stole it?"

"Did you drive that little blue Escort?" the man yelled out to me.

"Yeah. Where is it?"

"The cops just towed it about an hour ago."

I just put my head down. Man, this sucked! I went to the police station and they told me that they check the cars there occasionally. They said that when they ran my plates, they noticed it was towed three other times for having none of what I listed above. So now my car was not at a towing yard, but it was now the property of the police impound. To get it out, I was going to have to show up with proof of registration, insurance, and new license plates, all of which had to be issued from the state of Massachusetts.

"The charge to get it out is one hundred fifty dollars, plus twenty-five dollars a day, for every day that it's impounded," the cop said to me.

I had just lost my car for good.

Then I thought about my job. I only worked the next town over, but it was like a five or six mile drive. That meant I was going to have to walk almost twelve miles a day to go back and forth to work. But wait, there's more. It actually gets worse.

This biker guy walked into the shoe store one day looking for his money. He went by the name of Spanky. He was a huge truck driver who owned a leather repair shop and he had a lot of big biker friends. I backed into his Harley Davidson drunk one night and bent his frame. He was pretty cool when it happened. He said that it looked to be about three fifty in damage. I promised to stop by the following week to settle up when I got paid. That had been months before, though. Now he came looking for his money and was not happy. He gave me until the following morning, or else. So I decided to rob the shoe store I worked at and get out of Boston.

-1 Peter 4:15-
But let none of you suffer as a murderer, a thief, an evildoer, or as a busybody in other peoples' matters.
(NKJV)

This was a turning point in my life. What I did took me in a direction that I had not been before. I remembered well what my friend Jamie had taught me about committing robberies and burglaries.

I was the assistant manager, and the store manager would not be in until Monday morning, so it was my job to drop the deposit bags off every night in the bank drop box. It was Sunday night, and I hadn't dropped the bags off yet from Friday and Saturday. There were supposed to be two of us that went together to drop off the bags of cash. It wasn't much of a burglary though. I emptied all the cash into one bag, put it in my backpack, and dropped off empty bags to the bank. The way I saw it, I only had two options: steal the cash or wait around for Spanky and his crew to smash my head in. There was no way I was going to pay him his money. I had too big a cocaine problem. This is a perfect example of me not thinking things through. I was going to go on the run with a few thousand dollars and no plan. Before my shift ended that night, I had my dealer meet me at the store. I bought two ounces of weed, an eight-ball of cocaine, and that was that.

Donna and I shut down the store and I told her that I'd see her later. I walked to the Commuter Rail station in Woburn, took the train into Boston, caught the Red Line to South Station, walked to the Greyhound Bus Station, and bought a ticket to Albany, New York. I would switch busses there.

I bought a change of clothes and a bottle of peroxide to dye my hair. When I got to Albany, I quickly got a cab and took it to a cheap motel. It was there that I dyed my hair, took a shower, changed my clothes, and counted the money. I cannot remember the exact amount, but I think it was just over three thousand dollars. My nerves were now starting to get to me. I smoked a joint and did a few lines. I looked in the mirror and thought I looked ridiculous. My hair looked retarded. The peroxide did not do to my hair what it did in the movies. I thought it was going to dye it blonde, but it came out kind of multi-colored. There was some red, some yellow, some orange, some burnt orange, and some black patches that did not seem to want to change color. I thought I looked like a white Dennis Rodman. I was not about to re-dye it. I wanted to be on the next bus out.

Back at the Greyhound terminal, I bought a ticket to Salt Lake City, Utah. My bus wouldn't leave for a while, so I sat back and tried to count the minutes. The time to leave finally came, and I got on the bus with no problems. I settled in for the three and a half day bus ride that would take me across the country. The seat in the back was open, and there weren't that many people on the bus. I sat back, tried to relax, and snorted the rest of the eight ball that night. Every time the bus stopped, I went for a walk and smoked a joint. I walked around without a care in the world, smoking a joint in whatever city I was in.

When I got to Salt Lake City, I got a motel room for a couple of days. I decided to go shopping, bought a few changes of clothes and brand new leather jacket because, well, I had to look cool while committing interstate felonies. I stayed in the room the entire time and got high. I thought about where I was going to go. I wanted to drink, but was underage and couldn't find anywhere that would sell to me. I didn't like Salt Lake City, so I went back to the Greyhound Station and got a ticket to Sacramento.

You know, sometimes life just sucks. Even now, I'm going through some crap and want to run away. I just want to run and not look back. I do not want to be here anymore. I've seriously thought about putting a bullet in my head these last few days, really! I have a friend I work with who has a gun, and I've really thought about buying it from him and just passing a bullet through my brain. I just got back to work this past Sunday from being suspended. I have to pay seven hundred dollars to my job every month for child support to my first ex-wife, Eva. At my job, I get paid cash daily for driving a cab. Because I was suspended, I didn't think I had to pay the child support two weeks ago. Long story short, the cab company I work for had to pay my child support. So now, after my shift each morning, I have to drop and extra fifty bucks for eleven days.

Sabrina went to Welfare a week and a half ago to get food stamps and to have the child support I have to give her garnished. She never said anything to me about it. I had to pull it out of her. I was asking if she could give me until next month so I can get the other paid off. She said she tried talking to me about it, but she never did. Then she said that she thought it would be easier to have it garnished because she isn't getting it, which was a lie because I have all of my cancelled checks that I wrote to her that all say child support in the note area. The only time I had trouble paying her was when I was suspended. She said it was okay, but then she went behind my back without telling me. On top of that, I have no money for rent. I know it's my fault for getting suspended; I'm not trying to pass blame here. I'm just so pissed off because everyone thinks that Sabrina got a bad deal when she married me. I'm the jerk to everyone, and when we fight, she gets an attitude and will not let me see my kids.

I was wrong in a lot of ways, but it was not all me. She said that she wants me back but filed for divorce. Now she is facing some consequences herself from filing for divorce, and now her consequences are, of course, my fault. When I'm struggling with something, no matter what it may be, one hundred percent of the time, she says, "It's because you're not living right."

I just want to smash her face in sometimes. She goes out and buys a new car with a $350 payment, and it's my fault she has no food. Her cable gets shut off, and it's my fault. She said that she didn't have enough money to pay her rent, but that was my fault because she said that I abandoned my family. I AM NOT THE ONE WHO FILED FOR DIVORCE! So yeah, I have wanted to put a bullet in my head, quick and easy. I can't even sit here and say that I won't do it at some point. I just don't know right now. I'm on the edge of totally losing it.

I've prayed for God to take my life in a car accident. I've begged Him to take my life. I've pleaded for Him to kill me. I don't care how, just end my life, please. I've thought about how happy I would be if I found out that I had terminal cancer. I've smiled at the thought. I would not even do the chemotherapy. I would just lovingly accept it and wait to die. I'm not saying this for anyone to feel sorry for me. I'm really not. I'm honestly just trying to be as real as I can. I want to die. I try to imagine a better life. I try to imagine a life not on this earth.

"God wants to use our imagination in the painting of the picture of what He is leading us to dare to hope for and expect."
(Lloyd Ogilvie)

I have tried to dare to hope and dream, like writing this book. I've dreamt about it actually selling millions copies and touching people in a real way, that maybe it would bring some people to Christ. I'd love to have a DVD made of me giving my testimony at a church that seats thousands, not for my glory, but for His, to be able to tell people what He has done for me, how He can do for you as well, if you let Him. Am I asking for too much? Probably. I've got nothing to lose except some dignity and respect, and even at that, I don't care. Do I think this will ever happen? No, I do not. I feel like God is up there laughing at me. I feel like He's waiting for me to screw my life up more. I used to have dreams, big dreams. Now I just cling to the hope that maybe one day God will just stop messing with my life. Maybe I'm just meant to struggle the rest of my life. It even says in the Bible that some people are meant for suffering....

I wonder if I'll ever get published by a reputable publishing company. I've thought about the chances of that not happening. I'm going to make this a readable book. It may not, and probably will not, sell many, or any, books, but that's not going to stop me from writing it. I'm stubborn, and I'm going to do it anyway. At least I'm being real. I tell the truth about what I did, how I feel, how I reacted, and what I've done wrong. If nothing else, I'm finally being honest with myself.

Just seeing this as I write it all down gives me some clarity, and closure, on a lot of things. Some of it even makes me sick to my stomach. More than anything, though, I feel sad that a child was as lost as I was.

"A small God? No thanks. You and I need what Moses needed – a glimpse of God's glory. Such a sighting can change you forever. At that moment I realized something. I could look around and find fear, or I could look at my father and find faith. I chose my father's face. So did Moses. So can you."
Max Lucado

263

(It's Not About Me)

Don't get me wrong. I believe that He can, I just do not believe He will, for me. It doesn't matter how I feel inside or what I think God will or will not do for me. I will never stop telling people that Christ is the answer to all their problems, and that He is the only way that leads to life.

"Somewhere we have picked up the notion that if we live a faithful and obedient life, we will be spared the pain and sorrow that is so much a part of our fallen world."
(Richard Exley)

Even when I have done the right things for a time, things still come crumbling down. I have often wondered why God will not give me a sustained period of peace in my life.

-Philippians 1:29-
For to you it has been granted on behalf of Christ, not only to believe in Him, but also to suffer for His sake, (NKJV)

-Daniel 8:4-
I saw the ram pushing westward, northward, and southward, so that no animal could withstand him; nor was there any that could deliver from his hand, but he did according to his will and became great. (NKJV)

I did do as I pleased, and in fact, became very great in my own mind. I lived in the moment, a moment at a time, never looking ahead, back, or sideways. I felt as if I could handle anything, at any time, in any moment. I was superior. I was Steve Gray, damn it!

———————

When I got on the bus in Salt Lake City, my nerves were shot. I wasn't sure I could handle my emotions, never mind the consequences that came with felony grand larceny, burglary, and evading the authorities. I also felt euphoric. I was running, ducking, hiding, dodging, and evading the police. It wasn't that big of a deal to me. I wanted more.

The following evening the bus rolled into Reno, Nevada. We stopped at one of the local casinos, and I figured I had a few bucks to spare. We had an hour or so to do what we pleased. I blew a few hundred dollars playing craps, blackjack, and roulette. As I walked to get on the bus, I saw some dudes who looked like they wanted to kick the crap out of me. I was wondering if I had pissed anyone off in the casino. I brushed it off as just being in a bad part of town. It felt good to be back on the bus and we would soon be on our way to Sacramento. We were just about to pull out of the parking lot when I heard someone say, "Damn! Check that out! It's the police!"

For a split second I thought maybe the cops had caught up with me. How could they have known that I would be on this bus? I was nervous but couldn't do anything about it. A regular looking guy walked on the bus and pulled out a badge.

"Narcotics officers! Everyone just stay seated, and we'll be done here in a minute."

Cool, they were not here for me. I felt like the weight of the world lifted off my shoulders. I was able to sit back and relax. They were looking for someone who was trying to transport drugs, and that wasn't me. I had about an eighth of an ounce of weed in my jacket pocket, but the dogs were not allowed in the bus.

Three officers got on the bus and started from the rear, moving their way forward. They asked each person for their ID, bus ticket, if they had any luggage at all on the bus with them, and if they could search it. Everyone complied with the officers, giving them permission to search their luggage in the overhead compartment. For the most part the cops were cool; they only looked in the luggage of every tenth person or so. They came to me, asked me for my info and if they could also search me and my luggage. I complied, but they moved on to the next person. They finally finished and were headed off the bus.

"Thank you for your time everyone. We are just having the K-9 unit search the luggage compartment below, and you'll all be on your way. Have a good trip."

Cool. I could not wait to get going. It only took a few more minutes for the dog to sniff the luggage below. Just then another cop came back onto the bus and said, "I need everyone to look out the side of the bus. Whose bag is that that the officer is holding up?"

We all looked out of the side windows on the right side of the bus and as sure as the sky is blue, they were holding up my duffel bag. Perfect! Should I say anything? I didn't have any drugs in my bag. No one said anything, so the cop said, "We are going to open that bag and search it anyway. It would be a lot better if we knew who's bag it was. It will make my life, and yours, much easier if you tell me now."

Not one word came from anyone.

The cop walked off the bus and to the luggage that the dog sniffed out. My mind was going a mile a minute. I had no ID in my bag at all, but inside of my bag was a deposit bag from the shoe store that I kept to initially hold the cash in. It also had the checks in it that I forgot to get rid of and the paperwork I forgot to throw out. Damn! I didn't know what to do. I always scribbled my signature, so maybe they wouldn't be able to tell. I should have dumped that damn deposit bag. Why in the world I kept it, I have no clue.

As I sat there, I wondered how the hell the dog sniffed out my bag that had no drugs in it. As I sat there wondering, I remembered that when I did my laundry, I brought it back to my hotel room to fold because I wanted to get stoned. While I smoked, I folded my laundry at the same time. That's how the dog sniffed out my bag. I sat back down in my seat and tried to wait it out. I had my wallet on me, and nothing in my bag could identify me anyway.

"Wow! Check that out! There's a deposit bag in that luggage," came a voice from one of the passengers. My heart sank.

"It's a bunch of checks." Came another voice.

A few minutes later, one of the officers came on the bus and yelled out, "Steven Frederick Gray II!"

No one said anything.

"Is there a Steven Gray on this bus?" he yelled out again.

I kid you not, the officer was holding up my birth- certificate. I had forgotten that I had left it in my bag. So I stood up and said, "Yeah, that's me."

"Could you step off the bus, sir?"

I couldn't believe this. It hadn't even been a week, and I was caught. Actually, I could believe it. I was at a loss for words. I thought I was smarter than that.

"Is that your bag?" the officer asked me.

"Yes," I responded.

"Would you mind telling me what all that is?"

"Well, I'm on vacation. I'm the assistant manager of the store, and I forgot to drop that bag off at that bank before I left. I was in a rush. I guess I just forgot."

The officer looked at me like I was full of it, which I was, and said, "Give me your ID."

I knew I was going to be arrested. He patted me down and wanted to know what was in my jacket pocket. I was nervous and pulled out my pack of cigarettes. I still had the weed in the same pocket, but he didn't pat me down a second time. I didn't want to go to jail. They put me in handcuffs, and I stood there as he ran me. I was going to jail and was now feeling sick to my stomach. Then, after a few minutes had passed, I heard over his radio, "Steven Gray, New York State driver's license. Clean. No wants, no warrants at this time."

What? I couldn't believe this. How could I have no warrants? It had been at least four or five days since I ripped off the store. I had to be wanted by now. He gave me back my license, took me out of the handcuffs, and said, "I don't believe a word you said, Mr. Gray. Something's going on here, and I'm gonna find out what it is. But for right now, you're free to go."

He made me tell him where I was going and for how long, all of which I told him was false. I gave him a fake date on when I would be going home, and he just looked at me. He knew I was lying, and it didn't help that I looked guilty too. I got back on the bus, and we started rolling on down the highway. I sat and wondered how I was not arrested and taken to jail. There had to be a reason. As I thought about what just happened, the words on the police radio replayed in my head, "Steven Gray. New York State driver's license. Clean. No wants. No warrants at this time."

Oh my gosh! That was it! That's how I wasn't hauled in! I had moved from New York to Massachusetts and never switched my driver's license over. I never did what I was supposed to, therefore, when they ran me, they ran me in the state of New York and never made the connection to Massachusetts. All the paperwork in the deposit bags and all the checks had addresses on them from Massachusetts, but my ID was from New York. They never caught on. If they had only run me in Massachusetts, I would have a different story right now. I sat there dumbfounded, a small smile on my face. In the morning, the cops would know they had made a mistake. It was a very narrow escape, but I didn't care. The bus rolled into Sacramento in the wee hours of the morning, and I split. I was not about to wait around.

"I refer to them as miracles – although some may call them fortunate circumstances – because I believe there are no accidents or surprises with God."
Don Piper
(90 Minutes In Heaven)

Was this from God or the enemy? I believe, in one way or another, that this might have been, in some form, divine intervention.

-Exodus 14:3-
For Pharaoh will say of the children of Israel, 'They are bewildered by the land; the wilderness has closed them in.'
(NKJV)

I was confused, lonely, and didn't know what to do. I couldn't escape my desire to just roam.

When I got off the bus in Sacramento, I found a hotel room far enough away from the bus station that I felt was safe and paid for a few days. I figured I would just chill for a while and think.

During the day, I roamed the city. At night, I sat in the hotel room and got high and drunk. I found a tattoo shop and got some ink done: a naked red-head on my left inner forearm.

I didn't know what to do, and I did not want to stay in California. I remembered that my friend, Andre, whom I hung out with while I was in the foster home in Woburn, MA, had moved to Atlanta, Georgia. I still had his number in my wallet, so I called him, told him I was on my way to Atlanta for a few days, and wanted to hook up to get high.

-Ecclesiastes 8:14-
There is vanity which occurs on the earth, that there are just men to whom it happens according to the work of the wicked; again, there are wicked men to whom it happens according to the work of the righteous. I said that this also in vanity.
(NKJV)

Why does it seem sometimes that people who do the right things and follow The Lord with a pure heart suffer? Why does it seem as if some wicked people flow through life with no worries at all and seem to get everything their hearts desire? It sucks to see this happen. At the end of the day, though, why do I think I can follow The Lord and have no troubles?

A while back, I was sitting in a Bible study. We were talking about the *Left Behind* series. The focus of the conversation was the rapture. I used to know this guy, Ryan Omlie, a real man of God, a true believer in every sense of the word. He was someone I looked up to and wondered if one day I would ever have the kind of faith that he did. He said something that night I will never forget as long as I live.

"If I could, I wouldn't mind if God allowed me to stay behind on earth so I could bring other people to Christ."

This is the most selfless thing I have ever heard anyone say. To want to stay behind after the rapture to proclaim the name of Christ so others could have a fighting chance, that's the heart of a true believer!

———————

I made it to Atlanta without any problems. When I got there, I called Andre, and he came to meet me at the bus station. It was good to see him. We had not seen each other in a couple of years. We used to be tight. I didn't want to overstay my welcome, since I was on the run. His mother had been extremely nice to me already by letting me stay a few days. I bought a flight ticket to Tallahassee, then another bus ticket, this time to southern Arizona, less than ten miles from the Mexican border. I wanted drugs.

-Mark 2:17-
When Jesus heard it, He said to them, "Those who are well have no need of a physician, but those who are sick. I did not come to call the righteous, but sinners to repentance."
(NKJV)

———————

Have you ever felt like you're just not good enough? I have. Even right now, I feel like I'm just not good enough. Lately, I feel like I just cannot shake these demons out of my life. Even trying to pray them out doesn't seem to be working. Why do they keep messing with me? I wish they would leave me alone. At times, I feel like it's the way I am living. Other times, I feel like they love messing with my life because I'm easy prey. Sometimes I hope they're only messing with me because they know the plans God has for me. No matter what, though, they stay latched on. I feel like their claws are so deep in me that they couldn't let go if they tried.

I know that I go back and forth in this book. Sometimes I'm feeling good; other times I can't shake the feeling that my life is, and will always be, filled with crap. I look at this as I write and realize that this is just as much for me as it is for the world. I have my good days and my bad days, and right now, I'm trying so hard to fight. It's not that I don't care what you think. I just care more about the fight. If God came to call the sick and the sinners, then let me tell you something, I'm right at the top of that list.

"Any attempt to measure the value of our lives by comparison and contrast to others belittles our gifts and dishonors God by our ungratefulness."
Brennan Manning
(Ruthless Trust)

I made it to Sierra Vista with a couple hundred dollars left in my pocket. I was tired, in need of a shower, had nowhere to go, and didn't know what to do. I looked up the address of a girl I met on the bus, and to my surprise, she lived just a few blocks away. Her trailer was easy enough to find. I held my breath as I knocked on her door. A few seconds later, she was at the door.

"Hi Janet. It's me, Steve. I met you on the bus a couple of weeks ago."

"Oh, wow! Yeah, I remember you. How are you?"

"I'm okay. I was just rolling through Arizona, and I thought I would stop by and say hi."

When I met Janet on the bus, she was traveling cross country with her daughter, had two days left on her bus ride, and no money to feed herself or her daughter. I gave her fifty dollars and told her to feed her kid. I didn't want anything in return.

She invited me in and we talked for a few. She asked me what was really going on, so I told her I was robbed in Tucson. When I met her, I was sure to flash my wad of cash trying to look cool. I lied and said that I was on my way back home to Boston when I was robbed.

"What are you going to do?" she asked.

"I'm going to find a homeless shelter and try to get some work, try to make enough money to get back home."

"Well, I have a roommate, so you can't stay here for long, but I can let you stay the night so you can figure something out."

"That would be great."

"Where are your bags? Don't you have anything with you?"

"My bags will be at the bus station on Monday morning."

"Okay. You can stay here until Monday morning then."

"Thanks, Janet."

"No problem, Steve. Thank you for helping me out on the bus so I could feed my daughter"

"You're welcome. Don't worry about it."

Janet knew this family that rented out rooms to transients, and they said I could stay there for a while. I would have to do some yard work until I found a job and was able to pay rent. They lived in Hereford, Arizona, which was really far out. Who was I to complain? I had to hitchhike into town every day just to look for work. I found a job at a Burger King but was fired after a couple of weeks for not making it to work on time. I had to hitchhike over twenty miles just to get to work. I knew that job wouldn't last long.

The couple I lived with had three daughters: Chase, Dharma, and Ellen. Chase was around my age and pregnant. She lived in the house because she and her boyfriend were having problems, so we started hooking up. Dharma was sixteen, married, had a daughter already, and lived in town with her nineteen-year-old husband, Steve Mocco. Ellen was thirteen, lived at home, and had the most level head of the three of them. They were a seriously dysfunctional family. It wasn't long before I was kicked out of the house. For the next couple of months, I lived where I could, usually on people's couches and things like that. More times than I can count, though, I had to sleep outside.

I wound up meeting these two guys, Steve and Rob, not the kind of people I should have been hanging out with. We smoked and snorted speed all the time, as well as smoked weed and drank a lot of beer. They were the violent type. I was where I thought I was supposed to be.

I wound up finding some work with a fix-it guy through Steve and Rob. He got jobs now and then, and when we worked for him, he usually didn't want to pay us. A few times, the three of us would have to go threaten him just to get paid.

We ran twenty-four hours a day, non-stop, only sleeping when our bodies couldn't take it anymore. We hung out a lot at our friend Miguel's house. We all thought Miguel was the man. He was an older guy in his early fifties. Miguel had cancer. He was dying, but we never knew this at the time. He owned a house and had a never-ending supply of weed and beer. That was where we hung out.

It was at Miguel's house that I met Jason. Jason was a mechanic whose wife, Sherri, was sleeping with Rob. Jason knew it and could do nothing about it. He was small and weak, so he just took it as normal. I felt bad for him. Jason told me I could stay at his house as long as I didn't sleep with his wife. He was only going to charge me a few bucks a week for rent, so I agreed.

I didn't like Arizona, at least not where I was. There was trouble all over, and I always seemed to be right in the middle of it. At the time, I didn't think it was all that bad, but I saw that it could wind up ending badly for me. Steve and Rob loved to start crap all the time, and people usually did what they said. I didn't know why people were so scared of them. I had to get out.

Jason had just bought a brand new Camaro RS. He also had a gun he needed to fend off this other guy that his wife had cheated on him with who wound up turning into a psycho. I didn't want to stay here anymore. I don't just mean in Arizona; I didn't want to be alive anymore. One night, I was as high as I think I have ever been. I had been drinking and smoking speed while thinking about my life. I was on the run and wanted in two states. I would never amount to anything. I was a loser and destined to fail.

Then my thoughts turned towards Colleen. That was where it all started. I started thinking that if Colleen had never been my birth mother, then maybe things would have turned out differently for me. She was an alcoholic and a drug addict who cared about no one but herself. That's what I had become. I saw myself as Colleen, and I hated her for it. I made my decision. I was going to kill her, then kill myself.

While Jason was sleeping, I stole his .357 magnum revolver, the keys to his brand new Camaro, and the money from his wallet. He had just been paid and had over four hundred dollars. I knew that would be more than enough to get to New York to kill Colleen. If I was stopped on the way, I would shoot the cop who pulled me over, then put a bullet in my head. That was my plan. I took the money, the gun, the car, and took off for New York one night at about midnight. Colleen was going to suffer first. I was going to torment her. Shoot her legs, then her arms. When I finally saw true fear in her eyes, I would torture her even more. She would not die quickly.

<u>Chapter Nine</u>

-Ruth 1:17-
"Where you die, I will die, and there will I be
buried. The Lord do so to me, and more also,
if anything but death parts you and me."
<u>(NKJV)</u>

The following is song I wrote while in my Christian band, SEED. I hope you can see my heart in this.

<u>(He Cried)</u>

I can't think
Don't trust
Suffocating in my lust

Can't see
Eyes blind
Vivid thought of that life behind

Memories past
Pain revealed
Child's life left concealed

That dark room
Broke and bruised
Little boy left confused

Why do I run away from my God
Why do I duck and hide from my God
Don't you know that Jesus saves

On my knees
Chemical fade

Please just take this life away

Pipe down
Arms raised
Boy to man just needs to praise

He took my shame
I didn't know
Jesus bleed, He told me so

A door knock
I open wide
Just for me Savior died

When will I run to the arms of my God
How do I stand and fight for my God
Don't you know He's always there

Only one fight
In boys life
Trust Jesus day and night

All alone
No heroes known
His only tear, filled with fear

When I lied
He cried
Tell me why You died for my life

Second chance
At last dance
Came to me You set me free

Now it's time to live and tell about my God
This is the life of one:

Saved by grace
Who ran the race

Touched by light
Given sight

Redeemed by faith
Healed by God

Demons out
Jesus in
Blessed be forgiven sin

LET ME TELL YOU ABOUT MY GOD!

"Did God want me to know how real pain could feel so that I could understand the pain of others?"
Don Piper
(90 Minutes In Heaven)

I've thought so much about how God allowed me to go through things that are so difficult, painful, and heartbreaking. Maybe all these trials are not even for my benefit at all. To think I went through these things because God wanted to touch someone else through me is mind blowing. The whole time I'm just crying out, "Why me?" And it may not even be for me.

-2 Corinthians 3:2-3-
You are our epistle written in our hearts, known and read by all men; clearly
you are an epistle of Christ, ministered by us, written not with ink but
by the Spirit of the living God, not on tablets of flesh, that is, of the heart.
(NKJV)

As I drove on that night, I wasn't even concerned with the fact that I had just stolen a car, cleaned out my friends wallet, or had stolen a loaded .357 magnum revolver. I drove without a care in the world. Only one thing mattered to me: killing Colleen Jane Riley. I drove as safe as I could. I didn't want to get pulled over, but if I did, I was going to go out shooting. I drove through state after state, my thirst for Colleen's life intensifying. I drove across the country with the gun on my lap. I had passed many cops and wondered if I would get pulled over before I got to New York.

I don't know exactly where in the United States I had the car trouble, but along the way, the radiator started to overheat. I did not want to get stopped, so I pulled into a truck stop and parked the car. I went in to get something to eat so the car could cool down. I wasn't smart enough to check the water or coolant. After I ate, I sat there thinking about Colleen. After a while, I went back out to the car, started her up, and drove away. The car seemed to drive okay. I pulled into a rest stop later on that night to get some sleep and to give the car a rest.

The following day, the car continued to overheat, and each time, I pulled into a rest area for about an hour to let it cool down. That night though, I got a hotel room and I was worried about the car being seen. The hotel took the vehicle information and gave me my room key. I parked three doors away and backed into the parking spot so the plates could not be seen. I didn't get much sleep that night.

I was afraid the cops would be here to arrest me. I kept the gun under my pillow with my finger on the trigger. I woke up paranoid, peeked out the window, but didn't see anyone.

I finally made it to New York, but the car wasn't going to make it all the way to Colleen's house. I was on the highway when it started to blow smoke out of the engine. I pulled off the next exit and into a hospital parking lot that was just off the exit. The car wouldn't go any faster than about 5 m.p.h. I shut the engine off and it just blew more smoke. I didn't know what to do. I was in a stolen car with a stolen gun.

-Nahum 1:3-
The LORD is slow to anger and great in power,
and will not at all acquit the wicked. The LORD
has His way in the whirlwind and in the storm,
and the clouds are the dust of His feet.
(NKJV)

How big is my God? He's big enough to stop me from doing something that would have completely ruined my life. I didn't just want to kill Colleen; I wanted to torture her, slowly. God had other plans though. I do not think Colleen will ever fully understand how close she came that day to being murdered. God is always on time; He is never late. That car breaking down that night is what saved Colleen from becoming a statistic.

I sat there in the car and wondered why. What was I doing? What was I thinking? What have I become? The questions just kept coming. My eyes filled up with tears, and I started to cry, and when tears came, it was as if a river let loose. I could not stop crying. I just sat there for a while and cried my heart out. When I finally did stop, I took the bullets out of the gun, put them in my pocket, placed the gun in my hip, and walked into Saint Joseph's Hospital in Elmira, New York. I walked up to a guy that took information from incoming patients. He looked up at me and said, "Can I help you, sir?"

Then I started to cry again.

"Here, have a seat. It's okay."

I just could not stop crying again.

"It's okay, you're safe here. What's going on?"

My body was shaking uncontrollably.

"Try to relax. I'm here to help you. Just tell me what's going on."

"I was going to go kill her tonight, then kill myself," I blurted out.

"Kill who?" he said.

"Colleen. I was going to kill her and then kill myself."

"Well, I'm glad you came here instead. How were you going to kill her?"

After he asked me that question, I pulled the bullets out of my pocket and put them on the desk in front of him. His eyes widened, like he couldn't believe I just put bullets in front of him.

"Do you have a gun?"

"Yes."

"Would you be able to give it to me, please? I just don't want you to hurt yourself."

"Okay."

I pulled the gun out from my hip and put that on the desk in front of him as well. He looked astonished but also relieved.

"I'm just going to go put this in a lock box real quick so no one gets hurt. Can you sit here for a minute? I'll be right back. Is that okay?"

"Okay," I said.

He was looking past me at someone in the distance. He got up to go put the gun away, and I turned around to see another guy at a desk, not far away, looking at me like I might shoot him. He looked petrified. I turned back in my seat, put my head down, and started to cry again. When the guy I gave the gun to came back, he asked me if I wouldn't mind coming with him down the hall. He brought me to another room, and once in it, I realized it was locked. He sat with me for a few minutes, told me that he had to call the cops, and that they were on their way to take a report. He asked me if I was still suicidal. I said that I was.

"Do you have any other weapons on you at all?"

"No."

"Okay then; just sit still for a couple minutes. Are you hungry?"

"No."

"Okay, don't worry. You came to the right place. We're here to help you."

"Okay."

He left the room, and I sat there waiting for the cops. I figured I was going to be arrested, but I wasn't concerned about that. I didn't care at that point. I just wanted help. I really didn't want to kill anyone. This was the first time I can remember that something else was controlling me. That something else was God. He was taking me out of a situation that would have sent me to prison for the rest of my life. I know this for a fact. Without intervention, I would have killed that woman that night.

-Daniel 4:2-
I thought it good to declare the signs and wonders
that the Most High God has worked for me.
(NKJV)

About twenty minutes later, the cops showed up to take their report. They asked me a lot of questions about why I wanted to kill Colleen. I couldn't explain to them why; I just kept telling them that I hated her and wanted her dead. My mind was junk. They asked me how I got here from Arizona, so I gave them the keys to the car. I told them I parked the car outside. They would find out it was stolen as soon as they ran the plates. They kept telling me that nothing in life could be so bad that I should want to kill myself. I just looked at them through my tears and told them they didn't understand.

"Do you still feel like killing yourself?" they asked.

"Yes."

"Okay. Everything is going to be all right. You did the right thing and came to the right place." Then they left.

I thought I was going to be arrested, but I wasn't. Some other people came in and said that they were taking me upstairs to a psychiatric ward in the hospital. I was taken to a locked unit where they showed me to my room and let me be. As I sat on my bed, I wondered if there was a God at all. If there was a God, why did I have the life that I had. I sat and cried for a long while. Eventually, I fell asleep and slept the better part of three days.

> *"He wants to steal our joy and replace it with hopelessness."*
> **Don Piper**
> **(90 Minutes In Heaven)**

Things are kind of messed up right now, but aren't they always? Or, at least, aren't they always with me? I don't know what to do right now. I feel so helpless and hopeless.

The other day I saw a movie called *Bruce Almighty*. Morgan Freeman says something that I want to share with you. He plays the role of God, and when Bruce, played by Jim Carry, is talking with him, Morgan Freeman says,

> *"People want me to do everything for them, and what they*

don't realize is they have the power.
You want to see a
miracle, son? BE the miracle."

Be the miracle: that's what God spoke into my heart. You see, I have the tendency to mess up my life, as if you haven't gathered that already. I just always seem to do all the wrong things at all the wrong times, and what happens is I wind up messing up a big portion of my life. Then come the consequences from my decisions. Oh, what a joy. Directly after that, I'm looking up to God saying, "Help me, help me, help me! Can't You see what's happening? Help me, God! Why are You letting this happen? Why? I don't deserve this, God! Why do You hate me? Why are you letting this happen to me? Please fix this. Please, I need a miracle!"

And what He is saying to me is, "You want a miracle, son. BE the miracle!"

It's all about choices. The choices we make now will affect how He will be willing to work in our lives later. Right now, at this point in my life, when I say "No" to smoking crack, that's a miracle. When I say "No" to buying any beer today, that's a miracle. When I say, "Yes, LORD, today I am going to try to do things Your way," that's a miracle.

My point is this: sometimes I have the power to allow God to perform a miracle in my life by the choices I make. Don't get me wrong. I am not saying that I am God or that I can act on His behalf. What I am saying is that whatever I think, say, or do, can have a direct result on whether God will perform a certain miracle in my life at that point in time. That goes for you as well.

You want a miracle? Be the miracle!

Chapter Ten

-Psalm 27:14-
Wait on the LORD; be of good
courage, and He shall strengthen your
heart; wait, I say, on the LORD!
(NKJV)

I'm struggling harder than I ever have before. I'm in a bad way right now. I haven't written anything in this book in over a year. Right now I am facing two to ten years in prison. This is not good. Yes, I did something wrong, but I do not believe this is all my fault. Do not take anything I am about to tell you as me trying to justify myself or my actions to you. I am only telling you what has happened.

I cannot see my kids right now, per the court. When things were okay with my ex-wife Sabrina and me, she would let me have my kids on the weekends, per our divorce decree. If we happened to be arguing, she would not let me see, or even talk, to my children, Rhesa and Asher. I have been dealing with this crap for two years now. I'll shed more light on that later on. In November, my ex-wife and I got into a massive argument. After that fight, she would again not let me see, have, or even talk to my kids, again. The reason: I had used drugs again. I refused to call on the LORD for His help and fight for me. I simply became tired of Sabrina messing with my relationship with my kids, not telling about my daughter, Rhesa's, birthday party, lying to child support, lying to welfare, and not letting me see my kids whenever we had an argument. To cope with her crap, I turned to drugs again to numb my mind. I believe with all my heart that she knew what she was doing, and that by doing this, I would do drugs again. I truly believe that! I can blame it on her lying or any other number of things, but it comes down to me not trusting in God enough to take care of the situation. I just didn't trust His timing. Sabrina moved and committed child abduction. I even have the event numbers from the Las Vegas Metropolitan Police Department. I snapped and lost it, thus ruining my life and my relationship with my kids.

I even tried doing it the right way this time. I was driving to her house and calling the cops. I was getting event numbers to try to build a case against her. She moved! What else did she do? Sabrina filed for, and was granted, a restraining order. Awesome! There are so many things in the middle that you do not know right now, but that will come out later. I promise. Everything will be brought to the surface: the things she did wrong and the things I did wrong.

The bottom line is this: I broke the restraining order on Christmas because I was just so upset about not seeing my kids. The judge even told her what she did by moving was child abduction. I have a copy of the DVD of Judge Matthew Harter, telling Sabrina exactly that. I didn't know where my kids were. She blamed me for doing drugs again, and she was right. I only got high again because she was messing with my kids. I should have been stronger. I wasn't. On November 27th, 28th, & 29th, I got high. I failed. I lost in court.

On Christmas day, I called and texted Sabrina, telling her that I was going to kill her, and I truly meant it. I was arrested and charged with aggravated stalking, a class D felony. I reacted wrongly to her messing with my kids, and I messed up big time! I was released from jail on January 2nd, and she subpoenaed the family court to have me held in contempt of court for violating the restraining order. The judge would not put me in jail, because he was worried about double jeopardy. This woman will stop at nothing until I am out of the picture! Never going to happen, Miss Jones!

What I'm feeling right now, you couldn't possibly have a clue! I miss my kids! I love my kids! I love Rhesa and Asher with all my heart. I just want to die! I want to kill myself! You don't know how serious I am. You don't get it! Where's God? Where's Jesus? Why does He continue to mess with my life?

Because of the hate that two people have for each other, two children's lives are, and will be, altered and crushed, because I will never stop! I walked away from my first son, Sebastian. I will not do it again. One day, I will show Rhesa and Asher all my court papers, videos, and documents as to why I was not around when they needed me. It will take my death for this not to happen.

I hate God right now! I hate Jesus! Right now I have ZERO love in my heart!

-Zephaniah 3:8-
"Therefore wait for Me," says the LORD, "Until the day I rise up

for plunder; My determination is to gather the nations to My assembly of kingdoms, to pour on them My indignation, all My fierce
anger; all the earth shall be devoured with the fire of My jealousy."
<u>*(NKJV)*</u>

I cannot stop drinking right now. I get drunk every night until I pass out. Then I wake up for work the next day. I just don't want to feel anything. Nothing at all! I miss my kids so much it physically hurts! It is killing me on the inside. Women just don't understand that even though they are the ones that give birth, we, as the fathers to those children, also have a deep connection. It kills us and tears us apart when women play games with our children. Have you ever watched the Discovery Channel and watched what a lion, or any other male beast, does when he even thinks you're about to mess with his children? Just a thought. Yet, we're expected to stay calm, cool, and collected and sit and take it.

I've thought about killing Sabrina recently. Maybe taking her and keeping her in a hole while I torture her year after year, playing with her mind, giving her hope that one day she'll live, only to torture her even more. I could kill her entire family, everyone she loves, leaving only her alive so she could feel the gut wrenching pain I wake up to, live with, and go to sleep with at night, every day. I can't do that though. It's my children that stop me from going off the deep end. As much as I hate that evil, vile woman, I just will not do that to my kids. One day, Rhesa and Asher will know the truth, all of it. I won't stop until they know everything that has happened. It's the here-and-now that's killing me. I want to die! I wake up every morning in turmoil because God has not killed me yet. Sometimes I live my life wrong just so He has an excuse to kill me. Where are You, God? What are You waiting for? Take my life now! Give me a break and take my life. I have given You every reason to take me away, yet You still won't do it. I hate You right now! I HATE YOU! Sabrina is wrong right now, and You freaking know it! Yet, You still let it play on. How do I ever come back to You? How can I ever love You again? How do I believe in You? How? I need help! I can't stop drinking right now, and it's all Your fault!

I'm so mad because this all started when Sabrina wouldn't let me see my kids whenever we had an argument, so I messed up, and now she is being cocky, looking as if she was in the right to everyone. God knows! I got so angry with God that I made the accusations become true. Now, no one believes me.

My birthday was Monday, and not one phone call from anyone. No calls from my children, not that I expected to receive a call. Not one family member called to wish me a happy birthday either. Brothers, sisters, parents, NO ONE!

It's not that I need someone to call me. I don't think my birthday is a big deal. It's just that as the years roll by, I look and see how people make a big deal about people's birthdays. I'm thirty-eight years old right now, and I have not gotten a call for my birthday from anyone in seventeen years. Other than that, my court date in family court to see if I can see my kids is on June 3rd. I filed the motion two weeks ago. Now I'm just waiting, just waiting.

Today is January 29, 2015, and I still have not seen my kids. It has been almost fifteen months now. My feelings are still the same. I miss my kids more and more each day. When I walked out of my first son Sebastian's life, I was so wrapped up in the dope game, that the days, weeks, months, and years, rolled on by. I became numb. That doesn't mean I didn't miss him. I thought about him every day. I just got numb as time went by.

Sabrina, yet again, filed for another restraining order four days after the last one ended, and all I did was send a video text each day asking to see my kids. She took me to court for another restraining order saying she feels threatened. I haven't talked to her in a year. She is making me do everything through the courts, but the courts are on her side. I'm at a loss for words right now.

This was the very first time I ever knew her to outright lie in court. I really think she feels I won't fight for my kids, that I'll just give up, that I won't show my kids all the evidence I have that I got from my lawyer about all her lies: the lies to Child Support, the lies to Welfare, the 911 calls I made trying to find my kids, and all the videos from all our court appearances, both in family court, and in justice court.

I found my old phone the other day in my storage unit. I charged it and turned it on so I could watch old videos of my kids. I turned on the WiFi, went to the internet, and Facebook popped up. An old Facebook account I had with my old band, SEED, was showing some recent posts. It's been years since I looked at that page. The very first post was Sabrina saying, "I'm having Asher withdrawals," because I guess he was at a sleepover. I'm sitting here thinking about things and words I cannot write down here. You're having withdrawals?! How dare you! I was so mad. I saw a picture of Asher from two weeks ago and started to cry. One day, Sabrina will know what it feels like to not see her kids for a season. She's gonna look up at God and say, "Where are You, Lord? Why is this happening? What did I do? I miss my kids!" I just hope and pray that God will replay these last years in her mind while she's begging Him.

I'm scared to start writing again, really scared. I don't know why. I have a burning desire to write. I want to write. I'm just afraid of what other storms and trials God is waiting to throw my way or allow to be thrown my way. Does it really matter anyway? I am meant to suffer, and suffer I will!

Chapter Eleven

-Revelation 2:21-22-
And I gave her time to repent of her sexual immorality, and
she did
not repent. Indeed I will cast her into a sickbed, and those
who commit
adultery with her into great tribulation, unless they repent of
their deeds.
(NKJV)

"The immediate fear and suffering of the
humans is a legitimate and pleasing
refreshment for our myriads of toiling
workers. But what permanent good does it
do us unless we make use of it for bringing
souls to our Father below?"
C. S. Lewis
(The Screwtape Letters)

———————

Today is May 31, 2015 and it's 1:14 in the morning. I can't sleep. I've been having a hard time sleeping for some time now. When I lay down to try to sleep, I start having homicidal and suicidal thoughts. My thoughts are real. They scare me. The problem starts the second I lay down and close my eyes. I start thinking about giving up. I fantasize about going on a killing spree. I want to kill the judge in my family court case, the DA that prosecuted me in the county case, because he wouldn't give me a break, the public defender in that case, because he didn't do crap to help me, and then myself. People talk all the time about wanting to kill themselves. I have often wondered how close they really were, or was it all just a bunch of talk? I did not do anything so bad as to not see my kids for this long.

I have three years of probation to do. Every month I have to pay thirty dollars for supervision fees, complete sixteen hours of community service, and check in with my PO. This does not include the $1,000 fine I received or the $277 I have to shell out to Parole & Probation for all the beginning paperwork. On top of that, I have to do a mental health assessment that costs $100 that I don't have. I still have to do the drug patch program and drug classes for family court, so I can see my kids. The drug patch will cost me $350 to have put on and $100 a week to change. This is for nine months. The drug classes are $25 a week for nine months. I cannot afford any of this. I lost a good paying job due to this felony and currently work through Labor Ready, because no one wants to hire a felon. Everyone does background checks these days, and my felony is fresh, hot-off-the-press. I have looked and looked and looked for a job, nothing! I make minimum wage at Labor Ready, but the work is scarce. I take home less than $75 a week after child support. And get this, my license is suspended now, because I don't make enough for them to take out all the child support I owe, so they take out what they can, still getting deeper in the arrears every week. I'm also six months behind on my car payment. I'm just waiting for them to repo it. All this happened because I did not trust God to handle the situation the way He saw fit and refused to trust His timing.

I miss my kids so much. More than anything in the world, I miss them. I can't see them, because now it's literally become a money thing. I can't see them because I can't afford the things that are in place for me to see them.

Sabrina, satan's daughter, has filed for yet another restraining order. When this last one ended, I sent a video text to my children thirteen days straight, telling them that I miss them and want to see them, and then I got served again. In the first video I sent, I gave Sabrina my home address, and the addresses to both my jobs. She tells the court that I sent thirteen videos threatening her. I have the videos on my phone but was unable to show them to the judge. One day, one day I will show them to my children.

Summer 2015:

It's early Saturday morning. It doesn't matter, because I can't sleep anyway. My car has been repossessed by the bank. When I got up to go to work on Monday, it was gone. One less thing to worry about, I guess. Slowly, so ever-loving slowly, I just keep losing things in my life. It's summertime here in Las Vegas, and now I have to take a bus when it's in the 120s. Simply AWESOME!

Another issue I'm having is that work at Labor Ready has been dwindled. Now I have no car. I missed work on Monday, because I wasn't prepared to take the bus. I now have to get up at 2:00

in the morning, leave the house by 2:30 so I have enough time to take three busses so I can be at Labor Ready to see if, maybe, I can get some work. Because I do not have a car now, I usually just have to wait. I worked two days this week, and that will not cover anything I have to pay for.

Every day I think about reading my Bible. I wonder if I'll ever pick it up again. I just do not trust Jesus anymore. I do not believe God has a better, or even a good, plan for my life. Why should I read my Bible? Why should I pray when it's pretty darn obvious that He doesn't care about me, my life, or my relationship with my kids? What's the point? He doesn't care. He doesn't answer my prayers. He doesn't care about giving me what I need to survive. He doesn't care about my feelings. Most of all, why should I even think about trusting the God of this universe to do anything for me who has caused me nothing but pain in this life. I'm sober and have been for a while.

I still can't sleep, so I made a list of people I want to kill. When I do lay down and start to doze off, I dream of rattlesnakes and scorpions biting and stinging me, as well as demons taking me on a killing spree. My mind does not stop running. I'd rather be in prison for something I did do than my mind be in prison for something Sabrina is doing. The demons take me out, and together we kill the following people:

1- Judge Matthew Harter, my low-life, family court judge, for not giving me a chance to explain my side of the story. He took all my rights away seconds after he yelled at Sabrina for committing child abduction.

2- Bomb the Child Support office building in Las Vegas for almost suspending my license and for allowing any woman who says their child's father isn't paying child support without first doing an investigation. (The only reason my license didn't get suspended was because I went to two different banks to get copies of all the checks that said "Child Support" on them and brought them to their office.) Then my license got suspended anyway for actually paying my child support because I make so little and am unable to pay the full amount.

3- Bomb the Nevada Welfare office in Las Vegas for calling me to say I owe them over $5,000 for medical and food stamps for my kids, because Sabrina said I wasn't paying child support without first doing an investigation.

4- Doug Loman, the associate pastor at Valley Bible Fellowship in Las Vegas, for shaking my hand, smiling, and having a conversation with me, not eight hours after giving Sabrina his, and the churches, "blessing" to divorce me and never telling me one word about it.

5- Jim Crews, the lead pastor of Valley Bible Fellowship in Las Vegas, for continuing to employ a pastor who, in my eyes, is worthless and ruining a marriage without first seeking God.

6- Trey from Desert Cab, for telling Michael Tomlan Jr., who told Sabrina I failed a drug test.

7- Michael Tomlan Jr., for his lying e-mail to my former boss at Desert Cab, and his big mouth for telling Sabrina that I failed a drug test at work.

8- Chelsea Tomlan and her two children, because she's Sabrina's best friend.

9- Mike Tomlan, for not listening, responding, and saying that my divorce was mostly my fault.

10- Ben Little, my public defender, who really didn't care about my case and told me that if I didn't take the plea to "Have fun in prison." He also told me that the judge would just throw out all the evidence against Sabrina, and for telling me "The evidence doesn't matter because you still broke the law."

11- The District Attorney that prosecuted my case, for not caring about the evidence my public defender had against Sabrina and all her lying.

12- The second restraining order judge I had in family court in January of 2014, after Sabrina filed for another TPO, because I called her just to try to talk to my kids. The judge would not even let me speak in court.

13- Colleen Riley, for giving birth to me. She treated me like a burden, kicked me around, abused me, punched me, kicked me, slapped me, made my life a literal living nightmare, and treated me like trash.

14- Belinda, my blood sister, because she's just like Colleen.

15- The cop who kicked the crap out of me for shaking my head yes at a comment he made and wound up putting bruises on my ankles, wrists, waist, neck, and face. He told me the camera that sees this would be deleted by the time I got out of isolation at the Las Vegas jail. (I'll never forget his face, ever. I'll see him again one day; bet on it!)

16- The female cop that almost broke my wrist and whispered in my ear, "Come on you little bitch!" at the Las Vegas Jail. (I'll never forget her face. I'll see her again one day as well; bet on it!)

17- The cop that head-butted me on West Sahara while I was still in handcuffs. (I'll never forget his face. I'll see him again one day; bet on it!)

18- Tim Secession, the current operations manager at the Las Vegas Rescue Mission, because he runs it as if it's his own personal house and plays favorites. In doing that, he plays with people's lives.

19- Eva Hackett, my first ex-wife, for not giving my son Sebastian the gifts and cards I have sent him over the years, so now my son thinks I did nothing for him.

20- Dick & Jane Hackett, Eva's parents for being the a-holes they are.

21- Ty Chew, because he was once a great friend in Christ, but deleted me as a friend on Facebook and won't accept me as a friend. Thank you, my "Christian friend."

22- Diedre & Eugene Wallace, Sabrina's mother and stepfather, because it was okay to disrespect me the night before my wedding while telling me not to tell Sabrina.

23- Elise & Billy LaForge and their six kids, Sabrina's sister, brother in-law, and nieces and nephews, simply because they're fake, and seem to think they're better than everyone else, and that it would hurt Sabrina.

24- Chris Davis, because he tried to act tough, punk me out, and give me dirty looks at prayer group at church, because of the things he was hearing from, none-other-than Sabrina's sister, Elise.

25- Sabrina! I wouldn't kill her though. I would, however, torture her, making sure she was deformed for life, and in so much pain that she would never again be able to trust another man in her life, and never be able to hold our kids again. I would also see to it that she was unable to have children ever again.

That is how the enemy is messing with my mind. That's how my mind wonders. Not even prayer stops these thoughts and dreams.

I sat on my bed and cried two weeks ago, because it was my daughter Rhesa's sixth birthday on July 11th, and I couldn't do anything! My son Asher's birthday is in three weeks, and I won't be able to do anything for him either, unless I want to go to jail. I'm clean and sober, and there is nothing anyone can say to me that justifies me not seeing my kids.

I sit and wonder how much worse it can actually get? I'm sure it will get worse though. I keep having this nightmare that the cops are going to show up at my door and tell me that my kids are dead.

They say that God wants you to put everything aside and give it all up for Him, including your kids, but I just can't do that. I will never stop thinking of Rhesa and Asher. I'll never stop hating God for what He is doing to me now! If setting my kids aside while He works on me is a part of His wonderful master plan, then I guess I'll never grow or see my children again. As long as my kids are living and breathing, I will not be able to set them aside to put Him first. I will never understand why God is doing this.

I can't find a job. I miss my kids. I'm behind on rent, car repossessed, no money, and lost. I lost most of my stuff I had in storage because I couldn't afford $30 a month. I packed up three small boxes, just enough to fit in a small closet, and was forced to let everything else go. I still have the box of Christmas presents I got my kids, and their bikes. I won't let those go as long as I breathe.

I often sit here and wonder why God made satan, who rebelled against Him.

Chapter Twelve

-Isaiah 9:19-
Through the wrath of the LORD of hosts the
land is burned up, and the people shall be as
fuel for the fire; no man shall spare is brother.
(NKJV)

After a few days was when it hit me that I was in a locked unit of a psychiatric ward. I had stolen a car, a gun, money, and was going to kill Colleen. It had been on the news and in the newspapers. I'm in a hospital and not in jail? Cool. I was in awe. I wondered what would come next. What would I do?

I was getting restless and started walking back and forth down the hallway. I felt confined and wanted to get out of here. The nurses and doctors that worked the unit didn't say much to me. When they saw me, they looked at me with what seemed to be a little fear, like they didn't know how to react. This went on for a few days. I was surprised at how little was going on and was growing tired of wondering how long I was going to be locked in this unit. One day I walked to the nurses' station and started talking to one of the nurses. I didn't know how to approach them, so I was as straightforward as I knew how.

"Hi. How are you?" I said.

"How are you doing, Steven?" a male nurse responded

"I'm okay. How long am I going to be here?"

"Well, that's up to you, but it depends on how you react to things and what your assessment says about you. You scared a lot of people when you came in. You stole a car in Arizona and drove it here to New York. You went into the emergency room downstairs and handed the orderly a stolen .357 magnum revolver that was loaded. You were crying and said you wanted to kill your mother, Colleen. Do you remember that?"

"Yeah, but she's not my mother. My mother is Jean Gray."

He seemed confused by my saying this and tried correcting me.

"No, your mother is Colleen Riley."

I have never openly acknowledged Colleen as my mother. I only ever referred to that woman as the woman who gave birth to me. In reality, Colleen was a bad person and an even worse mother. I did not love her. I didn't even like her. She was just the woman who gave birth to me. My dad's wife, Jean Gray, is the woman who acted like a mother to me. She's the one who showed me love and tried her butt off to treat me like a person, not a punching bag. I never had to be worried if Jeannie was going to stab me, punch me, choke me, kick me, hit me with a pair of pliers, put a piece of coal on my stocking at Christmas, or call me stupid, worthless, and no good.

"No, she isn't! She only gave birth to me. Jean Gray is my mother." I became irate.

"Okay! I understand you." He looked at me for a few seconds. "How are you feeling?"

"I'm okay. How long do I have to be in here?"

"You were put on a 72-hour hold. You will have to have an evaluation. If you are ready to talk to someone, I can let the doctor know now. He'll have a meeting with you and go from there."

"Okay. When will that be?"

"Probably sometime tomorrow, but I'm not exactly sure when."

"Okay." I didn't know what else to say, so I just stood there for a minute.

He came around from his desk and talked with me for a while. He didn't bring up what happened at all. He just listened to me. He did say, however, that most of the doctors and nurses were a little on edge concerning me because of the whole gun situation. He said they wanted to make sure I was stable. I was growing extremely tired of being locked in a unit and was willing to do anything to get out, even if meant talking to someone. I just wanted to move on to the next unsure thing that waited for me in life. I sat down at a window at the end of the hall the rest of the day and wondered what was next.

The following morning I met with a psychiatrist. He didn't ask me about the car, the gun, wanting to kill Colleen, or anything like that. To my surprise, it was a very superficial meeting considering I was on my way to commit murder.

"Are you okay?" the doctor asked me.

"Yes," I responded.

"Are you suicidal?"

"No."

"Do you feel like you're ready to leave?"

"Yes."

"Are you going to hurt yourself or anyone else?"

"No."

"Are you eating?"

"Yes."

"Are you sleeping?"

"No."

Those were the questions and answers that got me out of the locked unit. Within an hour, I was moved next door to a much bigger unit where I could smoke. I only had to meet with a counselor once a day. I was game for that. I was nineteen and going nowhere fast. This wasn't the greatest situation to be in, but I could eat, sleep, and not worry about much for a little while. That was all I cared about. As I looked around, I saw despair. I saw loneliness. I saw people waiting for life to end. It was as if I almost felt compassion. Weird!

-Numbers 17:12-
So the children of Israel spoke to Moses, saying,
"Surely we die, we perish, we all perish!"
(NKJV)

It is our job as believers to share what The Lord has done in our lives.

One of the coolest, most selfless things I had ever heard someone say came from this guy I used to know, Ryan Omlie, during a Bible study one night. We were talking about what we could be doing more of as believers. Ryan said that after the rapture, he would love it if God allowed him to stay on earth to tell as many people as he could about Jesus Christ. Life on this Earth isn't going to be pretty after the rapture, and for someone to want to stay to be used by God to help as many people as he can become saved, to me, defines the phrase "cool dude!"

We all have eternal life; it just depends where you are going to spend it: heaven or hell. We will all kneel before Christ and acknowledge Him as LORD. We will either kneel before Him and go to heaven, or we will kneel before Him and be cast into hell. Either way, everyone will utter the words "Jesus is LORD!"

"You're absolutely right," I said. "We're willing to save someone in a visible crises, but a lot of folks are in spiritual crisis and we don't say a word about how they can get out of it. That's why I was crying. I've been convicted about my silence, my fear of speaking to people, my reluctance to SPEAK UP."
Don Piper
(90 Minutes In Heaven)

That's the kind of man Ryan Omlie is, a man after God's heart. He doesn't just have a passing thought of what it would be like to help save the lost; Ryan puts it into motion.

The days began to drift by. I had meetings with counselors and made a couple friends. I was doing as little as possible, the minimum requirements. I knew I couldn't stay there forever, and I was starting to wonder what I would do when I left. During one of my meetings, I saw in my file that I was due to be released the following week. I asked my counselor about it and she said that was just a target date and asked me how I felt about it.

"I'll be fine. I'll figure something out. I'll probably just go back home to Boston."

One of the people I met there was this guy Skip. He was older and not all there in his head. We talked a lot, and he didn't have any family. He lived on his own and did a stint in the hospital a few times a year due to depression, or whatever else, to get his medication adjusted. He offered me a place to stay when I got out until I could find a job and get my own place. He said he didn't have anyone to talk to and didn't mind helping me out. He said it would be nice for him to have some company. I was skeptical at first, but not only was he old, he couldn't move well. I didn't see him as a threat, so I accepted. Now I didn't have to worry about what to do next. Life seemed to be going my way for once. That was until a few days later when I found out I caught crabs from this girl, Misty, who I was messing around with in the women's wing. Not cool!

A few days later, I was told that I was set for release the following morning. I couldn't wait. I was ready to leave. I could have walked out anytime I wanted, but as always, I waited to be told it was time to go.

Sometime around afternoon that day I got called to the nurses' station and was told I had a visitor waiting in the hallway. I walked out, and there stood Jason, the guy who's money, car, and gun I stole. He had actually borrowed the gun from his friend, but you get the point. I was shocked to see him standing there. I didn't know what to say. He didn't even look mad. He just said, "What's up?"

I was embarrassed and shook my head. "Not much."

We walked to the visiting area and sat down.

"You stole my car, my rent money, and Ron's gun, Steve."

"Sorry, Jason." I was at a loss for words.

"Miguel bought me a bus ticket so I could get here to get my car from the police impound."

I said nothing.

"Ron is pretty pissed you stole his gun."

I had no words. This man let me sleep on his couch when I had nowhere to go, and I stole from him.

"What the hell were you thinking? I can't believe you made it across the country without getting pulled over."

"I was going to go kill Colleen." That was all I could say.

"Are you okay, Steve?"

"Yeah, I'm just confused right now."

"You really don't have anything you want to say?"

"I'm sorry, Jason. I really am. I don't know what else to say."

I was leaving the hospital tomorrow and just wanted Jason gone. I felt bad about stealing his money and his car. I just didn't have a good excuse and never thought I would see him again.

"The cops asked me if I wanted to press charges against you for stealing my car and my money, but if I do that, I have to come back here to New York if you take it to trial."

I just looked at him.

"So, I'm not pressing charges."

"Thank you." Boy was I happy. I thought it was weird that he came the day before I was getting out. If he had pressed charges, I was sure to be going to jail.

"Ron is flying here next month to sign some paperwork so he can get his gun shipped back to the Sierra Vista Police Department."

"I'm sorry, Jason."

"I hope you figure your life out." And with that, he got up to leave. He didn't say goodbye or even look back. I was glad he was finally gone.

All I could think of was, cool, I dodged that bullet. I was getting out tomorrow, and Jason wasn't pressing charges. When I saw my release date from the hospital, I had frequently thought about leaving on my own the night before, just in case I was to be arrested. I had even gone for walks with some of the other patients around the block and thought about splitting. Now I knew for sure that I was in the clear. Life was good.

The next morning I woke up, got dressed, and went to breakfast. It was a good day. The sun was out, the birds were chirping, and I had somewhere to go. Skip had given me a spare key to his apartment the night before. I ate and sat in the smoking room with Faith until my counselor, doctor, and nurse came in and told me it was time to go.

"Are you ready Steven?" the doctor asked.

"Yep," I said with a smile.

"Okay. We'll walk you out, hospital rules."

"Okay."

They walked me down the hall to a set of double doors. He handed me some paperwork and wished me luck. They buzzed the door to open it, and I shook all three of their hands and walked out the door straight into three Elmira Police Department Police Officers.

"Steven Gray?"

I was shocked and at a loss for words. I didn't comprehend what was happening.

"Steven Gray?" one of the officers said again.

"Yes?"

"You're under arrest. Put your hands behind your back, please."

They began to cuff me, and I could not understand why I was under arrest.

"What am I being arrested for?"

"You're being placed under arrest for third-degree criminal possession of a weapon and attempted murder." With that, they read me my rights and took me to the county jail. I could understand the weapon but was at a loss for the attempted murder.

"Why am I being arrested for attempted murder? I didn't try to kill anyone!"

"Is your name Steven Frederick Gray II?"

"Yes."

"Did you turn in a stolen gun to this hospital last month?"

"Yes."

"Do you remember the police officers that came and talked to you that night?"

"Yes."

"Did you tell them that you were on your way to kill Colleen J. Riley, your mother?"

"Yes."

"Okay then. That's attempted murder," the officer said.

Why the hell did I not leave the hospital the night before?

-Acts 27:42-
And the soldiers' plan was to kill the prisoners,
lest any of them should swim away and escape.
(NKJV)

———————

I don't feel like I hear God talking to me very much these days. Back in February, though, I heard Him clearly. I have a notebook I write in from time to time, so I can remember things that are happening. On February 20th, 2015 I wrote a few things down that I know God was speaking to me. The following isn't exactly word for word, but it's pretty much what I felt like God was saying:

"What's your focus on Steven? Time is running out. You're behind a lot of points right now, and you need to start making some moves. I've shown you some of what I have planned for you in your life, and you just refuse to believe it and you refuse believe that I Am for you and not against you. I have taken you down this road for a reason. I have allowed things to happen to you in your life for a reason. I have taken things from you that you feel weren't right for Me to take because you were doing the rights things. You blame Me for some of the things I have taken away from you without asking Me why, and for what purpose I Am doing these things. You act out and blame Me without thoughtfully and prayerfully trying to see the reason. You blame Me! You walk away from Me! You turn your back on Me! You cuss at Me! You tell Me you hate Me! You shake your fist at Me! You cry out but do not cry out TO Me! You have started to think that everything good thing in your life is a direct result from life for being "good" and then blame Me when I take them from you! You lash out and have no self-control! I took your kids from you for a reason, and you will not seek Me to find out why. Not every time that I take something from you is it because you are being punished. You think I Am trying to hurt you! You believe that! I know you love your kids. Your son Sebastian is YOUR fault Steven, NOT MINE! You

lost him because you were a bad father to him! I gave you the tools you needed, and you ignored Me and did things your way. You hurt Sebastian. NOT ME! You pushed your son away. NOT ME! You have to deal with that, Steven, but I can help you if you let Me! I know the feelings you have for Rhesa and Asher! You love them more than anything, and that's a problem! You love them more than Me! You would do MORE for THEM than you will for ME! Yes, I took them from you! I want NOTHING in between YOU and ME! You are a very stubborn person. I know; I made you. I took your kids because you refuse to seek Me! You refuse to follow Me! YOU REFUSE TO LET ME IN! YOU refuse My help! The love you have for those children isn't 1/100th of the love I have for them. I know you love them! I know it hurts! I know the pain you go through every day, because I Am with you and I feel it too! You don't think I do, but I DO! ITS NOT ABOUT YOU, STEVEN, IT'S ABOUT ME AND SACRIFICING YOURSELF TO FOLLOW ME! You have treated Me like garbage. One of your biggest problems is not thinking that I can do for YOU the same as I Am willing to do for others. You think your life with Sebastian is over, but it's not, if you let Me help! Rhesa and Asher are safe! Your time is now! You can take it, or you cannot take it! Either way, I love you! I need to be first your life! There IS a reason! I set before you a door to a life that I have prepared for you. I have given you the gift of leadership, DON'T WASTE IT!"

———————

We got to the jail and I was photographed, finger printed, and booked. I was petrified. I didn't know what to expect. I was young, immature, and very naïve. An officer asked if I was suicidal. I said that I was, hoping they would send me back to the hospital. I was not. I was sent to a unit called Post 20 for inmates who were suicidal, had mental problem, and were sex offenders. I looked for a way to be moved off of that post.

Within a week, I went to court and I hadn't seen a lawyer yet. I was brought over to court in shackles with a bunch of other inmates, placed in a locked room, and made to wait. Sometime late in the afternoon my name was called. I got up and walked toward the lady who called me, and she told me to sit back down and said, "You've been indicted by a grand jury and will be transferred to county court."

"What does that mean?" I asked.

She looked at me with a smug face and said very slowly, with attitude,"You-have-been-indicted-by-a-grand-jury-and-will-be-transferred-to-county-court." Then she shut the door.

"First felony, huh?" one of the other inmates asked.

"Yeah."

I was taken back to jail to wait for my next court date. A couple weeks later, my lawyer, Steven Forrest, showed up to meet with me. He wore a bad suit that had rips in the pockets, and he barely looked in my direction. I was just another number on his charity list.

"Steven Gray, I assume?" he asked blandly.

"Yes, that's me. Am I getting out soon?" I responded.

"No. You're charged with third-degree criminal possession of a weapon. You're very lucky, because the D.A. will not move forward, nor prosecute you, for attempted murder because of your mental capacity at the time. You went to the hospital to turn the gun in. Your friend does not want to press charges for stealing his car or money. However, in the state of New York, being in possession of a firearm is a very serious crime. You're looking at a sentence of three and a half to seven years in state prison. You've never been in serious trouble before, so I can probably get that down to one and a half to three years."

"What? Why?"

He didn't want to hear anything I had to say. He was busy with his paperwork.

"You'll have a court hearing sometime next week in which you'll plead not guilty and be issued another court date. I expect the D.A. to agree to drop it to no more than three years in prison, at which time you'll accept and wait for sentencing."

"No, I won't!" I said. He was trying to goad me into taking something I didn't want. This is how public defenders work.

He just looked at me.

"Colleen Riley messed my head up. She treated me like crap. If you think I'm going to just say, "Yeah, send me to prison!", then you're an idiot. Can't you get all the documents from the hospital? My sessions with the doctors? Or what about all the court documents from when I was a kid?"

"I'll see you at your court hearing, okay?"

"Okay."

"Good. I'll be in touch."

What a jerk, I remember thinking.

Jail was pretty much just that, jail. I learned some things: some good, some bad. I did learn how to keep my mouth shut though. I got into a couple of fights which promptly got my butt kicked for running my mouth when I shouldn't have, pretty standard stuff I guess.

I was eventually moved off the baby rapper unit, as it was called, and moved to a double tier, 120 cell unit called Post 10. It had an east and west side, sixty cells each. This is where I spent most of my time. I've never done so much reading in my life.

There was this guard I began to notice, Officer Michael Dancer. He was rough with the inmates that were out of control, civil and polite to those who showed respect. Most guards were jerks and threw their weight around because they could. Officer Dancer was different. You could even see the distaste in his eyes when a guard treated an inmate like garbage.

I was in my cell one day reading, minding my own business, when Officer Dancer stopped by. He was just looking at me without saying anything. I didn't know what to say. I thought maybe I was in trouble. I don't remember everything he said word for word, but he started talking to me about God and wanted to know if I believed in Him. He told me a story about his house that he and his wife were trying to sell before they moved to New York. Some things happened, and he told me that he and his wife really needed to trust Jesus in a time that seemed questionable. He said it was a tough time for his family to go through, but that they just had to trust Jesus, and because they had trusted the LORD, something wonderful happened. What looked like a failure wound up being a great victory for him and his family. I will never forget the conversation that followed, "The Lord is calling on you, Steve."

I didn't say a word. I just looked at him.

"Jesus wants you to know that He can change your life. He has a purpose for you, Steve. He wants to use you. But you have to be willing to let Him in."

I wasn't sure how to respond. Maybe Officer Dancer was on drugs or something.

"It's Jesus' desire that we all call on Him to be saved, but not all of us will. There are some of us, Steve, that Jesus specifically goes after, for a very important purpose, that only those of us He goes after can do. Jesus wants you to fulfill a purpose that only He can show you, that only you can carry out."

My heart was jumping inside my chest. My eyes were filled with tears.

"Jesus is going to use you, Steve, whether you want it to happen or not. It's only going to depend on how long it takes you to give in to Him. He's calling on you now. It'll change your life forever."

"I'll have a better life?" I asked him.

"I said it'll change your life forever. Walking with the LORD isn't always easy, but it's worth it in the end. God is going to use you, Steve. It just depends on how long you take before you're willing to let Him in."

I felt it in my heart.

"Are you willing to give your life to Jesus tonight?"

"Yes," I said.

Officer Dancer came into my cell, grabbed both my hands, and prayed with me the prayer of salvation. I felt warm. I never felt that before. That conversation happened twenty-four years ago as of this writing.

Relationships seldom die because they suddenly have no life in them. They wither slowly, either because people do not understand how much or what kind of upkeep, time, work, love, and caring they require or because people are too lazy or too afraid to try.
(Dr. David Viscott)

Just before Officer Dancer walked out of my cell, he turned to me and said, "Congratulations. How rough your walk with Jesus is depends how hard you make it."

He never smiled at me. He simply gave me a short testimony of what God did for him and led me to the LORD. He never gave me special treatment, never did favors for me. He was a tool that God used to start a fire. Over the years, that fire has flamed up, remained steady, or gone out completely. It didn't matter; the seed was planted. For the next few days, I couldn't get my mind off God and wondered how this thing worked.

I became a trustee who passed out the meals at chow time. Another trustee, Kurt, had a real issue with me, and I didn't know why. He committed armed robbery, had done time in the past, and was on his way back upstate. We just got done passing out the meals to the inmates, and us trustees were getting ready to sit down to eat. I went to grab my meal plate, and all my food wash mashed together. You could tell it was on purpose. I just figured that some of the kitchen workers were being jerks. I went to grab some bread, and Kurt grabbed it first.

"You want some bread?" he asked me.

"Yeah."

He threw it in the opposite direction on the floor and said, "Go get it, snitch."

"What the hell, bro? I ain't no snitch!"

He ran up to me about one inch from my face. "You like hanging out with the guards, huh?" he said through clenched teeth.

"What are you talking about, dude?"

"I ain't your freaking bro, snitch. You like hanging out with the guards in your cell."

"No, dude! He was talking to me about God."

"No, you weren't. You were snitching. I'm going to knock you in the dirt."

"Dude, I didn't snitch on no one."

I was scared and didn't know what to do. I was nineteen, small, and weak. I was literally scared for my life. When chow time was over, I went to my cell and stayed there. I did not come out for anything. I quit being a trustee and didn't even come out of my cell to take a shower.

He would yell out, "SNITCH IN 223! THERE'S A SNITCH IN 223!"

He would come by my cell, stand outside of it, and taunt me to come out. After a couple of weeks, I was getting tired of it and wrote a note to the guards, asking to be moved to a different unit because someone wanted to kick my butt. I never wrote his name on it, just that I was scared and wanted to be moved.

Kurt's cell was directly next to mine, and two days after writing the note to the guards a guard came to my cell during lock in and asked, "We got your note. Who is bothering you and threatening you that you want to be moved?"

"No one, never mind."

-Mark 5:5-
And always, night and day, he was in the mountains and in the tombs, crying out and cutting himself with stones.
(NKJV)

Of course Kurt heard, and now I was a dead man. I just could not catch a break. I was in my cell praying and asking God for help. The taunting became worse. This guy was determined to get me out of my cell. I was more determined to stay in it.

When the cells were popped, I would lock myself back in. For two months this went on. I was praying and trying to talk to God but felt like He wouldn't answer me. So one day I said, "Forget this. If following God is like this, I'm done."

The very next day, I was moved to a different unit. For over two months I locked myself in my cell and didn't shower, scared out of my mind and praying. All it took was me telling God that I wouldn't follow Him, and I was moved. That's all it took for me to justify that God was a joke and not worth the pain. I was on a new unit, able to shower again, and felt free once more.

———————

It kind of reminds me of this book I'm trying to write. I know without a doubt that God wants me to write this book. He told me so. He leads me through it, yet every time I get into a rhythm with my writing, it seems as if the devil comes at me full force. Bad things happen that make me stop writing. That's why it's taken me ten years so far since I wrote the opening page.

I still can't find a job, and I'm way behind on my rent. At one point, I was almost $2,000 behind, but Jack made it look like someone different moved in. He squashed how far behind I was, which was great. I'm writing again now, diligently, and I can almost bet my life that things will take a turn for the worse again. Just wait. I can almost feel it coming.

———————

Anyway, I don't know how many court dates I had, but it was a lot. At one such hearing, I was the very last case to be heard. When my name was called, the bailiff came to get me and walked me into the courtroom. I was in an orange jumpsuit and shackles, ponytail hanging, a huge chip on my shoulder, and walked in to see that the only two remaining spectators in the courtroom were, of course, Colleen and Nanny.

Nanny looked sad. Colleen just stared at me. My heart went out to my Nanny, but I wanted to strangle Colleen. I did the best I could to ignore her and get on with my hearing. When it was over, I was taken back to jail, and as sure as the sun shines, about twenty minutes later I hear, "Gray! You have a visitor!" I wanted to deny the visit, but I wanted to see my Nanny at the same time. I didn't know if I would ever see her again, so I went.

Colleen was wise as not to bring up what happened. She just asked the basic stuff: "How are you? Are you okay? How are things going in jail?" My Nanny just sat for the most part and let Colleen say what little she had to say. The visit didn't last long. When they got up to leave, Colleen had tears in her eyes. I think she wanted to hug me but knew better than to try. My Nanny hugged me and told me that she was praying for me. Colleen asked me if I needed anything. I told her I did not.

Later in the day, I received a receipt for one hundred dollars that Colleen put on my books. A week later, a package arrived. Colleen sent me some t-shirts, boxers, socks, magazines, books, another fifty bucks, and a letter, which I promptly tossed in the trash. Every month she would send me a few more books, money, and a letter.

I wound up taking a plea deal to do one year in jail. There was too much of an abusive history with Colleen for the D.A. to get a hard conviction, so I did my time and managed to wait it out. Time passed quickly for me, and soon enough, my year was over. I was called down to booking at eight in the morning one fine day, given my clothes, which in no way fit anymore, and was booked out. I had plans to get over to Faith's house on the other side of town at about ten or so. I was going to stay at her house that night to party. She would take me to Skip's house the next day. I couldn't wait to get loaded. I had my life all planned out. The door buzzed open, and I walked out of the detention center to see Colleen standing there waiting for me. I had a strange feeling she was going to kill me right there.

When you forgive someone for hurting you, you perform spiritual surgery inside your soul; you cut away the wrong that was done to you so that you can see your "enemy" through the magic eyes that can heal your soul.
(Lewis Smedes)

I thought it took a lot of guts for Colleen to show up. Not because she did anything wrong, but because she was visiting the boy she gave birth to, whom she treated like a disposable baby wipe, who just walked out of jail after a year, who was on his way to kill her a year ago. Yeah, that took guts.

"Hi," she said.

"Hey." We just looked at each other for a minute. "What are you doing here?" I asked.

She had tears in her eyes. She looked confused and hurt, but I really didn't care about her feelings. I didn't want to forgive her. I would not forgive her. Being angry and on the offense was familiar to me. It's what I knew. It's what made me feel safe.

"Listen, Steven, I know you probably don't want me here. I know I'm the last person you want to see right now. I'm sorry that you're so angry at me. I don't know what I did so bad for you to hate me this much. I did the best I could with you kids," she said. Always the victim. What a freaking joke.

Here we go again. She was delusional, and she did not see the pain she had caused me. Maybe she did and just didn't see how I could be that angry. She acted as if I was supposed to just shrug it off, as if it never happened.

"What are your plans?" she asked.

"I'm headed over to a friend's house for the rest of the day."

"What are you doing after that?"

"Why?"

"I was wondering if you wanted to come back home. You could stay with me until you find a job and get your own place if you want to. It's up to you."

"No, I'm going to stay here and see how it works out."

I was just about to tell her to go take a hike, when she said, "Well, can I at least take you out to eat? Your clothes look like they don't fit you. I'd like to buy you some new ones. I can give you some money to help you out. I came a long way, Steven. It's a four hour drive one way. Is that okay?"

She didn't have to say much more. All I heard was free food, new clothes, and money! I was sold. I could fake it for a little while.

"Yeah, fine."

I got into her car, and she drove me to the mall. We didn't say a whole lot to each other at first. She took me to lunch, then to a department store where she bought me three new changes of clothes. I wish I could say more, but our conversations were short. I felt awkward. I don't think she knew how to come at me. When we were done, she drove me to Faith's house. I think Colleen was looking for me to open up to her, but that was not going to happen. She had Faith take a picture of us, and then she gave me a hug. It was one of the worst feelings I've ever had.

"I love you, Steven," she said.

"Okay. Thank you for the clothes. All I had was what I was wearing."

"You're welcome." She gave me another two hundred bucks, wished me well, told me to keep in touch, and then drove off. That was that.

I got a job at a gas station owned by a couple, Butch and Kathy. Kathy, come to find out, was a police officer. Ironic, I thought. It wasn't long before

I moved out of Skip's apartment and into my own place, but not before I gave Skip a four hundred dollar phone bill for calling nine-hundred-number sex lines. Skip opened up his home to me, and I repaid him by abusing his telephone. He was on a fixed income and had to have his phone shut off.

I worked hard, was never late, and always went the extra mile. Soon enough, I got a better apartment on the other side of town, happy to be out of the ghetto. I even bought Faith's old car that she was selling. I worked, paid my rent, smoked a lot of weed, and drank a lot of beer. I thought this was success.

It wasn't long before Kathy found out I just did a year in the same jail she worked in. I couldn't believe it. I started noticing Butch was being short with me, and when Kathy came in, she gave me the dirtiest looks. I wondered why they didn't just fire me and get it over with. As always, things took a turn for the worst real quick. On the days that I was scheduled for the night shift, I would take the deposit bag with the day's cash and drop it off at the bank.

Faith asked me if she could use my car one night, so I rode my bike to work. I was beginning to despise this town. On my way home that night after work, I was stoned, aggravated, thinking, and not paying attention to where I was going. I looked behind me to cross the street when I veered off to the right and ran smack into a mailbox with my right hand, breaking it in three places. I lay on the ground for a few minutes in serious pain. I hit that mailbox so hard I knew I broke my hand. There was no question about it. I just didn't know how bad I broke it until later. I was so mad that I walked all the way home so I could drop my bike off first, then I walked to the hospital. My hand was completely jacked up. It looked like E.T.'s hand. It had a few bumps and bones that looked out of place. My hand was placed it in a cast, was given some pain pills, then sent home.

Things continued to get worse after that. Faith was cheating on me with the guy who lived next door to her, so I lost it and flipped out. I drove to her house loaded, kicked her door in, trashed her living room, and got arrested again, this time for D.U.I., breaking and entering, domestic violence, and petty larceny. For some reason, I thought a woman fourteen years older, who cheated on her husband and boyfriend with me, who lived on welfare, would be faithful. I obviously did not see things for what they were.

-Psalm 78:72-
So he shepherded them according to the integrity of his heart, and guided them by the skillfulness of his hand.
<u>(NKJV)</u>

I was shepherded directly to jail, which was the safest place for me to be. I went to court later that morning, then transferred to the Chemung County Jail, again.

The petty larceny charge was from some automobile fluids that were found in my car that I had taken from work without paying for them. The guards were rough with me because the gas station was owned by one of their own.

I was housed in a unit where all the inmates had, in some way, gotten into trouble with the guards. They did surprise cell checks on us all the time just to break our things. I was sitting on my bunk one day during lock down when a guard, Officer Gunnerman, came into my cell. He walked up to me and just stared at me for a minute.

"You like to steal from cops, huh?" Then he grabbed me by my throat, pulled me towards him, and smacked my head off the concrete wall. He laughed at me and walked out. My head hurt for a week.

Eventually, I was sentenced for my D.U.I. They gave me six months, and I was already two months in. I had to deal with crap from the guards for another four months with the added stress of not knowing what I was going to do when I got out. I was positive if I stayed in Elmira, Kathy would make my life a living hell. I had to get out, but I didn't know where to go.

I couldn't go back home to Boston, so I called Colleen, collect. I really didn't want to, but it was the only solution that could get me out of Elmira and off the streets. I waited a few days after I made the decision to call Colleen to actually call her. I was nervous but pretty sure she'd let me stay there. My plan was to use her as a stepping stone, getting the hell out as soon as I could.

-Job 14:14-
If a man dies, shall he live again?

All the days of my hard service I
will wait till my change comes.
<u>*(NKJV)*</u>

———————

I constantly think of all the things I could have taken care of in life but didn't. I think about all the things I could have done right the first time, all the things I could have corrected and fixed directly after messing up. I struggle with these thoughts daily.

———————

So, Colleen finally accepts the call.

"What the hell? You're in friggin jail again?! Don't you ever freaking learn?!"

"I'm in jail! I didn't call you to get freaking yelled at!" And I hung up the phone. I had a few months to figure out what I would do.

A few days later, one of the guards brought a note to me that said, "Call your mother." The note should've said, "Call satan's daughter!"

I tried to come up with a plan, but I didn't have any other options, so I called Colleen back a few days later. When I got her on the phone, she apologized for speaking to me that way. I told her what had happened, that I wanted to get out of Elmira, and didn't have anywhere to go.

I walked out of jail a couple months later to Colleen again standing there. I was moving back to a town I despised, where no one liked me, where I had zero friends, with a woman I wanted to murder.

Chapter Thirteen

-Psalm 109:26-
Help me, O LORD my God! Oh,
Save me according to Your mercy,
(NKJV)

Love conquered even the natural thirst for
life.
Rev. Richard Wurmbrant
(Tortured For Christ)

I'm pretty upset right now. I live in this sober house, but half the people living here are using drugs. It used to be that if you were caught using, you had to go to West Care Detox for three days, and then you'd be allowed back, but that's just not the case.

The house has sixteen beds for men who are supposed to want to be living a sober lifestyle. The manager lives here as well, so that makes seventeen guys under one roof. The house manager is someone I've known for years, Jack, who has had a hard time staying clean himself. Jack was on staff at the Las Vegas Rescue Mission after completing their Christ-centered recovery program, but was soon fired and kicked out for drinking on property. He now manages three sober living homes and has now taken up drinking and smoking weed in the house. This man is not a good leader and should not be in charge of other people's lives.

There are fourteen men currently living here, not including Jack. Of the fourteen men, two are on ecstasy, one is passed out drunk, one is messed up on pills, one is high on methamphetamines, one just drank his dose of methadone and is on his way to the bar to go drink, one is passed out on heroine, and Jack, the house manager, is locked in his room smoking pot. Aside from that, two others are sleeping right now but frequent the local Dotty's Casino to gamble and drink. Out of fifteen guys living here, ten are getting loaded. Steve Anderson, the guy passed out on heroine, just got back from the hospital yesterday after he overdosed on heroin a week and a half ago, and that's not the only time he's done that. About a month and a half ago, he overdosed on heroin in the bathroom and was taken to the hospital. He's allowed back because he's on SSI and can pay his rent. I can't move because I have no money, so this is the toilet I live in.

-Proverbs 26:11-
As a dog returns to his own
vomit, so a fool repeats his folly.
(NKJV)

"Are you ready to go?" Colleen said.

"Yeah, thanks for picking me up," I said. "You're not going to get nothing to eat or go to the bathroom?"

"Nope. We'll stop later. Let's get going."

"Okay."

She tried to make small talk, but I just wasn't into having a conversation. I was less than thirty minutes removed from spending the better part of the last year and a half behind bars. Between that and knowing this was a wrong move, I just wanted to put my head back. Within a few minutes, I was fast asleep. As much as I hated her, I had to give her credit. She was taking me to her house to live two years after I almost killed her, which took guts.

Would I ever get my crap together? I was twenty-one years old and couldn't take care of my own life. I could survive on the streets, sure, but that was about it. I didn't know anything about life.

We finally pulled into Colleen's driveway, and my stomach was in knots. She had a two bedroom, split-level ranch, with a full livable basement. It was deceiving because from the outside it looked like it could have had three or four bedrooms easy. There was also a big front yard, as well as a sizable back yard that ran into the forest of the Catskill Mountains.

Right off the bat, my older sister Belinda had a big problem with me being there. I didn't blame her. I wanted to kill her mother. Belinda and I had never gotten along. Her attitude towards me was just what I expected. She had been through some of her own crap with Colleen. I've always given Belinda a lot of credit. Colleen kicked her out of the house when she was sixteen, and she finished high school anyway. That took a lot of integrity. Colleen told me on the drive that she was dangerously close to kicking Belinda out of the house. No surprise there either. Not many people could tolerate either one of them on a regular basis.

My room was the basement. It was large with a stereo, television, and futon. Nice living quarters actually. I tried to relax the rest of the night. Colleen made dinner, during which Belinda was told to leave the table because of her attitude towards me. I don't think Rhonda knew how to react to me being there. Rhonda was always Colleen's openly favorite child. She was always treated well. Having to deal with the crap in the house with Belinda couldn't have been easy. Rhonda never got beat, talked down to, called names, or ever kicked out of the house. Rhonda was always loved.

"All growth that is not toward God, is growing to decay."
George MacDonald
(3 Reasons We Must Grow Or Die)

———————

No matter who you are, what you try to change, why you want to change it, or who you try to change it for, all means nothing if you're not changing first for Christ.

———————

As expected, Colleen was turning into the woman I knew she was: a self-righteous, dictating, controlling, tyrant. My fears had all come to the front of my mind and seemed to sit there marinating. I literally had to ask to do anything. I had to ask to go out, go for a walk, make something to eat, watch a movie. It felt like I had to ask to breathe.

Colleen's boyfriend, Ken, was married and cheating on his wife with her. How fitting. Things never change. His wife came over to the house one day asking her to stop the relationship she was having with her husband. Colleen did not care one bit. She even told me that it's her fault for not taking care of Ken the way he should be treated. She said that she was old and looked as if she could be his mother. Sure, that makes it okay then, huh, Colleen?

Rhonda had gotten into a really bad car accident. She was t-boned by a car that ran a red light at 55 mph. Her car was totaled, and she almost died. She had to have therapy, and was in pretty bad shape for a while. When she was doing well enough to go back to school, Colleen let her use her car. Usually, Colleen would have said to take the bus to school. Rhonda told me that she thought it was weird how she was letting her use her car to go to school and that all of a sudden Colleen was being real nice. I knew it before Rhonda even said it. There was a settlement involved. Rhonda got screwed on her settlement. Her car was never replaced, she had medical bills out the butt, and she almost died. All she got was eight thousand dollars. As soon as she got her settlement check, Colleen demanded four thousand dollars. She wanted half of Rhonda's money, because she let Rhonda use her car to go to school. That was a downright sleaze-ball thing to do. I asked Rhonda how she felt about it, and she said there was nothing she could do. What an absolute DIRT-BAG parent Colleen was, and is.

Belinda was kicked out within a couple weeks of me being there. Not only did she get kicked out, but Colleen threw her things in the driveway, again, breaking some of it for Belinda to see when she came home from work. Again, I felt this was a sleaze-ball way to treat your child. But then again, this is Colleen we're talking about.

-Nehemiah 1:6-
please let your ear be attentive and Your eyes open, that You may hear the
prayer of Your servant which I pray before You now, day and night, for the
children of Israel Your servants, and confess the sins of the children of Israel
which we have sinned against You. Both my father's house and I have sinned.
<u>*(NKJV)*</u>

I want to say something real quick. You may think all I'm doing here is bashing, slandering, and belittling Colleen. That may be true to some extent, but just hear me out. I know some of what I am saying is disrespectful, and although I want this book to reach and change millions of lives, I have never dealt with my feelings towards this evil, vile woman. The root of all my pain, hurt, and most of all: my anger, rage, and hatred, comes from how this woman treated me. I need to deal with it, no matter how it comes out. As much as I hope this book brings peace to many people, this right now is for me. I may not say the right things, but I do know God wants me to do this. Right now, this is for me and me alone. I need to do this.

———————

-Nehemiah 9:31-
Nevertheless in Your great mercy You did not
utterly consume them nor forsake them;
for You are God, gracious and merciful.
(NKJV)

Things at the house were getting bad. Every single day I was threatened to be kicked out of her house. I had to walk on eggshells. One day I was on the computer and needed to look for something. I wound up finding her Last Will & Testament. Upon her death, Belinda and Rhonda would each receive twenty-five thousand dollars. I was to receive one dollar. That's it. New York State Law requires that if you leave one of your kids something, you have to leave all your kids something. It's not about the money. It was the blatant disrespect. I would have to sit during the reading of her will, looking like an idiot in front of everyone. I never wanted her money. I still don't. When she dies, I am going to put a one-dollar bill in her casket.

A few other things were bothering me also. Colleen rented that house for six hundred dollars a month because she told the owner that was all she could afford. Yet, she received more than seven hundred a month in death benefits for Rhonda until she turned eighteen, because her father, who was also married at the time of Rhonda's conception, being more than twenty-five years older than she, had died. All the house expenses were split in three. Rhonda, who was in high school, Colleen, and I split all the bills in three and were forced to pay.

Don't have a third of the rent? Get out!

Don't have a third of the electric bill? Get out!

Don't have a third of the heat bill? Get out!

Don't have a third of the water bill? Get out!

She was getting death benefits for Rhonda, driving a school bus, and had no compassion. I made minimum wage and only worked twenty-five hours a week. She had a fire place and would order a cord of wood to make fires with. I made a fire one day and when she came home, she said, "What the hell are you doing?"

"What?" I really did not know what she was talking about.

"What do you mean, 'What?' What are you, a friggin light bulb? What are you doing with a fire going?"

"I made a fire. It's snowing outside. It's cold, so I made a fire."

"This is my house, and that's my wood," she said.

"I paid for a third of that wood. I wanted to make a fire."

She looked at me like she wanted to slap me but knew I wasn't a child anymore. I would not just take it like I did when I was a child.

"Listen here, ass-wipe. I let you dwell here. This is my house. That is my wood. That's my fireplace. Keep your friggin hands off it. When I want a fire, I'll make one."

I could not win no matter what I did or how hard I tried. I was walking in the snow every day to go to work, and she would drive right by me on the way to work and not offer me a ride, in the middle of winter, while it was snowing. Her job was less than a hundred yards from my mine. I was in a bad situation, with very little money, and nowhere to go. I had to put up with it until I could make a move.

I worked two jobs now and was barely home. Before long, I was able to afford to move in with a friend of mine. Finally, I felt like things would get better. I wrote Colleen a note telling her I moved out and that I thought she was an evil woman. She sued me for two hundred dollars in rent for not giving her a thirty-day notice. She won the judgment. I never paid it.

Knowing I had my tax refund coming, a friend helped me out by giving me a ride back and forth to work every day until my check came so I could buy a cheap car. When my refund finally did arrive, he took me to a cheap dealership in Catskill where I bought an old white Pontiac Grand Am for $700, which promptly caught on fire less than two miles down the road. I was able to put the fire out with some dirt and started laughing. The car was a major hazard, but it still drove somewhat okay. It didn't matter to me. I wouldn't be here much longer anyway.

I spent every penny I had to buy that car, so I couldn't afford to get it registered or insured. That wouldn't stop me though. Like so many of my "bright ideas," I stole some license plates off a car I found in a random parking lot. That's how much of a scumbag I was, no regard for anyone. Whatever I needed, I took. When I got back to Cairo, I put the plates on my car and felt like I was good to go.

No offense to anyone who lives in that area, but for me, Cairo, Catskill, Greenville, Hudson, Durham, and all surrounding towns are nowhere-towns. Nothing but bad memories. If you were born there, most of the time, you grew up and died there without seeing much of anything else in the world. I literally cannot think of one single good memory I have of anything to do with that place, none whatsoever.

"I continue to exist, and He continues to exist, but we don't exist together."
Colleen Hoover
(Hopeless)

God was there all right; no doubt about that. His existence was very real. I just chose not to have Him exist in my life.

I was going to get out of this town, but I was waiting for an opportunity to present itself. One day, I was with a friend when he needed to stop by his friend's house to pick something up. He knocked on the door and this girl Nichole answered, whom I went to school with. Nichole was tall, had blond hair, and to this day, is the most naturally beautiful woman I have ever met, but it was not about that. It was about beauty in general and how there was no beauty at all in my life. I never felt there would be. A child was so abused that all the beauty that should be, never existed. It was stolen by a woman, Colleen, who gave birth to him, me.

What I saw when she opened the door was my childhood. I realized that as we grow up, things change: some for better, some for worse. We learn, we fail, we get back up. One thing never changed though: me. Steve Gray never changed. I may have looked like an adult, but on the inside, I was still very much this scared, hurt, sad child with no self-esteem. I don't know why I saw that when she opened the door, but that's what happened. Up to that point, I hadn't made concrete plans to move yet, but after seeing what I saw when Nichole answered the door, I knew I was leaving that night.

I was scheduled to close the store I worked at that night. So I wouldn't get busted for the stolen plates on my car right before I was about to leave, I asked my friend if he could take me to work. When it was time to close the store, I stuffed all the cash from the safe into my backpack, set the alarm, left the store, and walked away with more than eight thousand stolen dollars.

-Romans 9:16-
So then it is not of him who wills, nor of
him who runs, but of God who shows mercy.
(NKJV)

I didn't just do something small here. I committed a serious crime, again. I was about to go on the run. I didn't like me. I was living a lie the entire time I was here. Most of what came out of my mouth was false, because the truth about me was not interesting. I felt broken.

I called a cab from a payphone down the street and had him take me to a motel in Hudson. Once there, I found a Wal-Mart and bought a few changes of clothes. After showering and changing, I called another cab to take me to the Greyhound Bus Station in Albany.

"Where you headed?" the driver asked.

"I'm just waiting for a friend coming in from Boston," I responded.

I figured I had until about 8:30 in the morning before things started to unravel. Once we got to the bus station, I bought a ticket to Syracuse, New York. Within forty-five minutes, I was on my bus and on my way out of town. Once I got off the bus in Syracuse, I was paranoid and had a hard time trying to think straight. I spent half the day taking different cabs and busses to different areas, hoping I wasn't followed. I must have paid for four or five different motel rooms that day. When early evening rolled around, I settled into a motel about an hour away from the Greyhound for three days trying to relax. It took at least a full day for everything to sink in and to come to terms with what I had just done. I couldn't change what I did. I needed to push forward. I spend the next couple of days checking things out. I bought a pair of black leather pants, dyed my hair with blond tips, tried to stay drunk, and got high.

I went back to the Greyhound Station after a few days and couldn't think of where to go next. I wasn't looking for somewhere to settle down. All I wanted to do was party. I was waiting in line for my turn and wasn't sure where to go.

"May I help you?" the lady at the counter asked me.

"Next bus to Las Vegas, Nevada please," I replied.

"Okay, and when would you like to return?"

"One way, please." I loaded the bus and settled in for a three-and-a-half-day bus ride across the country.

I met a couple people on the bus who also liked to party. When we rolled into Vegas, I rented a limo and we all hit the Strip. I was on a roll as soon as I got there. Right away, I hit jackpots at the MGM, Monte Carlo, and Harrah's for a total of about $2,000. With the money I had stolen and jackpots I just won, I was sitting on almost $10,000 cash. It's amazing what you can do when you have the money. I spent two weeks in Las Vegas doing nothing but drugs, living like a rock star. I've never been so strung out in my life. I lived in bars, strip clubs, and can't even remember the number of hookers I had sex with. I snorted enough cocaine on that trip to kill a horse. After two long weeks, I was busted. No money, no food, no shelter.

-Isaiah 37:27-
Therefore their inhabitants had little power; they

*were dismayed and confounded; they were as the
grass of the field and the green herb, as the grass on
the housetops and grain blighted before it is grown.
(NKJV)*

I don't know much, but one thing I know for sure: the enemy loves to replay my past failures. He likes to remind me of how worthless I am and tries to keep me in that mindset: that I'll never amount to anything. He doesn't remind me of any of the victories in my life unless it was quickly followed by a failure, in which he just reminds me that any victory I have, God will ultimately follow that with difficult times.

Just as real as God has spoken to me, satan has spoken to me, also. I vividly remember the enemy sitting me down and saying,

"Why continue reaching out to God, Steve? Can't you see that every time you think you are having a victory, your God just kicks you down again? Can't you see that your God is really hurting you? He does not care about you the way you want Him to. When your God tears you down, takes your kids, takes your job, and takes your life away from you, can't you see that that is killing you? Why suffer now, Steve? Suffer later, and let me give you what you really desire now. Give me your life and you'll see the real truth. I am the one who truly loves your soul, my friend. Feed into me, and you won't have to suffer the things you're trying to fight."

Many times in my life I have believed that lie from satan. I have given in to him time and time again. Even now, I want to give up.

Satan is not all-knowing. He is not omnipresent. He has to send demons to carry out most of his work, and I truly believe that I am called for such a great purpose by God, that satan himself, has visited me and messed with my mind and life. I have let him in by walking away from what I know to be the truth, and most of the time I tell myself that I just want to be happy. I can be happy if only this or that happens. Would I be happy if the struggles that God puts me through didn't happen? I don't know. Maybe for a time, but I do know this: satan doesn't necessarily want or need me to completely devote my life to him. He just wants me not to follow Christ. That's a victory in his eyes. There are many "good people" in this world who are headed straight for hell simply because they choose not to accept Jesus Christ. Satan won't mess with those people. He doesn't want them to think "God or satan." They can help all the people in the world they want to and volunteer as much as they wish. That isn't going to matter one bit. To enter the Kingdom of Heaven, we must choose to accept Christ.

"You can choose to live by choice, not by chance; to make changes, not excuses; to be motivated, not manipulated; to be useful, not used; to excel, not compete; choose self-esteem, not self-pity; choose to listen to My inner voice, which is not dependent

upon situations or conditions, not the random opinions of others." –God-

It can be tough to believe when you're struggling. For me, it's hard to find happiness in tough situations, like right now. Today is August 10, 2015 and Jack, the manager of the house, told me that I only have a few days to find somewhere else to live. I understand, because I'm behind on rent. I'm behind on rent because I cannot find a job. I could go on and on and on and explain things. I'm mad because those who are using in this house are allowed to stay, because they can pay their rent. I'm clean. I'm sober. I'm looking for a job. I am going to church. I am reading my Bible. Why is it that I'm struggling this damn hard? Why is God allowing this to happen?

When I read things that say that "Happiness is a choice and shouldn't depend on our situation," I wonder. The only thing I can say right now is that I'm not enraged about being asked to leave. I'm upset but not so mad I'll lose it. There are too many people using drugs here anyway. There is a small peace about it, but it's still frustrating. I feel it's another thing God is allowing me to go through for whatever reason, and I don't like Him for it. More crap on Steve's plate? Sure thing. Thanks, God! I expected nothing less. Can I get a double portion of suffering this time, please?

"I'm not going to worry about what I can't do.

I'm going to do what I can do well."
Blind Man Quote
(90 Minutes In Heaven)

What I can do well is foul up my life! Or, I could pray and see if God talks to me and leads me somewhere safe right now. I choose the latter.

Chapter Fourteen

-2 John 1:9-
Whoever transgresses and does not abide in the
doctrine of Christ does not have God. He who abides in
the doctrine of Christ has both the Father and the Son.
<u>*(NKJV)*</u>

After four long days on the bus, we finally pulled into Boston. I'd been stressing hard for the last few hundred miles. It felt good to be back in Boston, the only place I ever felt at home. Medford, Massachusetts: the only place I ever felt safe. The problem was that I was crawling back home to a family that didn't want me around. I had to make sure I showed up on a night that Jeannie was working, otherwise, I had no chance. I wasn't trying to be deceptive, I just wanted my dad to have compassion. Many times over, I had wished Jeannie were my real mother. My life would have been different if she had been. After months of no contact, I casually showed up as if nothing ever happened.

"Hi dad," I said when he answered the door.

"Hey Steven, come on up," he said.

He wasn't happy to see me, but he wasn't unhappy either. I'm sure he knew a story was coming. I would be out and about for months, even years at a time, then show up one day out of the blue. It's just how I was.

"Are you hungry? You want something to eat?" my dad asked me.

"Yeah, okay," I was starving.

A few things my dad always did for me whenever I showed up was let me come in the house, eat until I was full, take a shower, do laundry, and talk to me. So many times he wanted to write me off, but he never did. He did it because he was my father and he knew I was messed up. The one thing he was determined to do was love me. Everyone in my life either walked away or wrote me off. When I finished eating, I told him about Colleen, my trip to Las Vegas, leaving out, of course, robbing the store I worked at and the amount of drugs I was doing.

"Is there any way I can please stay here for a little while? I don't have anywhere else to go," I finally asked.

He knew it was coming. He looked at me, and I couldn't tell what he was thinking. He told me that he didn't know and would have to check with Jeannie first. He had my brother Justin call her at work then went into his room and shut the door. He was in there for a while. I knew she did not want me there. I have never been mad at Jeannie for not wanting me there. I was wild. She had Natasha, Jarred, and Justin to think about. My dad eventually came out of his room and sat at the kitchen table with me.

"You have thirty days, Steven. That's it. You had better start looking for a job. Thirty days goes quickly, and I don't want to hear that you need more time or that you can't find a job, because thirty days from now, you have to be gone. Do you understand? And you're not allowed in the house when no one's here."

"Yes. Thank you dad. I'll start looking for a job tomorrow."

"You better, Steven."

"I will. Is Jeannie mad at me?"

"Don't worry about that. You can stay here, but you better find a job. And don't bring any drugs in this house, do you understand that?"

"Yes."

"Okay then. Go take a shower. Do what you have to do. You can sleep on the couch in the living room, and you need to thank Jeannie when she gets home. Okay?"

"Yes. Thank you."

"Okay then. I'm going to bed now. Good night."

I was happy about the thirty days. It was actually more than I expected. I took a shower and hung out with Justin and Jarred in the living room while they played their video games. Natasha came home a little while later, said hello, and went to her room.

I was tired and wanted to go to sleep, but I waited for Jeannie to get home from work. I was at the kitchen table when she walked in.

"Hey." She was short, but cordial.

"Hi, Jeannie. Thank you for letting me stay here."

"Ah-huh. You have thirty days, Steven. That's it. You had better look for a job, and I really hope you find one. In thirty days you need to find somewhere else to go."

"I will." I remember thinking I wished I was Justin or Jarred.

"Are you okay? Did you eat something?" she asked.

"Yeah, I ate."

"Good. I'm going to watch my story. Have a good night. Get some sleep." And that was it. Her "story" was *Days Of Our Lives*. She's been watching that soap opera for like a hundred years now.

I immediately started looking for work but got nowhere the first few days. I didn't understand why I couldn't land a job right away. The one thing I was always able to do well was get a job when I wanted one. Around the fourth or fifth day of looking, I was feeling defeated, and I vividly remember praying a small prayer out loud. "Please, God, help me get a job today."

I was walking down Washington Street in downtown Boston and saw a "help wanted" sign on a t-shirt cart. I walked up to the guy working the cart and asked about the job. He called the owner and then asked me if I could stick around for a few minutes. About ten minutes later, the owner showed up and talked to me for a couple minutes. He needed the help and hired me on the spot. I went with him to his office and filled out all the necessary paperwork. He never questioned my ID or birth certificate, because neither were legal documents. I would find out later that he hired a lot of illegal immigrants from Europe, but I couldn't have cared less. He owned something like ten or twelve t-shirt carts. We worked twelve-hour shifts, six days a week. The t-shirt cart that I was assigned to was in the Boston Commons Park. I sat in a chair, under a tree, sold t-shirts, smoked pot, and got to people watch. I was happy.

"God don't shop at Costco. And sometimes we want a Costco size blessing. It hurts when we almost lose everything. We say, "God, I can't take no more!" And we ask God for a blessing to last a month, but we only get enough blessing to last for today. We get enough grace and mercy every day to last for that day. God does not shop at Costco, and He loves to take us to the ALMOST point."
(Pastor Paul Shepard)

How quickly I forgot about the blessing God had just given me with the job. I prayed for a job, and He gave me one. He gave me what I needed and wanted right then. I never thanked Him, never a thought.

I was working and having a good time. I got stoned and looked at pretty girls all day long. Boston is packed with universities. The women were all over the place. All of us who worked in the downtown area, no matter what company we worked for, all partied together. I wasn't saving any money. I spent everything I had on beer and drugs. I found a rooming house on Center Street in Lynn for $90 a week and decided to wait until my thirty days was up at home before I moved.

I had fun hanging out with Justin and Jarred too. To them, I was the cool older brother. I really did love them. They never knew how much I envied them and the family they were born to. I was jealous. One of my saddest moments in life came during that thirty days. Justin and Jarred knew I was going to be moving out soon, and one of them said that they could not wait to move out when they got older as well. When he said that, Jeannie said, "You're my son. You won't be moving out until I know you can afford it and can pay all of your bills."

Those words crushed me. "Steve's son": that's all I was. I moved out and into my little room in Lynn. I was having what I thought was the best summer of my life, though!

-1 Thessalonians 4:3-
For this is the will of God, your sanctification:
that you should abstain from sexual immorality;
(NKJV)

I was having sex with all kinds of women. There were all these women from different countries I was meeting. The best part was that all they wanted was sex. I thought I was the man. I was loving it. I even started keeping track. I was sleeping with women from Scotland, Ireland, Italy, Germany, France, Greece, Mexico, Brazil, Chili, Panama, Bermuda, Canada, England, Spain, Poland, and the Czech Republic. At the time, I couldn't imagine life being any better than that. I am not a good-looking man, and could not believe the summer I was having. They were all beautiful women, except for one ugly one from Europe somewhere, but I didn't mind.

The girl from Poland, Mija, was drop-dead gorgeous. She looked like a model. When I met her, I stopped going out with other women. People couldn't understand how I landed her. I couldn't understand it either. Mija turned heads. I loved it. She also soon realized that she turned heads and dropped me pretty quickly. She got a job as a cocktail waitress, illegally of course, so I called the bar she was working at.

"Hi. Do you have a lady working there named Mija?" I asked.

"Um, no I don't," the manager said.

"Yes, you do. My name is Steve. I don't mean to be a jerk, but I know she doesn't have papers to be working here in America. If she continues to work there, I'm going to report you. What you're doing is illegal."

"Well you sound like a real jerk!"

"Yes, I am. You have no clue. I'll be in from time to time to see if she's working there or at any of the bars in Fanual Hall."

"Boy, you really are a class-A jerk, you know that?!"

"Yes, I do. Have a good day, dude!" I have never been a ladies' man, not by a long shot. I was a reverse chick magnet at best, and I couldn't stand to see Mija doing well.

I soon moved in with a couple of friends, one of whom sold t-shirts on a cart in Boston as well.

They had pot plants growing in the closet and always had some sort of alcohol in the house. It seemed like a perfect fit for me. Things seemed to be going well, at least well in my eyes, that is, until one day when I stopped by my dad's house to say hello. He looked angry when I showed up and said that he needed to speak with me outside. Something was wrong, and I didn't know what it was. We went outside and he said, "What the hell did you do?"

"What? What are you talking about?" I asked.

"I got a call last night from a sergeant with The New York State Police saying that you robbed a store and got away with almost ten thousand dollars. You're lucky Jeannie was working. The phone rang, and as he was leaving a message I picked up the phone. What the hell did you do? And don't freaking lie to me, Steven!"

My dad seldom swore, so I knew he was mad. I told him the truth about what I did. I really didn't have a choice. I didn't lie at all and told him everything.

"Ah, Steven! What the...!" He just shook his head.

"What did you tell him?"

"Well, he said that he knew for certain that you had been here, but he didn't know if you were still here. He said you're wanted for grand larceny, burglary, and felony evading, because you crossed state lines. He knows you were in Las Vegas."

I was stunned, scared, and silent.

"You better not come around here for a while, Steven. I don't know if they have the phone tapped or what. You're in a lot of trouble."

"I'm sorry, dad."

"I don't know what to tell you, Steven. I told him that I would call him the second I heard from you."

"Are you going to tell him I was here now?"

"No! Of course not! But if I were you, I would leave now, and the last thing you better tell me as you walk away is that you're on your way to Tennessee."

"Huh? Why do you want me to say that?"

"Because I told him you spent a few days here and that you asked me for some money so you could get to Tennessee. I told him I gave you five hundred bucks and dropped you off at Wellington station."

"Okay. I'm really sorry, dad."

"Me too, Steven. Me too. I hope he doesn't call again and Jeannie answers the phone. I think it's time for you leave now."

"Okay. I'm sorry. I love you, dad."

"I love you too, Steven."

"Hey dad?"

"Yeah?"

"I'm headed to Tennessee."

He walked back in the house and closed the door on me and I walked down the street to Wellington Station.

I figured things couldn't get much worse, so I started to steal money from the t-shirt cart in Boston.

I would double up the credit card slips and slide it back and forth a few times, making two receipts. I would add a t-shirt or two to most of the credit card purchases and pocket the cash. I got caught. I wasn't arrested, but I did get fired. Now I was out of work again and looking for a job. To my surprise, I was hired at the first place I applied to, Pizzeria UNO's, waiting tables right in the middle of Fanual Hall. I wasn't going to run away from trouble again. I figured if I was going to get caught, then I was going to get caught.

I did okay waiting tables. It was in the middle of all the tourists, so there was plenty of money being spent. I was clearing over $700 a week in tips, good money back then. As always, I worked hard, and thus received better shifts and was eventually promoted to bartender. That's where the real money was. More money meant more drugs. I started doing a lot of cocaine, pills, ecstasy, and acid. I even tried a little heroin. The first time I did heroin, though, I overdosed.

-James 3:15-
This wisdom does not descend from
above, but is earthly, sexual, demonic.
(NKJV)

_____

As I write this, I'm amazed at how I could not see what I was doing to myself, how out of control I was at the time. I read what I write and feel sorry for that man. I see a boy in a man's body, hiding.

One night, my roommate asked me if I wanted to go smoke some weed with a cab driver. He had taken a gypsy cab from Dorchester and wanted to pay the driver by smoking him out.

"Sure. Let me grab a knife first in case he gets weird."

"Okay. I'll get the weed."

I grabbed a long butcher's knife, went downstairs, and hopped into the back of the gypsy cab. I had the knife in my hand while my roommate loaded the pipe. I felt like someone was watching us and thought I kept seeing someone out of the corner of my eye. I tried to put it out of my mind when two cop cars came racing up the street and stopped in front of the cab.

This was it, I thought, I was finally caught. I knew I was going to jail and shipped back to New York. The three of us were placed under arrest, my roommate for possession of marijuana, the cab driver for operating a gypsy cab, and me for an outstanding warrant. We were taken in and booked. After a few hours, a cop knocked on our cell,

"The bailsman is here. Anyone want to bail out?"

"How much is it to bail out?" my roommate asked.

"You and Mr. Gray can bail out for twenty-five dollars each."

WHAT!? I could not believe it! I was able to bail out? Something had to be wrong. There just had to be a mistake.

"Do you have enough to bail us both out, Steve?"

"Yep."

We bailed out and walked home to Jamaica Plain in Dorchester from West Roxbury. I was still in shock. How did they miss me being wanted in another state? We got home, smoked some weed, and went to bed. A couple of nights later, when I got home from work, my roommate seemed a little upset, shaken, confused, and scared.

"Hey, Steve, the cops were here looking for you today?"

"What?"

"They didn't come in though. They knocked on the door, so I went down to open it. There were two cops at the door asking if you were home. I told them that you didn't live here anymore. They asked me if I was sure you didn't live here."

"Did they tell you why they were looking for me?" Now it was my turn to feel shaken and scared.

"No, but there were two more cops in front of the house, one each on either side of the house, and two more in the back. That's eight cops, Steve. When I came back upstairs, I looked out my bedroom window and there were two more in the backyard looking up at our apartment. What the hell are you wanted for, dude? Steve, I grow a lot of weed here, man."

"I have no clue what that was all about. I wonder what's going on."

"I don't know, man, but I took your name off the mailbox. What the hell is going on?"

"I really don't know, man. I got arrested with you. We bailed out together. I really have no clue what's going on." I knew very well what was going on. The only answer I could think of is my name must have come back on the NCIC check. They must have only done the local check when we were arrested.

"Steve, I can't have that, dude. I friggin grow weed in this house. I could really get busted."

"Okay, don't worry too much. I'll look for another place. Just give me a few. Move the plants into my closet, and I'll be careful coming and going. But I'll look for a different place to live, okay?"

"Yeah. Let me know what's going on though, okay?"

Damn. I knew I couldn't stay here much longer without getting busted.

The following week I was introduced to the new Assistant Manager at work, Eva. We hit it off great. Eva was a big drinker and loved to party. We would talk a lot and stay late at the restaurant, drinking and getting high. She was engaged to a guy named Mike who came in a few times.

Eva started out as CPA, following daddy's footsteps, but didn't want to continue on in that field, so she began managing restaurants. She rented a house in Quincy, just a couple blocks from the beach. We started to hang out a lot outside of work.

Soon, we started messing around, even though she was engaged. She said that, although she loved Mike, she didn't want to marry him.

As you can probably guess, Mike found out that we were messing around and was pretty upset. He came into UNO's one night. I thought he was going to kick the crap out of me. He followed Eva a few times while she was giving me a ride home after a night of drinking and hooking up, and he wanted some answers. All I could tell him was that we were drunk. I told him that I had a girlfriend, which I did not, and he dropped it and let it go. That's when I realized that Mike was a very mentally weak person. I would never let that crap fly. He did though.

Things calmed down a little between Eva and me. We stopped hanging out as much. A couple weeks had gone by when Eva asked if she could talk to me.

"Hey, do you want to come to my bachelorette party with me next week? I talked to Mike, and he said he was fine with it. We're all going to my parents' house in Richfield, CT. Me, you, Mike, and my friend will all drive down. Then you could come out with us to the party. You wanna come?"

"What? Mike is okay with that?" I was shocked.

"Yeah, come on. It'll be fun."

"Sure, but I don't know if I can get those days off though."

"I do the schedule, so I'll make sure you have those days off."

"Sure, I'll go. Why is Mike going?"

"He wants to hang out with my parents while I have my party."

"Wow." What a loser I thought.

The following week came, and the four of us drove down to Connecticut to Eva's parents' house. As we drove through her town, I noticed this was an extremely rich area. When we pulled into Eva's parents' house, I couldn't believe my eyes. The house was huge.

"Eva, you didn't tell me your parents were rich."

She smiled embarrassingly and said that her dad just worked hard. She said they were not rich, just well off. (Yeah, right.) We all went into her house and met her parents, Dick & Jane. How lovely is that?

Her dad seemed like a nice enough man. He was quiet, minded his own business, and let Eva entertain us all. Her mother was very different. She definitely had an air of arrogance and ignorance about her, and she acted as if she was better than most. We played pool upstairs and joked about what a snob she was.

Eva had about eight of her girlfriends or so, plus Mike, me, and her friend that drove down with us. At one point, Eva came over to me and asked if I could somehow watch my language. Her mother had pulled her aside and told her that I had quite the foul mouth.

-Obadiah 1:4-
"Though you ascend as high as the eagle, and

*though you set your nest among the stars, from
there I will bring you down," says the LORD.*
(NKJV)

"I do not agree with what you have to say, but I'll defend to the death your right to say it."
(Voltaire)

-*Psalm 31:1-5-*
*In You, O Lord, I put my trust; let me never be ashamed;
deliver me in Your righteousness. Bow down Your ear to me,
deliver me speedily; be my rock of refuge, a fortress of
defense to save me For You are my rock and my fortress;
therefore, for Your name's sake, lead me and guide me. Pull
me out of the net which they have secretly laid for me, for You
are my strength. Into Your hand I commit my spirit. You have
redeemed me, O LORD God of truth.*
(NKJV)

The party with Eva and her girlfriends was about to begin. Mike stayed at her parents' house, while I went out to party with ten women. Eva's dad drove half of us to the city. Now, I'm a pretty wild guy and am no stranger in taking risks, but Eva's dad scared the ever-loving-crap out of me with the way he drove. That man drives like he not only knows the roads, but also owns them, you're not supposed to be on them, and if you are on them, you're his guest. I never wanted to drive with him again after that.

I don't remember much of that night specifically. Things got fuzzy quickly. I forget the girl's name, but I wound up hooking up with one of Eva's friends. We were talking and drinking, then decided to go find one of the quieter corners of the bar. She had just broken up with her boyfriend, so I was there to agree with how right she was about everything. She was hanging all over me, and I was all over her. Eva got pissed!

"What the hell are you doing?!" she asked me.

I was confused. I had no clue what she was talking about. I wanted to say to her, "Trying to get laid."

"What are talking about?" I said.

Her friends pulled Eva away, and I could see them all in a heated conversation. One of her other girlfriends came up to me a few minutes later and asked me, "What the hell is going on with you and Eva?"

"Huh? What are talking about?"

"Is something going on between you two?"

"What? No! Of course not!"

"There better not be. She's getting married in two weeks, you know."

That was it. The party was over. We all somehow got back to her parents' house. Her friends left, and it was just Mike, who was sleeping, Eva's friend, who was now laying down in a spare bedroom, Eva, and me.

"Want to go for a ride?" Eva asked me.

"Sure," I said. She sure had a lot of guts.

We left the house and went and parked somewhere. I did not care that she was cheating on Mike. To me, this was a fantasy. I was hooking up with the bride-to-be after her bachelorette party. We were gone a while, and when we finally pulled into her driveway, Eva's friend, along with Mike, came out of the house holding my bag.

"Damn!" That was Eva's comment before we got out of the car.

Mike threw my overnight bag in front of me and said, "You got to go!"

"What? I'm in Connecticut, dude!"

At the same time Mike was trying to get me to leave, Eva's friend was yelling at her about us being out. Then Mike stepped up to me, pushed me back and yelled, "Get the hell out of here!"

This is where I partially blacked out. The next thing I remember is pushing Eva's father. He was yelling at me saying, "Get the hell off my property. Now!"

I responded with a slew of curse words, and the next thing I remember was being held up against a cop car.

"What's going on?" the cop asked me.

"That's Eva! Those are her rich, a-hole parents! That's her friend! That's her fiancé! She had her bachelorette party tonight! We're all from Boston! And I'm banging her!" I blurted out.

The cop shook his head, unable to digest what I just told him. This was a rich neighborhood. Things like this don't happen here.

"And they're trying to make me walk back to Boston!" I continued.

"Okay, calm down. We'll get it figured out" the cop told me.

"Are you going over there to talk to them?" I asked.

"Yes, in a minute."

"Good! Tell her fiancé that I've been banging Eva for two months now!"

"Boy, you sure got a mouth on you," the cop said to me.

The next thing I remember was the cops waking me up in the back seat of the cruiser.

"Get up!" the cop yelled.

I got up thinking I was about to be booked.

"Where am I?" I asked.

"This is the train station. It opens in the morning, and you can get a ticket back to Boston."

"Huh? How come I'm not in jail?"

"You want to go to jail?"

"No. What happened?"

"Well, Mr. Hackett didn't want to press any charges, to save his daughter the embarrassment."

"Okay. What time does the train run?" I asked.

"I don't know exactly, but it does start running in the morning. You'll be okay here. Just crash out on one of the benches."

"Thanks, man."

"Take care of yourself. Good luck to you. And you should really change that attitude of yours."

I fell asleep on the bench and woke up to the sun in my eyes and a killer headache. I walked into the train station and asked to buy a ticket.

"Where to, sir?"

I looked in my wallet to count my money.

"As far as twenty-six dollars will take me," I responded. I would figure out the rest when I had to get off. I couldn't imagine a train to Boston being more than thirty to forty dollars.

She printed my ticket, and I waited for my train. When it came, I got on, fell asleep, and waited to be kicked off. I woke up to the conductor telling me that I was at my stop. I looked around and had no clue where I was. Nothing looked familiar. The name of the town I was in made no sense to me. I never heard of it before. I went in to ask someone and what I found out was this: I FREAKING WENT TWENTY-SIX DOLLARS IN THE OPPOSITE DIRECTION! I mean, really? I was in the middle of nowhere-country-town-U.S.A. and had zero dollars. I expected that when I told the lady, "As far as twenty-six dollars will get me" meant closer to Boston. This sucked.

I went into the station and asked a lady if I could use the phone to call someone in Boston, but she said no. I had no pride left. Even if I was willing to swallow it, I couldn't, because I had none! I broke down and told her the entire truth about what happened. I think she felt bad when I got to the part about going twenty-six dollars in the opposite direction. She had mercy and let me call my job. I chose to call UNO's, because I knew the manager who was working. He was a pot-head, and I thought he would love to hear the story, plus get me my ticket. When I got him on the phone, he said, "What's up, Steve? How was Eva's party?"

"Crappy! And I'm stuck in Connecticut somewhere!"

He had himself a small laugh, because he knew my life was never dull and usually came with a wild story.

"What happened?" he asked as he continued to chuckle.

"Okay, I got caught messing around with Eva, got kicked out of her parents' house, almost got arrested, dropped off at a train station, and went twenty-six dollars in the opposite direction from Boston."

Oh how he laughed, and then continued laughing.

"Wow! You got caught messing around with Eva? The same Eva that works here? Your boss Eva?"

"Yes, Jason."

"Wow! You got to tell me what happened."

"Jason, I have no money, I'm supposed to work tonight, and I'm stuck in upstate New York somewhere. It's a real great story that I'm sure you'll find amusing, but I need help getting a ticket back to Boston. Can you help me, please? I'll pay you back tonight with my tips. Now's not the time to make fun of it, Jason. I'm really pissed right now."

He just continued laughing. I would have too if it were someone else.

"I'll get you the ticket if you promise to tell me the entire story when you get back."

"Yeah, fine."

"How do I get you a ticket back into Boston?"

I handed the phone to the lady at the counter, and she processed my ticket. She handed me the phone and said, "He would like to talk to you again really quick."

I took the phone and hung it up without saying anything. All he would have done was ridicule me anyway, and why not? I would have.

-Song Of Solomon 1:7-
Tell me, O you whom I love, where you feed your flock, where you make it rest at noon. For why should I be as one who veils herself by the flocks of your companions.
(NKJV)

I got into Boston and thought about not going to work that night. A really good reason I had was that Eva was working, but I told Jason I'd be there. I needed to pay him back for the ticket. I walked to Downtown Crossing, hopped the Orange Line to Haymarket, and then walked to UNO's.

Eva tried a few times to walk my way to talk to me, but each time I walked the other way. I guess I was pissed at her because I felt like she should have owned some of the responsibility but didn't. I wanted nothing to do with her, and I could not wait to get a different job. I couldn't work with her as my boss after everything that just happened. I'm not sure if I was starting to really like Eva, or if it was the fact that she was willing to give up so much for me. She cancelled her wedding a week before she was to be married. We started to hang out, and much more, after that.

Eva was a rich girl. She was the captain of the cheerleading squad in high school and went to an Ivy League college. I was the bad boy from the other side of the tracks that her parents could not stand. It fit. At that point in my life, I had never had someone give up so much for me. I loved her for it. One of the biggest problems though was I truly did not know how much of a "good girl" she really was. She never understood how much of a bad boy I was either. This was nothing short of a toxic relationship.

It wasn't long before Eva and I got caught in our relationship at work, and it was the District Manager that caught us. We tried to deny it, but come on, when you're caught kissing each other, it's hard to lie. The company made a big deal out of it. Eva almost lost her job, and I was transferred to another location.

We soon moved in together and this just proved to be a violent decision on both our parts. Eva drank hard, I did a lot of drugs, and the arguments never seemed to stop. Neither one of us seemed to want to let the other one go though. In Eva, I wanted the stability she had. In me, she wanted the rebellion. It was the perfect storm. The cops were called more than a couple times, always with me being hauled off to jail. Still though, we just wouldn't let go of each other.

-Matthew 14:30-
But when he saw that the wind was boisterous, he was afraid;

and beginning to sink he cried out, saying, "LORD, save me!"
(NKJV)

"The most common way people give up their power is by thinking they don't have any."
(Alice Walker)

The fighting just never stopped. There was never any peace, ever. She was tired of my drug use, and I was tired of her drinking. We were abusive towards each other, never respecting each other's space or feelings. She would never come clean to her parents about our relationship. I was tired of being her dirty little secret. Every time her mom came to visit, I had to either sleep in the car or get a motel room. Neither of us knew how to understand the other. One day, we finally figured out that it just wasn't working anymore and decided to fix it. We eloped to Las Vegas. Of course, this would fix everything.

-Ezra 9:14-
should we again break Your commandments, and join in marriage with the people committing these abominations? Would You not be angry with us until You had consumed us, so that there would be no remnant or survivor?
(NKJV)

"Some people think that to be strong is to never feel pain. In reality, the strongest people are the ones who feel it, understand it, and accept it."

A few months went by with a promise from Eva that she would eventually tell her parents about me, but it never happened. I was sick and tired of feeling as if I wasn't good enough. I spent my entire childhood feeling that way, and I was done, so one night I called her mother and told her that we got married in Vegas a few months before, then hung up the phone. Eva could not believe I did that, and that truly pushed her over the edge. She was now, with her mother's help, looking into divorcing me.

"They don't like you, Steve. We have to get divorced," she said.

"So, just because they know we're married we have to split up?"

"Yes. It's the only way."

-Ezekiel 38:10-
Thus says the LORD God: "On that day it shall come to pass that thoughts will arise in your mind, and you will make an evil plan:
(NKJV)

I was so mad at her. I was pissed at her parents for having such a tight hold on Eva, so I decided to get a little satisfaction of my own. I found out the alarm code to her parents' house, and when they were away, I drove to Richfield, CT, stole one of her dad's credit cards, along with all his information, and racked up over $10,000 in charges. Screw them! I didn't care when they would find out.

*"I'm an angel, I'm a devil, I am sometimes
in between.
I'm as bad as I can get, and good as it can
be.
Sometimes I'm a million colors, sometimes
I'm black and white.
I am all extremes. Try to figure me out you
never can,
There's so many things I am.."*

Then the bottom dropped out: Eva was pregnant. Change is inevitable; progress, though, is optional.

I was happy and looked forward to the opportunity to give my child something different than what I had experienced as a child. However, Eva was scared and wanted to get an abortion. It was weeks of arguing over whether or not she was going to abort what would eventually be our son, Sebastian. Every day I was nervous Eva was going to come home and tell me she had an abortion that day. Multiple times a day, I called on the God I did not know, begging Him to intervene. He did. Eva came home one day and seemed as if she found some peace.

"Listen, the only way that this is going to work is if my parents don't know. For this to happen, we have to move. I'll tell my parents that you left and I don't know where you are. I'll tell them that I'm sick of Boston and that I'm moving somewhere with one of my girlfriends to get away for a while. They can never know. They'll disown me, Steve."

Eva had a good job managing a restaurant. I held down two jobs, so we had a little saved. I didn't care anymore that I was her little secret. I was just happy that she wasn't going to get an abortion.

"How about we move to Las Vegas then?" I suggested.

"Yeah, let's move to Las Vegas," she replied.

Chapter Fifteen

-3 John 1:11-
Beloved, do not imitate what is evil,
but what is good. He who does good is of
God, but he who does evil has not seen God.
(NKJV)

I am now managing two sober living houses. I'm not paid for the job, but I also do not have to pay rent either. I have my own room and need to look after the guys to make sure they're working, staying sober, and paying their rent. Jack asked me if I would manage the houses because they are known as sober houses where it's okay to get loaded. Right off the bat, God showed me three who people were using. The first guy tried giving me apple juice for a urine sample, so out the door he went. The other two admitted to using when I told them I needed to drug test them.

This one kid tonight, Dylan, I felt bad for. I told him I needed to test him, and he said okay. He then got on his phone and went outside. After talking to him, he told me that he had been using heroin and gave me five needles, one of which was loaded and ready to go, plus a little baggie of heroin. I could literally see the struggle in his eyes. My heart broke for him, but I cannot play favorites. I told him that he had to leave, but could return if he went to West Care Detox and did their three-day evaluation. I saw myself in this kid. He is only twenty-two with his entire life ahead of him, but cares about nothing other than doing dope. All too well I know this struggle. I've felt the pain. I've lived the hurt.

_____

"I used to think a drug addict was someone who lived on the far edges of society. Wild eyed, shaven headed, and living in a filthy squat. That was until I became one..."
(Cathryn Kemp)

Eva and I hit the road knowing we were making the wrong decision. We had five thousand dollars, a bag that contained forty pre-rolled joints, and a will to make it to Las Vegas. We were both amped up and wondered how far we would make it our first day on the road. As it turned out, we did not make it that far as we only drove about three hours from Boston. The sky was getting dark with rain clouds. It looked like a thunderstorm was on the way. So where did we go? We went to Eva's parents' house. They were away for a few days, and Eva said it would be just fine to stay there. I thought it was a great idea because it felt like a big screw-you to her parents. There were no thoughts of stealing anything else. They would eventually find out about the credit card. Eva was a little nervous about staying there, but after all, it was her idea. She also had another good idea.

"My mom keeps gas cards in her glove compartment. Let go see what kinds of cards she has. We can take one with us so we don't have to pay for gas."

"That sounds like a great idea, Eva. Let's go look!" I said.

We looked inside Jane's glove compartment and found a slew of gas cards. Eva grabbed the Shell card, but I told her no.

"Take the Texaco card. There are Texaco stations all over the country," I said.

"No. We should take either the Shell card or the Sunoco card."

"That's a bad idea Eva. I'm telling you. Just grab the Texaco card."

She did not listen and took the Shell card.

"Whatever we have to spend on gas, my mom will send me a check for," she said.

"Okay, Eva. I'm telling you though, we won't find that many Shell gas stations. Everything on the interstates are Texaco's."

We got up the next morning, showered, ate, and hit the road. We fought the entire way about everything under the sun. You name it, we fought about it. Most every argument was about her parents. I would just not let that one go. The one thing that made the drive nice was the bag of joints I rolled before we left. I drove for fifteen hours straight the first day, only stopping for gas. I took a couple of wrong exits, but it was an adventure just the same. Can you guess what happened? We didn't see a single Shell gas station. Most everything was Texaco. I made sure to throw that in her face every chance I got. At one point we almost ran out of gas looking for a freaking Shell station. We got to St. Louis and had to get off the highway because the gas light in the truck came on. We didn't see any gas stations around, so we stopped on the side of the road not far from the Arch, in the middle of the night. Eva and I continued screaming and yelling at each other. I told her to screw herself and got out of the truck to flag someone down. As soon as I opened the door, Eva's cat, Ernie, jumped out and ran towards the Arch. Now she was pissed. I told her to stay with the truck while I looked for the damn cat. I saw him, but he wouldn't come to me. Then I heard Eva behind me. She was calling for him too. Then I looked up and saw that she had left the door to the truck wide open with all our cash in there.

"Are you freaking stupid, Eva?!"

We were stuck in the ghetto, and the chances of getting robbed were pretty high. I love the city life. I have been in my share of ghettos, but this place was on another level altogether. I ran to the truck to make sure the money was okay. A few minutes later, Eva came walking up with her damn cat in her hands.

"A-hole!" she said.

"Witch," I responded.

I stood on the side of the road trying to flag someone down, but no one stopped. A St. Louis Police Officer even drove by and refused to stop. If a cop wasn't going to stop for us, then we really didn't need to be there. We drove on and luckily found a gas station a few miles away. We were both tired and aggravated. After filling the truck with fuel, we found a hotel and crashed out for the night.

-Romans 12:19-

> *Beloved, do not avenge yourself, but rather give*
> *place to wrath; for it is written; "Vengeance*
> *is Mine, I will repay," says the LORD.*
> *(NKJV)*

The next day we were driving down the highway somewhere in the middle of Oklahoma. We were stoned and enjoying the ride when I saw a car broken down on the side of the road. I thought it was the funniest thing to see someone having car trouble in the middle of nowhere. They had smoke coming out from the hood, and I made a bunch of snide comments about it to Eva, which she did not think was funny.

"Sucks to be them," I said with a smile.

Then I heard a pop. I looked in the side-view mirror and saw black rubber coming out the side of the truck. Damn! I slowed down to pull over and got out of the truck. I had just blown out a tire on the car-hauler. Right away I thought of all the jokes I just made about the people on the side of the road. Eva drove the truck off the next exit, and we called Budget Truck Rental to tell them about the tire.

"We'll be right out to get that tire changed," they said.

Well... Nine hours later someone did come to change it.

"It took you nine freaking hours get here to change the tire?" I said to the guy.

He didn't say anything as he continued to work. He got the tire changed and we hit the road again. After three more days of driving and the never-ending arguing, we finally pulled into Las

Vegas. We got off the 95 on Tropicana and headed west towards the Strip. We were here. We stayed at a Holiday Inn Express on Sahara and Durango, the same hotel we stayed at when we eloped. Eva wanted to go see the apartment I rented for us, but I didn't tell her how bad of an area it was in.

"We'll check it out tomorrow, okay? I don't think you're going to like it. It's in a really bad area. I was figuring we could look for a different one tomorrow."

She looked at me as if to say, "Really, Steve?" It was just like me not to give all the details.

We got checked in, took the car off the carrier, and went out. The following morning, I took her to the apartment I rented on East Bonanza Road. She just had this look of disgust on her face. I didn't blame her. It was a bad apartment in a shady area, not somewhere you want to raise a child.

It did not take long to find a new apartment. We found one that same day on Decatur and Pennwood called, The Emerald Park Apartments. It was still ghetto, but with fewer gunshots.

We offloaded our things into the apartment, returned the truck, got our deposit back, and just like Eva said, her mother reimbursed her all the out-of-pocket money we spent on gas. (By the way, just a side note, we were only able to use that Shell card twice in over 3,000 mile of driving. About ninety-five percent of the gas stations were Texaco. Just saying.)

We both got jobs within a couple weeks through temp agencies. I worked at a warehouse packing boxes and loading trucks. Eva got a job having something to do with time-shares. Neither job paid much, but between the two of us, we were able to survive.

We continued to argue non-stop. Sometimes it was bad; sometimes it was bearable. When we didn't argue, we were bickering. It sucked and stressed us both out. We needed to find some weed. We went a couple months before we found any. What a relief that night was. We didn't fight at all. We just got high, ate pizza, and had sex.

It was nice watching Eva in her pregnancy. That much I did enjoy. We both looked forward to Sebastian arriving, and soon enough, he was here. Sebastian was born on August 28th, 2000 at 1:25pm, weighing 5 pounds 9 ounces and 18 ½ inches long. It was one of the happiest days of my life. I was a father. Eva was a mother. Sebastian was our son.

Eva stayed home with Sebastian for six weeks while I worked. It was tough, but God sure did supply us with everything we needed. I was only making minimum wage and had to pay the rent, bills, diapers, and formula. It was God, and only God, who brought us through that. I wasn't a believer then, but I knew God was providing.

One day while I was working, I got a call from Eva. Eva never called me at work. I thought something bad had happened.

"Hello? Eva?"

"Steve! I got a call from my mom. She said that you stole their credit card and raked up a ten thousand dollar bill. Is that true?"

I paused a long moment before answering, "…Yeah."

"What did you do?" she asked me.

"I don't want to get into it over the phone, Eva. What happened?"

"She said that she and my dad went to buy a new car, but when the guy ran their credit, it came back all messed up. So my dad looked into it and said you changed all his information on one of his credit cards to our address in Hingham, and that you spent ten thousand dollars."

"We'll talk about it when I get home Eva, okay?"

"No, it's not okay, Steve. You had better leave. My parents are pissed off. They said they're going to press charges against you."

"Where am I gonna go, Eva?"

"I don't know, but if you come home, the cops will probably arrest you."

"Okay. I have to get back to work right now. I'll call you later." And I hung up.

Okay, so how I saw it was like this: I had two choices. I could run or not run. That was it. I saw Eva's parents making one of two decisions, and I was prepared to call their bluff. They were pissed! I believed that if I ran, which I know they both hoped and wanted me to do, then, and only then, would they press charges. It would make sense. I would run and thus be out of the picture, so they could press charges and get Eva back. The second scenario was that I stay and not run. If I stay, and they pressed charges, they ran the chance of losing their daughter and grandson if she chose to stick by me. That was how I saw them seeing it at the time. I could have been completely wrong, but I stayed and called their bluff. I got home, and I told Eva everything I did in regard to Dick's credit card and told her why I did it.

"They're going to press charges against you, Steve. I'm scared," Eva said.

"No, Eva, they won't. Trust me on this."

She was mad and had every right to be. Every day I was scared I was going to be arrested, but it never happened.

-Proverbs 13:25-
The righteous eats to the satisfying of his soul,
but the stomach of the wicked shall be in want.
(NKJV)

At Eva's six-week mark, she had to go back to work, so we found a cheap daycare. Every morning I would drop Sebastian off, then pick him up after I got out of work. I felt bad that Eva had to go back to work so soon, but I just didn't make enough money by myself.

One of the women Eva worked with was looking for someone to find an apartment with so she could move out of her parents' house. The three of us got an apartment at Crystal Cove Apartments on West Desert Inn Road. Eva and I had one room with Sebastian, while her friend Kenya had the second room. This situation did not work out all that well, and Kenya wound up moving out within a couple of months.

My friend Brian is in the hospital right now with multiple problems. He lost his wife and kids, just as I have, but for different reasons. He is currently detoxing from alcohol, and is in rough shape. Brian is a man's man, but he is very lost at this moment. I can see the enemy working overtime in his life. I am dedicated to praying for this man. I am really asking God to step in and to not allow demons to access to Brian right now. He wants to be clean and sober. He's just struggling, hard. I'm glad he's in the pain he's in right now. Because of that pain he is now willing to try. I want him to give his life to Christ, but he just doesn't believe in salvation.

"Quietly endure, silently suffer and patiently wait."
Martin Luther King Jr.
(Why We Can't Wait)

Eva and I were both getting tired of each other. Our fights were becoming extremely physical as well. I had never hit a woman in my life until this point. I am in no way trying to justify hitting a woman at all. Please don't think that. But one thing I could never understand was why it seems to be okay for a woman to hit a man, but unacceptable for a man to hit a woman. Yes, I hit Eva, and that was wrong. I never hit her until she hit me first. I know that sounds like justification, but it's really not. I'm just telling you like it is. I do not condone hitting any person. The issue I have is that when I am hit,

388

whether it's a man or a woman, I don't see male or female. All I see is red. I go blank. In my mind, I go somewhere else. I honestly don't understand what is going on until it's all over.

I remember the first time I hit Eva. As always, we were arguing. We were both upset and both hated to be living a lie with each other. From her parents not knowing, barely making it financially, to just not wanting to be around each other, we were arguing, and she punched me directly in my face. I turned around and punched her right back without thinking about it. She landed on the bed, grabbed her face, and as soon as she pulled her hand away, I could see that there was already a welt forming. I felt bad, really bad. She looked at me like she couldn't believe I just hit her.

"You just hit me!" she said.

"I told you before, Eva, that if you hit me, I will hit you back."

Eva had a huge black eye. That's how things continued to go for us for a while. We would argue, fight, she would hit me, and then I would always hit her back hard enough to leave a mark.

After a few months of that routine, we just ignored each other and that seemed to help. Eva got a job waiting tables at Sammy's Woodfire Pizza, and I had finally landed a good job at a local steel company. Eva did pretty well in tips, and I was working hard and taking home a nice paycheck as well. We both enjoyed being parents to Sebastian.

-Proverbs 21:9-
Better to dwell in a corner of a housetop, than

in a house shared with a contentious woman.
(NKJV)

Soon, Eva and I started doing meth. I was picking up a couple of eight balls every Friday after work for us, and it would be gone by Sunday night. I would go to work on Monday mornings tweaking and trying to come down. We did this every weekend for months. It soon started to affect my job. I had lost almost thirty pounds and people noticed. I also found out that Eva had long since started cheating on me with the bartender she worked with named Travis. It hit me like a ton of bricks: I was the bartender she cheated on her ex with. It all came full circle. I found out that this guy was in my house doing my wife while I was working.

We were arguing one night, and she went to take Sebastian and leave. She was drunk and high on speed, so I grabbed Sebastian out of her arms and said, "You're not taking my son away from me!"

I was holding Sebastian as he was crying when Eva bit my back hard enough that I started to bleed. I put Sebastian down, bit her right back, dragged her outside on the porch, grabbed her by her hair, and slammed her face into the wall. I slammed her so hard that I knocked her out cold. I was scared because I thought I killed her, for real.

"Eva! Eva, wake up! Eva, are you okay?"

I picked her up, brought her into the house, and laid her on the couch. She had blood dripping down her face and looked bad. She came to and remembered exactly what happened.

"I'm calling the cops!" she yelled as she ran out of the house.

She went to our neighbor's house and knocked on their door, so I split. I went to the pool area and tried to relax for a few minutes. I waited for what seemed like an hour or so and thought I would walk back to our apartment. I was thinking things would have calmed down by then. As I turned the corner, there were three cop cars and two cops standing right there. One of the cops looked right at me and stopped me in my tracks, "What's your name?" he asked.

"Steve Gray," I said.

"Put your hands behind your back." I was placed in handcuffs.

As he was putting the cuffs on me, he saw the blood dripping down my back and asked me why I was bleeding.

"I'm bleeding, because she bit me on my back." It was the truth.

They wound up arresting Eva because they considered the bite wound on my back a defenseless wound.

I had to call off work the next few days because Eva was in jail, and I couldn't find a babysitter. I worked days, and Eva worked nights, so we never needed someone to watch Sebastian. Her parents came out the following week and hired a lawyer to start the divorce proceedings. I was not fighting the divorce at all. I wanted out of this marriage as much as she did. We were not good together. We were two different people, from two different worlds, who had no right getting married. I was the "bad boy" she rebelled with. I was the "bad part" of her life. To her parents, it was all my fault. I didn't care about her parents though.

Eva wanted to go back to Boston, but I didn't want to let Sebastian go. I really thought about it and wound up signing the paperwork from her lawyer giving Eva permission to move back with my son. It was painful, but I knew it was the best thing for Sebastian. I had plans to move back myself as soon as I could, but all I did was get deeper into drugs.

I remember dropping Eva and Sebastian off at the airport. I walked them both to security and watched as they walked away. I started to cry and left the airport. When I got home, I got as high as I could and stayed that way. I was trying to numb my feelings. I had never loved anything in my life before the way I loved Sebastian. I wasn't in the right frame of mind. People were making fun of me at work because I had become a junkie. I was called into the office a week after Eva moved back to Boston.

"How are you doing?" my boss asked me.

"I'm okay, I guess."

"We're gonna let you go, Steve." He was straight forward.

"Okay," I fought hard to hold back the tears, and he knew it. I knew this was coming.

"I know you're going through a hard time right now, Steve. You used to be one of our best workers. That's why we promoted you, but…" He let his words trail off.

"I know," I said.

"Here's your final check. I'm also putting in that we laid you off so you can collect unemployment. You're in no position to work. You need to figure your life out. You're headed in a bad direction, Steve. I hope you're able to pick yourself back up."

"Okay. Thanks, Todd."

I took my final check and walked out.

"Thank you for all your hard work, Steve."

I just kept walking. I could hear everyone laughing as I walked off the property. I didn't care really. I was used to being made fun of. I was used to being laughed at. What I could not believe, was that I was given a lay-off so I could collect unemployment. I had worked very hard at Century Steel. I gave everything I had to working my butt off there. My boss was right though; I had become a huge liability to the company. I went home, packed a small bag, and moved into the cheapest weekly I could find, in one the most drug-infested neighborhoods in Vegas.

I would get so high that I could hear people who were not there talking through the walls about wanting to kill me. It was driving me crazy. The more I heard it, the more dope I did. I got so scared at one point, because I thought I heard people outside my door talking about how they were going to break in my room to beat and stab me. So I crawled out my window, went up to the roof, and started yelling at the top of my lungs, "Help me! SOMEONE HELP ME! THEY'RE TRYING TO KILL ME! HELP ME, PLEASE!!!"

About five or six cop cars came with guns out, yelling for me to get off the roof. They searched my room but didn't find any drugs. I was doing so much dope, for so long, that I just looked like some guy who had mental problems. Why they didn't arrest me, I have no clue. I had an eight ball of speed in a vile hidden in my dirty laundry bag. The cops wound up leaving, but I was still hearing the voices that wanted to kill me. I snuck out of the weekly early one morning and roamed all over Vegas, ducking and hiding from people who were not there. I know now that I must have looked like a freak.

I finally ran out of drugs and found an ally to crash in for a few days while my body recovered. My unemployment checks were delivered to a friend's house that I used to work with at the steel company. He knew I was whacked out on drugs and suggested that I save a couple of them and move back home to Boston, so that's what I did. I was receiving a little over three hundred dollars a week and decided to save two checks and get out of Vegas. I slept in parks, dumpsters, alley ways, sidewalks, wherever I could, but I made it the two weeks without doing drugs. I picked up my two checks from Greg's house, cashed them, and bought a one-way bus ticket back to Boston. I would crawl home, yet again, and ask if I could stay there for a while. Although I was extremely relieved to be away from the drugs and safe on the bus, I stressed the entire way across the country on my way back to Boston.

I kept thinking of one of the happiest times in my life: the Christmas before, when Eva and I went to Boston. I went to my parents' house, and Eva went to her parents' house. We were splitting up but wanted to see our families. I remember sitting in the kitchen while holding Sebastian who was only a couple months old and talking to Jeannie. The kitchen phone rang, she picked it up and started talking to whomever it was. She told whoever it was that she had to go, paused to listen, then looking at me, said, "Because, I'm talking to my son."

I wanted to cry right there. It was the first time Jeannie ever referenced me as her son. That's all I ever wanted from her. Then she said, "No, Steven," meaning that whoever she was talking to thought that she meant Justin or Jarred. That's my happiest memory. It's one that still gets me through some difficult times today.

"Three grand essentials to happiness in this life are something to do, something to love, and something to HOPE for."
(Joseph Addison)

Hope, that's something not many people have anymore, but something happened the other day that gave me a little bit of hope.

I'm managing these sober houses right now, as I've already told you. I take a no-nonsense approach to it. I'm not being a jerk, but the old manager knew about and let people continue to get high. I, on the other hand, am not letting that happen. I have drug tested and kicked out seven people so far for using. I give them all one option and one option only. They can go to West Care Detox for three days and come back, or they can pack their things and leave now. I've had two guys tell me, "Thank you for what you're doing here."

That means the world to me. What I'm trying to get at is this: the other day I found a meth pipe on the porch loaded with dope. I threw it in the trash, but someone got it back out. There is this guy here, Darren, who has stage four liver cancer who's going to die soon. I was talking to him about the pipe I found. Darren is a good man who is sober and plans to stay that way. When I told him what happened, he said, "You know, Steve, I've done speed for twenty-three years. I've been clean for over a year, and I'm just not ready to see a meth pipe yet. I just want to die sober."

Can you believe that? This dude is going to die soon. Within a few months, Darren will be dead. He has a nurse come once a week to change the needle in his chest. He pukes all the time and is often a pale shade of either grey, yellow, or green. Not that there is any acceptable excuse to get loaded, but if there was one, Darren would have it.

How many times have any of us addicts said that we just want to live a sober life? Darren, though, said he wanted to die sober. To me, that is what hope is! It really did something to me on the inside. I've said over and over, "I want to live a sober life." I've never said that I want to die sober.

-Malachi 3:6-
"For I am the LORD, I do not change; therefore

you are not consumed, O sons of Jacob."
(NKJV)

I'm really glad the Lord doesn't change His mind. He really is the only compassionate and loving person I have!

Well, I made it to Boston, again. I went to my parents' house, again. I asked if I could stay there, again.

My dad wasn't too happy this time, not that he was happy any other time I showed up out of the blue, but he seemed particularly perturbed this time around. Again, I was given thirty days to find a job and move out. I often wonder if I looked strung out to my parents. I must have looked as if I just crawled out from a sewer. My dad never mentioned anything about my state of mind or my drug use, just always if I was okay.

I hit the job trail again and found a job in Medford, this time at a cabinet company. I was still collecting my unemployment checks from Nevada, so I was doing okay and was able to move out quickly.

Things were looking up for a change. I had reconciled with Eva, enough so that I was getting Sebastian on the weekends. I wanted to stay clean this time. I was doing all the right things and loved being a dad and spending time with my son.

One of the guys I worked with, Bob, was a big drinker. He loved Johnny Walker Black Label, and that was where it started. Then I went to smoking weed. Then I went from smoking weed to doing cocaine, again.

Eva and I started to fight even though we were not in a relationship. She felt that she could dictate when I could and could not see my son. This pissed me off to no end, and things just fell apart a lot quicker than they normally did. I could only see Sebastian when she didn't send him to his grandparents, so I numbed myself by drinking more. I will say this though: when I did have Sebastian, I never drank, smoked pot, or did any other drug, which was why I was so confused. When I had him, my life seemed full. When Eva played her games and I couldn't see him, I went deeper into my addiction.

My drinking got the better of me, and I was fired the day after Christmas for yelling at the owner's daughter in a drunken state. Now I was without a job again, so Eva said that I could not see Sebastian until I got another job. I couldn't understand why she was being so difficult. I thought about it, told her she could screw herself, and decided to leave. The only thing that crossed my mind at the time was that I did not want Sebastian to have to go through the same crap I went through as a child. I know that that may sound like a lame excuse, but in my mind, I was protecting him from the childhood I had. In my experience, women always won and got what they wanted, whether they were right, wrong, or indifferent. It was okay for Eva to drink and smoke pot, but not me. I just didn't want Sebastian to be pulled in two directions. I honestly felt it would be better to just leave rather than fight and have him affected by it. To stay and fight for what was right could end up with Eva and her family just talking crap about me to Sebastian. If I just left, he would forget about me and not have to hear garbage like that. There was also no way I could fight the money that Eva's parents would wind up spending to fight me back, so I decided to walk out of Sebastian's life.

My roommate had since moved out, because I started having sex with his ex-girlfriend. I never had any respect for anyone's stuff, even their girlfriends, if they so chose to be with me. I had no boundaries. When my roommate moved out, he took all the furniture with him, so I filled the place with stuff from Rent-A-Center. With no job and no way to pay for my stuff, I decided to sell it all. I was able to pocket close to $2,000 .

I called my dad one day while he was working and asked him if he could come over to my house so I could talk to him. He said he would, and when he came over, I told him I was moving. I forget where I told him I was moving to, but that was probably a lie also. I just wanted to give him the respect of telling him that I was leaving. As always, he didn't judge me. He never did. He just asked me if I was okay and if I really felt like I was making the right decision, even though he knew I was making the wrong one. He gave me his opinion and laid out what it was that he felt I should do.

"I love you, Steven. Be careful," he said.

When my dad left, I called my sister Rhonda, who was living in Arizona, and I told her that I was moving to Sierra Vista that coming weekend. At that point in my life, I never really thought I would see Sebastian again. I was walking out on him. I was leaving.

Sebastian, if you are reading this, I am so sorry for being a bad father to you and not being there when you needed me. I know that this may sound strange and that you probably don't want to hear it, but I LOVE YOU, SEBASTIAN! I always have. I always will. I was just too immature and too wrapped up in drugs to be able to want to show you what I was feeling inside. I love you more than you will ever know, Sebastian. I would love the chance to get to know the man you are today, the man your mother showed you how to be. I miss you. I would like another chance to be your dad. If not, I understand your anger. I will never stop praying for you, son...

Chapter Sixteen

-2 Corinthians 11:3-
But I fear, lest somehow, as the serpent deceived
Eve by his craftiness, so your minds may be
corrupted from the simplicity that is in Christ.
(NKJV)

So there I was, on another Greyhound bus, traveling across the country, living another lie. Why was it that I always felt the need to lie about my life and run away from what was going on, rather than be a man, stay, and fight. I became accustomed to running. That's just what felt comfortable.

———

I've been so nervous about continuing to write this book lately. I'm scared, and I don't know why. Telling the truth hurts! I've heard that expression many times in my life, but I never really understood it until I started writing this. I've tried to sit down and write, but nothing seems to come out. Things are going okay, I guess. I'm still managing these sober houses, but they've proven to be a full-time job. It's like babysitting adults who don't know how to act like adults.

I miss my kids so much it hurts. It's almost like they're the only things in my life that I have been unwilling to walk away from, yet that is exactly what everyone, thanks to Sabrina, thinks that I did. I've come to a point in my life where I don't want anyone to feel any kind of pain. There is this piece of me, way down deep inside, that can't wait for all the truth to finally be revealed, specifically about Sabrina, my relationship with my kids, and the truth as to why I am not in their lives right now. The only thing I've been willing to fight for are my children, but it just gets harder the more I try to. It's a crappy feeling. I have walked away from so much in life. The one time I really tried to fight for what was right, I get screwed.

I wonder what God has planned next. I really do. I don't want to go back to the old me, but at times, trying to fight for what's right, well, just plain sucks.

"Miracles start to happen when you give as much energy to your dreams as you do to your fears"
(Richard Wilkins)

It's only now that I believe that I'm putting in the work and energy to the things I dream of. I dream of being a strong man of God like Ryan Omlie. I dream of my kids calling me daddy, knowing I did not walk away from them. I dream of holding them, hugging them, them hugging me, and telling me they love me. I dream of touring the world giving my testimony. I dream about this book reaching the hands of millions of people, giving them hope, real hope, knowing that Christ really is the answer to all their problems. I dream that one day God will look at me and say, "I am proud of you, Steven." I dream of one day being able to see my kids again: Sebastian, Rhesa, and Asher. I also dream of Sabrina getting arrested for child abduction, losing her job, and having to cop-out to a felony. Hopes and dreams.

I rolled into Sierra Vista after my four-day bus ride and was tired. I had some money and paid for a month at a weekly/monthly motel on Fry Blvd. I unpacked and called my sister Rhonda. We talked for a little while and made plans to meet up the next day. It really sucked trying to keep up this lie about Sebastian being gone. I am ashamed of myself.

For the first few days, I lounged around and did nothing. I had plans to look for a job, and I would, just not right away. Rhonda came and met me on her lunch break the following day. I tried to keep the conversation short about my son. We made small talk and made plans to meet up at her house. She was married and had a life of her own to live.

I was hungry one night and just across the parking lot was a Subway, so I walked over to grab something to eat. When I walked in and stood in line, one of the girls making the sandwiches looked very familiar. I knew that I knew her from somewhere, but I couldn't remember where. Her name tag said Ellen, and I wracked my brain trying to remember. About an hour later it hit me. She was Ellen Hammond, the youngest of three daughters of the family I stayed with when I lived here seven or eight years earlier. I never thought about her back then, because she was so young. I remember feeling sorry for her, but my gosh, she grew up into a truly beautiful woman.

I went back a few days later to get another sub, and Ellen was working again. When it was my turn to order, she asked me what my name was, so I told her. She remembered who I was, and we wound up talking for a little while. I gave her the same bull crap story about my son passing away that I gave Rhonda, always the victim. One night, I bought Ellen a dozen white roses and had my sister deliver them to her at work. I don't know how it happened, but we started hanging out a little bit. She had a daughter named Lindsay, who was also a beautiful little girl.

Ellen was an awesome woman, truly amazing. She had gotten married, then divorced, at a very young age. She worked hard and took care of her daughter all by herself. She lived alone, and I gave her so much credit for the way she worked and took care of her child. She didn't do drugs and didn't drink. She really was just trying to do her best.

Soon after we started hanging out, Ellen asked me if I wanted to move in with her. Normally, I would have jumped at a situation like that, but when she asked me, I wasn't too sure. It wasn't because I didn't want to. It was because I didn't want to ruin her life. I knew enough that my track record proved to be one of a destructive pattern, especially when it came to women. It took a couple of weeks before I told her that I would move in with her. To be honest, the reason I did say yes was because I wanted to give her a little financial relief. She didn't make much money, and her mother and two sisters,

Chase and Dharma, all lived in Tucson. Ellen was a good woman. I respected her.

I moved in and things were good for a while. We both worked hard. I worked days. Ellen worked nights. I was able to watch her daughter while she worked, but watching her daughter made my heart heavy for Sebastian. I missed him so much and thought about him every single day.

Ellen and I seemed to be in a good groove. She made me happy, and it seemed I made her happy as well. The thing I loved the most about Ellen was that she didn't drink or do drugs. She always put her daughter above everything else. I don't have a lot of good memories in life that I can call on when things are rough that'll make me feel better and give me hope. One of them, though, was from Ellen. I still think about it to this day.

One day she came home from shopping, and for no apparent reason, she bought me two packs of boxer shorts and ten Chap-sticks. I'm a guy who can't live without Chap-stick. I have to have it. I was a little confused and asked her why.

"Because I noticed that your boxers were getting old and these were on sale. I know you always worry about running out of Chap-stick, so now you don't have to worry about it." Then she just smiled and gave me a kiss. "I love you."

"I love you too, Ellen." I had a good woman.

-John 10:10-
The thief does not come except to steal, and to kill, and to destroy. I have come that they may have life, and that they may have it more abundantly.

(NKJV)

One night, Ellen and I were sitting outside her apartment enjoying the night. As we were talking, I saw a man walking around the complex who looked very familiar. He started to walk our way when I recognized who he was. It was Steve Mocco, and I immediately felt his evil. I hung around Steve and his friend Rob when I lived here previously.

Steve was bad news. However, he was also the kind of guy that made you happy he was on your side, although terrified if he was against you. He walked up to Ellen and me, and he remembered who I was.

"What's up?" he asked me.

"Not much. How you doing, Steve?"

"I'm good. I just got out of prison. I'm trying to order a pizza, but I need a coupon. Do you guys have any pizza coupons?"

"No," Ellen responded without even looking in his direction.

"So, your back, huh?" he asked me.

"Yeah. I moved back about a month ago. I heard Miguel died."

"Yeah. Well, I'll see you around," he said walking back to his apartment.

"Yeah, I'll see ya. Have a good night, Steve."

Steve lived with his mother, who was a head case herself. He used to be married to Ellen's sister Dharma, but treated her like crap. He was less than a week out of prison and bragged about doing one year in an Arizona prison for assault. Ellen didn't like him at all. She did not want him around and didn't want me hanging around him.

It wasn't long before I got fired from my job. I had long become complacent and arrogant at work. I just could not find a job where I made more than minimum wage. Ellen even believed me when I lied to her about why I lost my job. Because I was now out of work, Steve Mocco and I started hanging out, a lot.

> **"A river cuts through a rock**
> **not because of its power,**
> **but its persistence."**

Ellen was determined to be satisfied with whatever life gave her. She took things as they came and dealt with it. She had a tough life growing up. She never dwelt on that though. She was successfully raising her daughter on her own. I loved her, I really did. But I was no good for her. If I could describe Ellen using only one word, that word would be integrity!

-Isaiah 28:8-
For all tables are full of vomit
and filth; no place is clean
(NKJV)

What was going well with Ellen and me soon started to dissolve. Since I was having a hard time finding a job, I gave up looking altogether and wound up hanging out with Steve every day. All that did was lead to drinking and doing dope. Ellen knew that I was drinking, but I was able to hide the fact that I was doing drugs for a little while. As always, the drugs took over and dictated my life. At one point, I was up for about three days or so and started thinking that people were after me wanting to kill me. I tried to convince Ellen not to go outside, so the people who wanted to kill me couldn't get in. She freaked out and wanted me to leave immediately, but I was stuck on stupid. She was crying and wanted to protect her daughter.

"I just want you to leave, but I'm scared of what you'll do." she cried.

She was truly afraid for her life. I went outside, because I really did not want to scare her. I felt bad that she was that scared for herself and her daughter. I was going to lose the first woman that had ever really fallen in love with me for who I was, who wasn't looking to change me.

While I was outside sitting on the picnic table, Steve came out, and we talked about what was going on. To cheer me up, we went to his house and started drinking and doing dope. Ellen called a few people to come to her apartment to help her pack up. Within hours, Ellen had quit her job, packed up her things, and moved to Tucson, literally that quick. She was not about to put up with any drugs in her house or around her daughter. To this day, I commend Ellen for doing that. I think about her from time to time, hoping she is okay, doing well, and happy. To this day, I still miss her.

Ellen, if you ever read this, I am so sorry for hurting you. You did the right thing by leaving. I am so sorry and very ashamed that I put you in that position.

With Ellen gone, I sank deeper into drugs. Steve and I wound up hooking back up with our old friend Rob. Talk about a toxic relationship of people who just did not care about anything. The thing about Steve and Rob was that the two of them were extremely feared in Sierra Vista. When the two of them got together, people did what they said and wanted. It was that simple. I was friends with both of them and noticed a certain level of respect shown my way now as well.

"The tragedy of life is not death, but what we let die inside of us while we live."
(Norman Cousins)

What little good was inside me then was quickly dying.

I moved in with a friend of mine named, Tune, and his wife. It was fun, because we all did dope together. Tune was an old friend of Steve's, who sold pot by the pounds. It seemed a good fit at the time. I slowed way down with hanging out with Steve and Rob. Rob manufactured meth, thus he was always under surveillance, getting arrested for petty things until the cops could get something hard on him. Rob didn't care too much. His house was set up with video surveillance as well. Steve, on the other hand, proved to be more than I could handle. He was off the chain. At no time did he care about anyone or anything. He did what he pleased. I didn't want to get on his bad side, so I stayed away.

One night while I was sleeping at this girl's house, Steve came and knocked on the door repeatedly until I opened it.

"Come on, dude. Let's go start some crap!" Steve said.

"I can't, dude, I'm tired. I'm trying to sleep."

"COME ON, MAN! LET'S GO START SOME CRAP!!!"

"Steve, I can't tonight. I really can't."

"Oh, never mind, man. I'll go do it myself then."

"Okay, Steve. Be careful, man."

Two days later, Megan, Steve's ex-girlfriend, showed up at my place and handed me a newspaper article that described Steve perfectly. As I read the article, it said that Steve was wanted by the police for a number of felonies. Megan was scared and wanted to know if I knew anything. I told her I didn't. It was the truth. People who had known Steve, Rob, and me started talking a lot of crap. I was confused, because I had no clue what was going on. I still could not get ahold of Rob, and that bothered me. I heard from some people that Steve raped some woman, but I didn't know if this was the truth or not. Knowing Steve, though, I wouldn't put it past him. My time in Sierra Vista was closing quickly. Like always, I had lost so much here. I lost Ellen, and even at that time, that was all I cared about. I needed to leave.

———————

About two months ago, I started thinking about Steve Mocco. I knew that I would be writing about him soon. I couldn't remember much, just that he had gotten into trouble at the time. I only remembered that and that Rob seemed to be MIA at the time.

The only place I knew to look for the two of them was the Arizona Department of Corrections, so that's where I started. I could not find anything on Rob. I'm pretty sure I wasn't spelling his name correctly, so I tried every combination I could think of, but still came up empty on him. I do know that the cops wanted Rob put away for a while. They were on him like white on rice.

My search for Steve was different. I couldn't find him at first, but the difference of one letter in his last name proved to make all the difference. His face and inmate number came right up. There was no mistake. The man I was looking at on my computer screen was the same Stephen J. Mocco I knew sixteen years earlier. He hadn't changed. The look in his eyes from his prison mug shot, to me, still said, "Screw you all! I don't care." I saw a very lost man. I saw a man I used to call my best friend. What I found on my former best friend was this:

Stephen Joseph Mocco
(Arizona DOC Inmate Number 169300)

1st count Burglary in the 1st Degree: 12 years

2nd count Burglary in the 1st Degree: 12 years

1st count Aggravated Assault: 9 years

2nd count Aggravated Assault: 9 years

3rd count Aggravated Assault: 11 years

1 count Attempt to Commit Armed Robbery: 9 years

1 count Armed Robbery: 10 years 6 months

1 count Attempt to Commit Sexual Abuse: 1 year

1 count Attempt to Commit Sexual Assault: 7 years

1st count Sexual Assault: 14 years

2nd count Sexual Assault: 14 years

3rd count Sexual Assault: 14 years

4th count Sexual Assault: 14 years

1st count Kidnapping: 15 years

2nd count Kidnapping: 21 years

3rd count Kidnapping: 21 years

Steve received a total of 193 years and 6 months in an Arizona state prison. It doesn't matter the story I heard. This is a man I once called my best friend.

If you sit there and hope he rots in hell, then you have a lot to learn about being a Christian. My Bible tells me that I should pray for this man and that he comes to believe that Christ died for his sins. If he were to do that and truly have a heart of repentance, then Steve should enjoy the same benefits of heaven as every other believer in Jesus Christ. Should he not? Think about it. It doesn't matter whether it's Adolf Hitler, Jeffery Dahmer, Timothy McVeigh, Dennis Rader, Arthur Shawcross, Ted Bundy, Pedro Alonso Lopez, Ed Kemper, Charles Manson, David Berkowitz, Elmer Wayne Henley Jr., Paul Bateson, Wayne Williams, William Pierce Jr., Richard Speck, Jerry Brudos, Montie Rissell, or any other person who had done something wrong. My Bible tells me to pray for all and that all can enjoy heaven if we believe in our hearts. It's the truth. It's what God's word tells us. No one, and I mean no one, is exempt from the love that Jesus Christ has to offer. He is the Messiah. His Word is Truth.

-Colossians 1:28-
Him we preach, warning every man and
teaching every man in all wisdom, that we
may present every man perfect in Christ Jesus.
(NKJV)

I needed to get out of Arizona, or else something bad was going to happen to me. I figured out a way to steal twelve hundred dollars from a friend of a friend. With the money, I bought a bunch of meth and a bus ticket back home to Boston, Massachusetts. My plan was to get back to Boston, and hopefully be allowed to stay at my parents' house. Maybe sell a little bit of the dope I had, but things didn't work out the way I had hoped.

I got on the bus and tried to settle in for my four-day bus ride to Boston, again. The problem was that I started snorting dope a couple days earlier and hadn't slept in a few days. I was edgy. Somewhere in the middle of nowhere, while driving through Texas, I got into an argument with some people on the bus. I can't even remember what it was over, but we were in a pretty heated exchange of words, threatening we were going to kick each other's butts at the next stop. Well, the next stop was this town called Monahans, Texas, and when the bus stopped at the convenience store, there were three cop cars waiting for us. The cops pulled me and the two people I was arguing with off the bus to question us.

After questioning the three of us and running our IDs, the cops concluded it was not me who started it, but asked if I wouldn't mind catching the next bus in the morning, because the two people I was arguing with had a child with them and needed to get to Dallas on time. I wasn't happy about being asked to stay and catch the next bus, but I had a bunch of dope on me and didn't really feel like getting searched. I couldn't believe they didn't realize I was pretty high, so I just counted my blessings. They were nice enough and just wanted to make sure the child was taken care of.

There was a motel across the street, so I walked over and got a room for the night. Two busses a day stopped at the convenience store: one each in the morning and evening. No big deal, I thought. It was better than arguing with the police and risking real trouble.

I couldn't sleep that night, because I had been up for while snorting and smoking meth. The next morning I realized I was too high to get on a bus. I was now gacked. I should have realized I was so messed up and needed to come down, but of course, I didn't. What I did do was get the motel room for another two days, figuring I would be okay enough to continue my bus ride then. That didn't work out either. As most of us addicts know, I wasn't able to put the dope down. I got to the hotel room for another two days, then another two days after that.

By this time, I was hearing voices. I heard the DEA talking about how they were going to bust me for all the dope I had. I heard the FBI talking about how they were waiting for me to come out of my room so they could rush in and arrest me for the dope. I heard the CIA talking about how they had a computer chip in my head and how they were tracking my every move and thought. I was hearing the Secret Service talk about how they needed to watch me and track my every move so that they could protect the President from me. I was hearing the local police talk about how they know I'm in here getting high and were waiting to bust me. I was hearing Joker, the dealer I stole two pounds of weed from, telling someone he was glad that he found me. I had to shut the TV off, because every channel I turned to was talking about me and how they just couldn't believe I was still continuing to get high while the cops were waiting to bust me. What set me off, though, was hearing the people in the next room talk about how they were going to bust into my room and kill me for being such a dirt-bag and stealing two pounds from Joker.

One night, I even went to the room next door, the room filled with people trying to kill me, and started kicking on the door and yelling at them for them to come out and fight me now. The room was empty. I was tweaking hard. Very hard! I couldn't tell the difference between reality and non-reality. That's how deep I was into drugs. I called the cops on myself that night. I called 911 and told them that I had gotten into it with some people from the hotel and that now they were threatening me with guns and trying to kill me.

"I've got 99 problems and 86 of them are completely made up scenarios in my head that I'm stressing about for absolutely no logical reason."
(Author unknown)

The cops came deep. I couldn't even tell you how many there were. They had their guns out, searching the motel for people who were not there. I had been so high for so long, that my eyes looked normal. They just figured that I was a mental case. They told me my skin looked pasty and asked why I was sweating so hard. I told them that I didn't know. I had a 12 pack of Budweiser on ice in the sink and they told me to try to have a few beers and relax. They never searched my room, but they did look around, searching for a reason for them to go through all my stuff. They didn't see anything that gave them probable cause. All my dope was hidden in the bottom of the trash can, under the trash bag, so they left.

I got higher and higher, and the voices never went away. They became louder and more convincing. The voices were telling me that they were pissed that I had called the cops on them, that they would find a way into my room to torture me, slowly, before they killed me painfully. I was freaking out bad and knew enough that I couldn't go outside the hotel room. The cops were most definitely watching for anything unusual. I did not want to be the reason that gave them an opportunity to search my room.

By the time the sun was coming up, I was freaked out and called 911 again. When the cops showed up this time, they found my dope just sitting on the table. I forgot it was there. I was arrested for possession of methamphetamine and taken to the Ward County Jail, booked, and placed in a medical cell, naked, so I wouldn't hurt myself. I was so paranoid that I thought that the cops were in on it all. I thought they were letting people into the jail, the people who were trying to kill me. It was not a good scene at all. All they could do was let it run its course.

It took me almost five days to come down enough to where I could be placed in a holding cell with my clothes on. I was so tired and just wanted a bed to sleep in. The cops in the jail told me some of the things that I was saying. I didn't remember any of it. They told me that they had never seen someone that wacked out on dope before and never saw someone take that long to come down. Finally, I was taken to a cellblock. I was able to take a shower and then passed out on my bunk and slept for a while.

The Ward County Jail was old-fashioned. We wore black and white striped prison clothes. About a week after I was in my cellblock, a public defender came to see me. He said that I didn't have a court date yet, because it took me so long to come down. He also told me that my charge was a mandatory two-year sentence. He was very short and left after a couple minutes.

I sat and waited for my court date to come. I waited, and waited, and waited! I sat in that jail for over five months and never went to court. I never even had a preliminary hearing. Every day I heard names called out for court but never heard mine. I asked one of the officers for my public defender's name and address so I could write him a letter asking him why the hell I haven't gone to court yet. A few weeks after I sent him the letter, he finally came to see me.

"Hello, Mr. Gray. How are you?"

"Well, I've been sitting here for over six months now and haven't had a court date. How would you be feeling? You came to see me a week after I was arrested and haven't seen you since."

I feared they found out that I was wanted somewhere else. Maybe going to court here really didn't matter in my case.

"I'm very sorry about that. Your file, somehow, slipped through the cracks at my office, and I completely forgot about you."

I just looked at him and wanted to punch him in his face, but then he said, "The good news is that you're getting released today."

"What?" I asked. This just could not be true.

"The cops cannot find the drugs you were arrested with. The meth you were arrested with was picked up to be taken to a lab and tested, but somehow it never made it to the lab. Between that, sitting here for six months without a court date, and no bail, you'll be released today on habeas corpus."

"What? How long until I get out of here?"

"You'll be released within the hour."

"Really?"

"Yes, we're finalizing the paperwork as we speak. We just have to have a judge sign the paperwork. It's a good thing it took you so long to come down off the drugs. You were so high that we couldn't take you to court. The judge told the jail to inform them when you sobered up so you could have a bail hearing. But there are so many federal inmates in holding here that they forgot about you."

"Thanks, man." I wanted to be upset, but how could I? I should be getting a minimum two-year sentence in a Texas prison, but instead, I was released, free and clear.

I went back to my cell to pack. Before I was even finished packing, I was called for release. While they were booking me out, I had this strange feeling I was going to be arrested just outside the doors for something else. They gave me my property and buzzed me out the door. I looked around and walked away from the jail, free.

I found the convenience store where the Greyhound bus stops. It was a long way away, and by the time I got there, it was dark outside and very cold. I walked to the cashier and asked her about the bus. She told me I just missed it. The next bus comes at eight the following morning. I found a dumpster across the parking lot and tried to get some sleep. I could see the hotel I was arrested at and couldn't believe what had happened. What had my life come to? I had my bus ticket in my property and a Greyhound bus ticket is good for one year. I shouldn't have any trouble getting on the bus in the morning.

"Life without faith in something is too narrow a space to live."
(George Lancaster Spalding)

The only thing I had any faith in was never knowing what the next day in my life would bring.

I was up way before the bus showed up that morning. I was cold, tired, and hungry. Finally, I saw it coming off the exit from the highway. The destination plate on the front window read: Dallas. The bus came to a stop on the side of the store. The driver looked at me, and I handed him my ticket. He wanted to know why my ticket was six months old. I reminded him that the ticket is good for one year from the purchase date and explained that six months earlier I had gotten into a fight on the bus, was then arrested, and had just gotten out of jail. He let me on with a warning, and I found a seat and settled in. I was broke, hungry, and needed money.

I don't know what time we got into Dallas, but was surprised I slept the entire way. I found a pay phone and called my dad, collect, again. It took me a few times before getting through, but I got ahold of him and explained everything that happened with my release and told him that I was stuck in Dallas. He wasn't at all happy with me. He asked me if I was okay and said that he would wire me some money so I could buy a ticket to Boston. He wired me a couple hundred dollars. Greyhound bus stations are notorious for being in bad areas and are havens for drug addicts. I was able to find a dealer, buy some weed, then headed for a bar and drank for a few hours until my bus was ready to leave. Finally, drunk and stoned, I was ready to load my bus. I settled in and tried to relax.

-Exodus 10:10-
Then he said to them, "The LORD had better
be with you when I let you and your little

ones go! Beware, for evil is ahead of you."
(NKJV)

We were somewhere in Virginia, passing a NASCAR Racetrack, and stopped at a small bus station. We all got off so they could clean and refuel. I found the bathroom, went into a stall, and smoked a half a joint. Just as I was coming out of the stall, the bus driver was coming in. Knowing exactly what I just did, he stared at me.

Soon, it was time to leave. After we were all on the bus, three cops got on and pulled me off. The one cop told me that he knew I had marijuana on me and was going to find it, so I had better give it up. This wasn't my first go around with the police, so his threats just fell on deaf ears. I would never just give up my drugs. You were going to have to work at finding it.

"Boy, you have one hell of an attitude about you," the cop said.

"No, I don't. You think I have something on me, and I don't. So, please just search me, my bag, and run me so I can get on the bus and get back home."

"You're going to jail as soon as I find your marijuana," he said.

"Well, search me then." I handed him my paperwork from the Ward County Jail.

"Sounds like you got a pretty good deal, huh?" he said after he read it.

"Yeah."

"I'll keep you so long that you'll miss your bus."

"That's okay. This is a bus station, and I have a bus ticket. I can wait for the next bus. Then I'm gonna sue Greyhound for this crap, and I'll get a few bucks."

The cops searched all my things and ran me through their system. I came up clean. The bus driver was not happy, but nonetheless, I gave him a big smile as I got back on the bus. I had one full joint left that was hidden deep in my sock. I was not going to touch that until I got home to Boston.

Eventually, my bus rolled into Boston. I quickly got on the Orange Line and took it to Wellington Station. As I walked to my house, I smoked my last joint. I knew everything was going to be okay. I would be given thirty days to get a job and move out. I really needed a shower and wanted to get something to eat. When I got to my house, Justin answered the door. We said hello and went upstairs to talk to my dad. He was sleeping. I woke him up to tell him I was home. He told me he'd be out in a minute. I sat in the kitchen and started to take off my boots when he walked in and told me to put my shoes back on, get in the car, and that we were going for a ride.

"You can't stay here anymore, Steven. Jeannie is afraid that you'll influence Justin and Jarred. You can't come by anymore. You need to figure your life out. You can't even just stop by anymore unannounced. No more calling collect from jail. You have to go and really figure out what it is you're doing. I'm not saying that you can't come by to visit ever. I'm saying that you need to go and not come around again until you really figure your life out. Do you understand me?"

I was blown away, but knew this day would come eventually. I was silent for a few minutes, wanting to cry.

"Yeah." I did understand him. I really did. I just didn't see this coming tonight. The one thing I could always count on was coming home for at least a month to get right again. Now that was over. I couldn't even take a shower or make a sandwich. I just had to go. I didn't blame my dad. I understood.

"Do you have any money, Steven?" he asked.

"No."

He didn't say anything to that. He just kept driving and eventually pulled into his bank. He went to the ATM, and when he came back, he drove off.

"Here, take this."

It was five hundred dollars. I did not know how to react or what to say.

"Thank you."

He didn't say anything until he drove me back to Wellington Station. I think he thought I was going kill myself one day doing drugs.

"Take care of yourself, Steven. Be safe. I love you."

My eyes filled with tears. I could not believe this was happening. I wanted him to change his mind. I looked at him, but he was firm.

"I love you, Steven. Goodbye," he said again.

"Yeah, I love you too, Dad." And I walked away. I went in and caught the T into Boston. I didn't know what I was going to do, but I knew I was leaving Boston for a very long time.

Chapter Seventeen

-Genesis 4:14-
*Surely You have driven me out this day from the face of the
ground;*
*I shall be hidden from Your face; I shall be a fugitive and a
vagabond*
*on the earth, and it will happen that anyone who finds me will
kill me."*
(NKJV)

I cannot remember much of the next few years of my life. I know I did a lot of drugs and lied my way through much, if not all of it. It's just that the next few years are a blur. I lived in dumpsters, cemeteries, stolen cars, homeless shelters, and sidewalks. I was a drug addict to the core.

"Like a roller coaster ride,
I'm elevating towards my high.
Adrenaline absorbed, on the edge of me seat,
I'm anxious to reach the peak.
Endorphins screaming and pores pouring,
*the moment freezes. I feel the tension breath upon
me,*
face to face with a dangerous high,
I push forth trying to hide the fear I feel inside.
*Never satisfied, I always want more – just enough
to hit that peak.*
*This ride never lasts long enough. It's a devil in
disguise,*
robbing me blind with no will to stop yet,
I'm always anticipating another adventurous ride."

426

(Author Unknown)

———————

That is such an accurate description of what it's like to live the life of a dope fiend. You always want more. You'll give up anyone, everything, at any time, just to get that next fix. The truth is: it'll never be enough. You know it, but your mind tells you differently. You start to believe the lie. The lie becomes a truth in your life. No one can understand the lie you're trying to pass as a truth, because in your mind, you're trying pass a truth that's really a lie. You don't understand that it's a lie anymore. People don't get it. They don't understand it. I'm not saying it's right. It's not. It's wrong. It's just what your mind is caught up in at the time. All you want is to feel right again. The only way to do that is to lie your ass off to get what you think you need. The problem is that you just can't see reality any longer. You want to. You think you do. You want the help but don't know how to ask for it. You're too far gone. The people that do see you see a dope addict who just wants to get high. What they do not see is your heart!

One person: that's what I wish. I don't care if all of you throw me to the side. If I could reach one person, just one, who changes their life because of what I went through, then I have succeeded! Whether any of you think different is a distant second. I care about reaching the hurting, the lost, the broken, the unlovable! Those are the people I'm aiming to reach.

427

The greatest pastor I have ever known, Pastor Jeff Chaves, once told me, "There's a difference between believing in Christ and believing IN Christ! Which one are you?" and, "We all have eternal life, Steve. It just depends on where you're going to spend it."

I never understood those words until now.

———————

As I was saying, I lived on the streets over the next few years of my life: sidewalks, dumpsters, under bridges, anywhere I felt I could be safe. I worked day labor for drug money. One thing that never changed was my work ethic. I worked hard, and more often than not, I found the work I needed to keep my drug habit alive. Rarely did I look homeless. I kept clean by using public restrooms throughout the city of Las Vegas. I had one backpack with a few changes of clothes while trying to not bring attention to myself. When I couldn't find work for the day, I would go to donut shop dumpsters and wait for the previous days donuts to be thrown out. I thought about my son, Sebastian, every day. I wondered what he was doing. I wondered what he looked like. I wondered if I would ever see him again.

I knew this other homeless guy, Larry, who, like me, lived on the streets and worked to get high. We almost had the same story as far as walking away from our kids. He walked away from his daughter in Colorado and was a serious drug addict. We would do our own thing with finding work during the day, then meet up at night, hang out, and get high. We each knew that we weren't trying to scam each other. We worked for our own dope and looked out for each other.

One day we were sitting in the Woodlawn Cemetery, getting high. It was a Saturday afternoon, and I had just gotten two hundred dollars' worth of crack cocaine. Larry had a bunch himself. I was lying on the grass getting high, and for some reason, I started to think about God. He just popped into my head. I looked up to the sky and thought about God for a while. I turned to Larry and said, "Hey Larry, do you believe in God?"

"No," he answered quickly.

He was very matter-of-fact about it, so I just continued to lie there looking at the sky, getting high. About an hour went by, and for the life of me I could not stop thinking about God. It was as if He was invading my mind. I couldn't enjoy my dope. I couldn't get comfortable. I couldn't hold a thought other than God. I tried my hardest to push the thought of Him out of my mind, but it wasn't happening.

"Larry, you really don't believe in God?" I asked.

"No."

"Why not?"

"I don't know. I just don't."

I stood up and walked away. He never asked me where I was going, and I never looked back. I just did not want to live this way anymore. I didn't know where I was walking to. I just started walking.

I was coming down and wanted so badly to get high. I couldn't hold any thought at all now. I found an alley behind a McDonalds in a bad part of town and just sat there for a while. I found a cement hole in the wall with a pillow and some blankets and decided to lie down. It was December and getting cold at night. I stayed in that hole for three days. I was coming down hard and wanted to get high, but didn't. After spending three days in that hole, I was hungry. I couldn't sleep anymore and felt God telling me to go for a walk. I left the hole and started walking with no destination. After a couple hours of walking, I looked up and saw a big blue cross that said JESUS SAVES. God had taken me to The Las Vegas Rescue Mission as they were serving the evening meal to the homeless.

-Genesis 45:11-
"There I will provide for you, lest you and your
household, and all that you have, come to poverty;
for there are still five years left of famine"
(NKJV)

There was what looked to be about a thousand people or so lined up around the block waiting to eat. I found the end of the line and waited. I was so hungry, not to mention strung out, cold, and tired.

I waited in line, and eventually it was my turn to go into the kitchen and eat. Everyone got a bowl of hot beans, and the tables had all the bread that you could eat. I can't stand beans at all, but I wasn't upset. I was grateful to be eating something in a warm kitchen. Each table had jugs filled with ice water, and I just sat there, eating my bread dipped in bean juice and drank my ice water. I could see the other homeless people coming in were wet and found out that it had started to rain. Just great. I did not know where I was going to sleep tonight. I would try to find a dumpster later to stay dry.

On my way out of the kitchen, I was told that we could smoke on the patio before we walked off the property. It was cold and raining, so this would give me another few minutes before I had to walk out into the rain. I found a few cigarette butts in the butt can and tried to hunker down out of the rain and take a few drags. As I was looking out at the rain-soaked city, I thought, "tonight is going to suck." It didn't look as if the rain would let up any time soon. In Las Vegas, it doesn't rain much, but when it does, it rains for a few minutes and then clears right up. We get about five days out of the year where it rains all day and night, and this night just happens to be one of them. I had just finished smoking, was ready to go walking in the rain, when this man came up to me and tapped me on the shoulder.

"Excuse me, sir?" he said to me.

"Huh?" I said.

"Sir, do you need a bed for the night?" he asked me.

"Huh? What are you talking about?"

"Would you like a bed tonight? We have one open bed left. You can have it, if you want. We called out all the bed numbers on the veranda and one of the homeless men never answered for the bed number he was issued. Do you want the bed?"

I didn't realize it was God moving.

"Listen, this is a Christian drug and alcohol program. We also feed the homeless and have an overnight shelter where we house homeless people for up to seven days. All we require is that you check in each evening by 5:30 p.m., attend our chapel service every evening, and you get a bed every night for seven days."

I didn't know what to say.

"Yes, please," I said thankfully.

I had to show my ID to security and was shown the way to the overnight dorm. I was given a towel, a bar of soap, and directed to the shower area. All homeless people that stayed in the overnight shelter had to take a shower before receiving bed sheets and a blanket. I went to take my shower and stayed under the water for a while. What a great shower it was. I had not taken a shower in a few years. The most I had done was wash up in gas station bathrooms, or the occasional water hose I would find on the side of a building. I felt so clean afterwards. I put on a fresh change of clothes and received my bed sheets.

I wasn't expecting all that much at the chapel service. I figured it would be the same old crap that was spewed at most churches that most people really didn't want to be bothered with. The pastor that night was an old-fashioned preacher. His name was Pastor Merrill.

As Pastor Merrill preached, I began to cry. It was as if something let loose inside me. My heart was hit. That's the best way I can explain it. It wasn't like I was all boo-hooing. I just sat there and listened while God spoke to my heart. For the first time in my life, I knew God was talking to me. He told me the reason my life had always felt cold and empty was because I didn't have Him in it. I heard Him say to me, "It starts now." I swear on everything I have that I heard Him speak those words to me that night.

Pastor Merrill's sermon was about turning your life around. It was about being sick and tired of being sick and tired. If we, as in the homeless at the service, really wanted to change, it would take making a choice and doing some work. The choice was ours to make. I wanted the drugs and the life I was living, gone. I didn't know how to though. Just then, I thought back to when Officer Dancer prayed with me in my jail cell back in the Chemung County Jail. He told me that I could have a better life with Jesus. He asked me if I was willing to give my life to Christ and if I believed that He died for my sins. Back then, when he asked me if I was ready to give my life to Jesus and if I was ready to follow Him, I said, "Yes." I did not believe it in my heart though. I believed Jesus was real. I just didn't believe IN Him.

"There's a difference between believing in God, and believing IN Him!"
(Pastor Jeff Chaves)

When Pastor Merrill finished his sermon, he prayed for those of us who wanted some prayer. When it was my turn to talk to Pastor Merrill, I just started to cry.

"It's okay, young man." he said as he held his hand on my shoulder. I continued to cry for a few minutes. When I finally slowed down enough to talk, I said, "I want to change, sir."

"Well, many people want to change. Are you willing to do the work it takes?"

"I don't want to live like this anymore."

"You can want to change your life all you want, young man, but if Christ is not the foundation of that change, it will never work."

When we finished talking, I went to the overnight dorm and tried to sleep. That night, all I thought about was Jesus Christ. I hadn't yet been saved, but God was working.

The following evening when I checked in for my bed, I asked about their drug program and was told I had to go to the back gate at 8:00 a.m. to sign up. Once signed up, I needed to come back each morning at the same time to keep my spot in line. If I missed a day, I would lose my spot and have to start over again. Every morning I was at the back gate, without fail, waiting to see if today was my day. I spent my seventh and final night in my homeless bed. I was worried, because my name hadn't moved up enough to get into the program, and I really didn't want to go back to the streets. I was fourth on the list, but they averaged just a few intakes a week.

The following morning, as usual, Bob came to the back gate, took our names, and announced how many available spots in the program there were. Four spots were open. Four men got in. I was the fourth.

"Welcome to The Las Vegas Rescue Missions Christ-centered drug and alcohol recovery program," he said.

Every time I try to get this book done, the devil comes at me in ways I cannot believe. These sober houses I'm managing are getting shut down because the owner is a crack head who wants control back. His name is Brian McGilvery. Two years ago he went on a serious crack binge, giving control of his houses to this guy, Mike Allen, who owns The Palms Sober Living Home.

Mike took over, got Brian's house out of foreclosure, and saved his other house from getting taken away. It's been two years since then, and Brian still hasn't come to his senses. About a week and a half ago, Brian was selling our donated food outside of a local bar.

When I took over managing these houses, the biggest issues I had was that I was not able to collect rent from Brian, because he was allowed to live there rent free. I also was not allowed to kick him out for his continued drug use. Everyone that lives in these houses are supposed to pay rent, except for Brian. Everyone who lives in these houses has to be willing to take random drug tests, except for Brian. Well, it all came to a head, and now the houses are getting shut down. Brian was asked to leave for selling our food and his continued drug use, so he called the police to have Jack and I kicked off the property, but due to the contract between Mike and Brian, he was unable to do so. What Brian did then was call my PO and tell him that I was selling cocaine out of the houses with the hope that I would be arrested, and thus, be out of the house.

Now I have to go back to the Palms Sober Living House that Jack manages. I don't know what to do. I hate this life. I can't find a job. I have no way to pay my rent. Jack told me not to worry about it for now, but how long will that actually last? I can't see my kids, and I just really want to give up. I am not using. When does it end? When will the blessings start? I would really just like to kill Sabrina and her entire family right now. She probably tells my kids, "I don't know where Daddy is." And if people ask about Rhesa and Asher's daddy, she probably says, "I don't know."

People wonder why guys just freaking lose it. It's because of the fouled up system like this! I think about my kids every day and wonder if they think about me at all. I wonder if they truly know in their hearts that I love them and want to be in their lives, but between the system, and their mother relying on her feelings toward me, I am blocked at every avenue.

I am beginning to think that this book is more of a suicide letter to my children than anything else. I just cannot take this bull crap anymore. When I'm done writing this, I'll probably just take my life, quietly, so I don't have to put up with it any longer, with instructions for my brother, Justin, to find my kids when they are of age, and give them each a hard copy of this book/suicide letter. Then they can read it, look up in the county record all the things I have filed, and how Ms. Jones goes for one restraining order after another once they end.

I pray, LORD, that You close Sabrina's womb, to never bear children again. I pray You destroy all her romantic relationships. I pray Doug's son, Seth, is never called up to the majors. I pray You show Doug that what he did was devious and wrong. I pray You, O LORD, give me the strength not to kill myself until I am finished writing this.

-1 Peter 1:3-
Blessed be the God and Father of our LORD Jesus Christ, who
according to His abundant mercy has begotten us again to a living hope through the resurrection of Jesus Christ from the dead.
(NKJV)

So the four of us were accepted into the program that morning at The Las Vegas Rescue Mission. We completed our intake paperwork, were given a small tour of the property, then shown to our rooms so we could unpack what little we had. We were in four-man rooms, but I was happy to be somewhere safe. I had a bed, three meals a day, clothing, and a daily shower.

The program was simple: we had to go to a few Bible studies a week and some other recovery classes. We had three one-hour classes a day. We were also assigned a job on property. If our job was during the day, then our classes were at night. If our job was in the evening then our classes were in the day. We had to meet with a counselor once a week and go to Chapel every night, seven days a week. My job was working in the kitchen for breakfast.

In my spare time, I tried to read my Bible. I can truly say that I wanted a life change. I wanted this God I heard about to change my life. My counselor, Bill Smith, gave me a Bible in one of our first meetings and told me, "Everything you'll ever need to know is in this book."

So, I got into it and started reading. It soon became more than just reading. I could feel God speaking to me. I didn't do anything but work my assigned job, go to my classes, and read my Bible. It was during my time with The LORD that He spoke Luke 9:62 into my heart:

-Luke 9:62-
But Jesus said to him, "No one, having put his hand to the plow and looking back, is fit for the kingdom of God."
(NKJV)

I love that verse! That was the first verse I ever memorized. It's true. Why put my hand to the LORD and follow His ways if I'm only going to look back, right? That's what it said to me. It was as if a light came out of heaven and lit up my world. I just knew that God was Truth. Everything I read was coming from Him. I knew that what He had for my life was better than anything I could ever imagine. Slowly, things started to click. I was cruising through the program. I was thirty days in and felt great. I felt invincible, like I could take on the world. I was praying all the time and could see God working in every direction. I wasn't just going to my classes and Chapel service, I was enthralled with what I was learning. I wanted more.

After thirty days in the program, you could sign up for a spot job off property where you could make a few bucks. You had to give the Mission ten percent and put some in your personal Rescue Mission savings, but you were able to keep a few bucks, so I signed up and waited my turn. Two weeks later, I received a spot job and was told to be ready outside the Chapel doors at six the following morning.

My job was to offload a container truck at a warehouse. I worked hard all day, and the owner was impressed with my work ethic. When I finished the container, he paid me and asked if I wanted to make a few more bucks putting together some equipment for him. I accepted, of course, and worked until early evening. When I was all done, he gave me a ride downtown and paid me $300.

I still had a couple hours before I had to be back at the Mission, so I went for a walk. I was praising God for His greatness..., then decided to get high. It happened that quickly. I called the dope man, bought three hundred dollars of crack-cocaine, walked back to the Mission, went to my room, loaded my pipe, got high, and was kicked out of the program just as I ran out of dope. I was now on the street again, homeless and hungry. I chose to forget everything I learned, everything God was doing, everything I wanted. I wanted drugs.

I am sitting here in the kitchen of the Palms House, writing. No job, no way to pay rent, not sure of what the future holds. I think about Rhesa and Asher every day and just want to die. Literally, I want to die. I keep hearing God telling me to write. Why? Nothing will come of it. God won't bless me when I am sober, job hunting, and trying to do the right things, so why try? What's the point? Kill me, please. For the love of God, just end my life!

I went to Catholic Charities the next morning and got into their program. I was surprised at how simple it was to get in. I waited in line for about an hour, and by lunchtime was already in my bed and reading my little Bible.

At Catholic Charities, you automatically get food stamps for six months and you had to work a job on property. On your day off, if you wanted to make some money, you had to get in line at two in the morning to wait. I was there about two weeks before I started to feel the itch to get high again, so I got up to wait in line to see if I could get a job for the day. I scored a job working for this guy who needed someone four to five days a week to remodel his guest house. He was willing to pay $100 a day plus buy lunch. That was all I needed. There was no need for me to go back to Catholic Charities. I worked all day and was able to live in the house I was remodeling and get high. This went on for about six months or so until the work was finished, at which point I roamed the streets again, living in the Woodlawn Cemetery. Sometimes I wrestled with my demons while trying to do the right things. Sometimes I just snuggled with my demons, loving them while they continued to destroy my life.

All I did was think about what could have been... I thought about Sebastian. The days blended together. Everything was a blur. Life was non-existent.

"There's never enough time to do all the nothing you want."
(Bill Watterson)

It was around this time that I started to see snakes all around me every time I got high. The second I took a hit, I saw rattlesnakes trying to bite me. I was starting to lose it, but it never stopped me. I was back to sleeping on my dirt pile in the cemetery and didn't care.

I got hooked up with this guy, Jonathan, who ran a small moving company. I had gotten cleaned up enough and looked somewhat presentable to work. I was his best worker, so he started giving me more and more moving jobs. He knew I lived in a cemetery, but I was at work every day, on time, and worked hard.

One day he asked me if I had a driver's license, because he needed someone to drive a U-Haul truck for one of his customers to Memphis, Tennessee. I told him I did, when I didn't, and he told me he would pay me $500 to drive the truck to Memphis then get me a Greyhound bus ticket back to Vegas. With no driver's license, I drove the moving truck cross-country. I made it in a few days, and the people were at the storage place to meet me on time. I helped them get all their things into storage, and they drove me to the bus station. When we got to the bus station, the wife turned to me and said, "Do I write the check out to you or Jonathan?"

"You write it out to me," I said.

She wrote out a check in my name, and I got out of the car. I looked at the check and it was for $1,000. I called Jonathan and told him that I was at the bus station, and he told me that my ticket was waiting for me.

"Did they give you a check for me?" he asked.

"Yeah, it's for $1,000," I responded.

"Okay, good. Just call me when you get back into Vegas, and I'll come get you."

"Okay."

When the bus got into Vegas, I walked directly to the bank, cashed the check, never called Jonathan, got a room for three days at the Downtowner, and bought $700 in crack cocaine. I stayed in the room the entire three days, got high, and saw snakes everywhere. I even started hearing the television talk to me. I couldn't get comfortable. Every station I turned to was talking to me through it. I heard Jonathan through the walls telling me he was going to kill me. Snakes were trying to bite. All I wanted was to get high and find some porn to watch. I wasn't losing it anymore, I was now mentally gone. Something broke.

When the three days were up, I struggled to leave and waited until exactly check out time to go. I was paranoid and high. I still had a few rocks left, but I could smoke them in the cemetery. As I was walking, I ran into someone I knew.

"Dude, Jonathan is looking for you. He was at the cemetery a few times with some people and a baseball bat. He said that you ripped him off. If I were you, I wouldn't go there."

Damn! Man was I in some serious trouble. I went further down Freemont Street and looked for another, cheaper hotel. I had about $80 left and a few rocks. I found a piece-of-crap motel for $20 a night down Freemont. I paid for three days and got a twelve pack of Budweiser. I was so paranoid.

So there I was, in a seedy motel room getting high on my last few rocks, paranoid, hearing voices, and trying to masturbate. The voices in my head were telling me that they wanted to kill me. I kept seeing rattlesnakes trying to bite me. I kept hearing Jonathan through the walls telling me he was going to beat me with his bat. The women on the porn station were telling me to keep getting high and that they couldn't wait to have sex with me.

I finished my rocks and tried drinking away the snakes and voices. I was sweating bullets and couldn't get comfortable. I shut the television off and drank my warm beer until I passed out. The next thing I heard was someone knocking on my door. I looked through the peephole and saw it was housekeeping telling me it was time to go. I didn't even have time to shower, so I grabbed my things and left. I smelled to high heaven and was so scared of running into Jonathan. It was time I got out of that part of Vegas for a while.

For the next couple of months I roamed Las Vegas, sleeping in dumpsters again, trying to stay out of sight. I didn't even work, because I was scared Jonathan would find me. I ate whenever I could find food and got kicked out of many business stairwells. It was tough. After a couple of months of this I wondered if it was safe enough to go back to the cemetery. I headed that way and tried to keep a low profile. I was on my dirt pile, worked day labor, and it seemed the heat was off me. Some of the people I knew said that Jonathan had been looking for me for a while, but had not been around in a couple weeks. I really tried my best not to be seen too much. I worked, got my crack, and kept to myself when a few disturbing things happened.

I was walking down the boulevard early one morning to go to the Chevron station to get something to eat and walked up on a dead body. I kid you not. It was right across the street from Jerry's Nugget, in front of a pawn shop. I walked into Jerry's Nugget, found a security officer, and told him. He looked at me like I had two heads.

"Well, call the damn cops then." he said.

"I don't have a phone, and I'm hungry. I'm going to the Chevron on Lake Mead and Las Vegas Boulevard." And I just walked out.

I went to the Chevron, got something to eat, and started walking back to the cemetery. The security guard was by the dead body with the cops pointing at me. The cops pulled me aside to question me. They couldn't believe I found a dead body and walked away.

"I told a security guard. I didn't just not say anything," I said.

I told them I lived in the cemetery, and they took my info and let me go.

One night while I was walking around the cemetery getting high, trying to dodge the snakes that weren't there, a car drove up and parked not far from where I was standing. No one drives in the cemetery in the middle of the night. Then two guys got out with baseball bats. One of the men was Jonathan. Damn! I flat out ran with everything I had in me.

I stayed away again for a while. When I came back again, I found that the homeless friends I had were having sex with each other when they got high. They even propositioned me to join them, telling me that they weren't gay, it was only something they did when they were getting high. Not a chance! This was freaking nuts! This was too much for me. I needed God. I had read that little New Testament from time to time. I didn't want this life no more. Things had finally gotten way too weird and out of control for me. I was scared out of my mind. This time, though, I wasn't running to get away from the trouble I was in. The difference was that I was literally running to God, because that was the only place I knew to be safe. All I wanted was Jesus.

I found a dumpster to hide in for the night, and in the morning walked back to The Las Vegas Rescue Mission and sat at the side gate.

The program manager, Bob Kirkwood, came to the side gate and told me that I couldn't line up till after one. I broke down and started crying. When I looked up, he remembered who I was. He asked me what was going on and I said, "I'm done! I'm really done, Bob! I can't do this anymore! I just need God back in my life!"

He came out and sat with me for a while as I cried. He asked me what was going on, and I didn't lie. I told him the truth about everything. He squeezed my shoulder and said, "Well, it looks like you're running to God and not away from Him this time. Just stay right here. I'll take you into the program when we open the gates, okay?"

"Okay," I said.

"Just hang in there for right now. You're in the right place."

I sat there for hours waiting, and right at three, Bob came over and let me in to the program.

"Thank you so much, Bob! Thank you very much!"

"Don't thank me, thank God. Welcome back."

"As you grow older, you'll find the only things you regret are the things you didn't do."
(Zachary Scott)

The other day I was thinking about people who have followed their dreams: people who really took a chance on themselves to pursue a dream that only they believed in. I wondered how they did it and how much they struggled to attain their dream. Not everyone on this list followed a Christian dream, but they all did something that people thought would never happen, something that at least one person said they were crazy and wouldn't happen.

Sylvester Stallone: He wrote Rocky, but had to sell his dog so he could eat. Once he tried selling his script; he was offered $350,000 but said no because he wanted to star in it as well.

Erin Brockovich: She fought a huge company for dumping chemicals that caused people cancer.

Vince Papale: A thirty year old rookie in the NFL for the Eagles who tried out as a walk on.

Jim Morris: A thirty-five-year-old relief pitcher who threw in his first big league game for the Tampa Bay Devil Rays at almost forty.

Eminem: Grew up in the ghetto and left that life to go to California to make it in the music industry.

Billy Bean: The general manager for the Oakland A's who built a winning team with no payroll.

Tobias Wolff: Lived a rough life with his mother and abusive step-dad. He grew up and wrote a book about his life.

Beverly Donofrio: She got caught up in drugs and married a heroin addict. She turned her life around, raised her son on her own, and then wrote a book about her life and struggles.

Micky Ward: A boxer who came back to win a world title after crushing his hand.

Coach Harold Jones: The coach who stood up for a kid, James Robert Kennedy, who had mental problems and stopped him from getting bullied. He taught people that we all should be treated with the same respect. They made a movie called *Radio* about it.

Ronnie Milsap: A blind piano player whose mother did not want him, then grandmother did not want him, because he was blind. He grew up in a state run school for the blind, was told he would

448

become a "failure" and a "liability" to the state if he pursued music as a career. He went on to have forty number one hits and seven Grammy Awards.

United States Master Chief Petty Officer Carl Brashear: He became a Master Diver for the Navy, with only one leg, after being told he had to retire due to the injury he sustained.

What I thought about was this: why can't Steve Gray be on this list as well?

<u>Chapter Eighteen</u>

-Psalm 63:1-
O God, You are my God; early will I seek You;
My soul thirsts for You; My flesh longs for You
in a dry and thirsty land where there is no water.
<u>*(NKJV)*</u>

So here I was, back at The Las Vegas Rescue Mission again. I was seeking God as I never sought Him before. I was broken in every way and willing to do whatever it took to get Him back into my life.

Bob brought me into the program, but I had to sleep in the homeless dorm until a spot opened in the residents building. I didn't care though. All the satisfaction I needed was to know that The Lord was holding me, and He was!

Soon enough a bed opened in the men's dorm, and I was able to officially start the program. Many things had changed. It had become a year-long program, and the classes were more intense. I liked it. I was going to all my classes, Chapel services, and even going to extra classes when I had free time. I just couldn't get enough Jesus.

"Being a Christian isn't for sissies. It takes a real man to live for God – a lot more man than to live for the devil."
<u>*(Johnny Cash)*</u>

My time in the program did not come without troubles, but I believed in my heart that God was in control of everything. That's one of the things I loved about Pastor Jeff the most. He always tried his best to instill in us that God is always in control, all the time!

Things aren't fair? God is in control!

Oh, there's an injustice happening? God is in control!

This isn't right? God is in control!

Can't you see what happened here? God is in control!

Can't you see that's wrong? GOD IS IN CONTROL!

That was Pastor Jeff's motto: that no matter what, God is ALWAYS in control! That's such a hard thing to understand as a new believer in Christ. We want to justify and take matters into our own hands, thinking were doing the Lord's work, when all we are doing is making matters worse when we try to control a situation.

Through my ups and downs in the program, I stayed focused on the Lord. I prayed constantly throughout the day. My knees hit the floor every morning as well as every night before bed. I did all my homework and was constantly reading my Bible. I welcomed new people into the program, staying away from those who were not acting as though they wanted Christ. Some of the residents called me a holy roller, brown nose, and a fake. In reality, I just wanted Christ. I wanted nothing to do with anyone who did not want Him at the center of their lives. One day I was walking to the kitchen when one of the residents said, "Bro, every second of every day doesn't have to be about God."

"Yes, it does." I said, and kept walking.

This church, Valley Bible Fellowship, would come to the Mission every Sunday. They would serve both the homeless and residents meals. They would play Christian music, have a small service, and have several people available to pray with us. I thought it was great. Each Sunday afternoon, this same lady continued to invite me to their church. It started to bother me because I felt she was singling me out, so I stayed in my room on Sundays when they came. Little did I know, though, this time spent in my room was from God. I had been so busy doing everything I could. Whenever there was a chance to help, I would. I was burnt out and didn't realize it, so on Sundays, I stayed in my room, laid down on my bed, and just listened to it all. I was upstairs and my window faced the veranda. For four or five hours every Sunday, I opened my window and listened to everything. I loved it! I needed to check out this church. I chose Valley Bible as my home church.

"Good works do not make a good man, but a good man does good works."
(Martin Luther)

That is what Valley Bible Fellowship was all about at first. This is the reason I originally fell in love with that church.

The time had come to start looking for a job. I was both scared and happy. I had been in the program for over a year and was set to graduate soon. I needed a job now. I looked forward to it but wasn't sure how to go about it. I didn't want just a run-of-the-mill job. I wanted a good job. There was still something I had to make right, though, my son, Sebastian!

Sebastian was always on my mind. Every day I thought about him. Every day I prayed for him and for God's direction on how to go about my relationship with him. I wanted Sebastian back in my life. Child Support: I hadn't paid child support to Eva in years.

One day I was called to the Chapel office. Lisa Marks, the Vice President of Human Resources for a local oil company called Haycock Petroleum, had contacted the Rescue Mission because she felt like God was leading her there to hire someone. The staff chose me, and an interview was set up for the following day. The Terminal Manager of Haycock Petroleum, Kevin, came to interview me. He told me that he had had his own struggles with alcohol in the past. I responded with complete honesty to all his questions. Long story short, he hired me and brought me to the oil plant I would be working at to show me around. I filled out the paperwork and was sent for a drug test. What a great feeling to not worry about a drug test. Within a few days, Kevin called me called me to give me my start date.

I loved this job. I loaded oil and fuel into transport trucks by the thousands of gallons. I worked with the pumps, tanks, drums, and rigs. It was a dirty job and extremely tiring, but also very rewarding. I did this job as if it was God's oil and fuel. I was working for Him.

With my very first paycheck, I bought two cell phones: one each for Sebastian and myself. I wrote Eva a letter and told her that I wanted Sebastian back in my life. I told her a little of what I had been through, and a lot of what was happening in my life now. On a separate sheet of paper, I wrote out all the child support I owed her, and told her that I was going to pay all of it. I said that once I paid off my child support, if I had not heard from her, then I would contact the courts and go that route. I didn't have an address for her, so I was sending all the mail to her brother's address. I was only making $10 an hour, but I was determined to do the right thing. I was due to be leaving the Rescue Mission, but they let me stay so that I could pay off my child support and regain a relationship with my son. Every single payday, I cashed my check, tithed my ten percent to my church, and sent Eva $750. I didn't have much money left, just enough to get my cigarettes and maybe a soda or something. I knew that I needed to honor God by tithing, and I was going to pay my child support off. No matter how tough things seemed to get during this period, I always just looked up towards the sky and said, "Thank You, Jesus."

My plan was to get caught up on my child support and move out of the Mission. A few months after I started paying off my child support, I went to the Chapel office because my name was on the mail list. I told the desk that I was there to get my mail and was handed a purple envelope addressed to me, with Eva's name as the sender. Wow! I was scared to open it, but when I did, it was a blank card with three pictures of Sebastian. That was it; nothing else. It was a start. I put my head down, cried, and prayed to God, thanking Him for His righteousness. I was overwhelmed with the presence of the Lord in my life at that moment, and I could not stop crying. I took the pictures to my room and hung them. I wanted to drop everything I was doing and get a flight ticket to go see Sebastian. God told me to be still and continue doing what I was doing. I listened.

The first week of October, my phone rang on a Saturday while I was helping in the kitchen. I grabbed my phone and saw the call was coming from the phone number of the phone that I sent Sebastian. I froze! I was scared and didn't know what to do. I walked out of the kitchen as fast as I could, said a quick prayer, and answered the phone.

"Hello?" I said.

"Yeah, hi. Is Steve there?" It was a man's voice.

"This is Steve."

"Hey Steve, I'm Rob, I'm Eva's boyfriend. We've been together for a couple years. Eva doesn't want to talk to you yet, but she's right here. She's been getting all the money you've been sending and wanted to say thank you."

"Okay."

"We started showing Sebastian your pictures. He's a really good kid. We've been talking to him about you, and he knows who you are."

"Okay."

"What are you plans with him?"

I went on to tell Rob exactly what I told Eva in the first letter I sent her: that I planned to pay off all my back child support then go to court to get my rights back.

"I don't say that to sound cocky, Rob. I thank you so much for being there when I wasn't. People change. I've grown up a lot. Sebastian is my son. I gave him his name. I've made a lot of mistakes in the past. You were there when I wasn't, and I thank you for that, but I'm his father, not you, and I'm going to do whatever I have to do to get him back in my life, even if that means I have to go to court. I don't blame Eva for anything. I just want my son back. I won't stop fighting for him until a judge tells me I can't."

He was silent, and I refused to speak until he responded.

"Sebastian is right here. He wants to talk to you. Do you want to talk to him?" he asked me.

"Yes, I do," I said.

"Here he is."

There was a very long pause where nothing was said.

"Daddy?" Sebastian said, and I lost it! I started crying like I never had before.

-Malachi 3:10-
"Bring all the tithes into the storehouse, that there may be food in
My house, and try Me now in this," says the LORD of hosts,
"If I

will not open for you the windows of heaven and pour out for you such
a blessing that there will not be room enough to receive it.
(NKJV)

"Hi Sebastian! I love you so much! I miss you!" I choked through the tears.

"I love you too."

"I'd rather die in the will of God, than to live outside of it."
(Jack Hyles)

Our conversation was mostly superficial in the sense that it was just how things were going for him right then, but it was the topping on the cake. Not only did I get to talk to my son again, but he called me, "Daddy." I was overwhelmed. After a few minutes, we said goodbye, and Rob got back on the phone.

"Thanks, Rob. I really appreciate that." I was so happy right then. "Did Sebastian open the gifts I sent him?"

"Not yet. He got them, but he didn't open them yet. Eva and I were thinking he could open them with you if you want to come out and see him."

"YES! That would be awesome!"

He went on to tell me that Eva wanted it supervised right now, because she didn't feel comfortable with me having him alone yet. I didn't have an issue with that and told him I would get with my job and see when I could get some time off. We ended the call, and I went straight to my room, got flat on my face, and cried out to God, praising Him for my life, for His blessing me so much, and for His second, third, fourth, and fifth chances.

The week leading up to my trip was the longest week of my life. I could not wait to see Sebastian again. I missed him. I loved him. The day came soon enough, and I was all packed and ready to go to the airport on a Friday morning. I couldn't even sleep that night, because I was so excited.

I got to Boston, checked into my hotel, and made my way to Fanual Hall in Downtown Boston, where I was meeting Sebastian. I got there early, found a bench to sit on, and waited. Then I saw Sebastian carrying the box of gifts I sent him, walking towards me. I got up off the bench, walked over to him, picked him up, and held onto him for a long time. I tried not to cry that much and just told him that I loved him.

"Can I open my presents now?" was the very first thing he asked me.

"Yeah, you sure can, buddy."

We sat down, and he opened everything up. I said hello to Eva and shook Rob's hand. For three days in a row, Friday, Saturday, and Sunday, they met me early each morning and let me just do my thing with Sebastian. We usually separated around six or seven at night. I did everything I could think of with him. I took him to the aquarium, went to eat, took the duck tour. I mean, you name it, we did it. We had so much fun together. He called me "Daddy," and I called him my son. The only thing that bothered me about the trip was that every time I hugged Sebastian, Rob hugged him right after. Every time I kissed Sebastian, Rob kissed him. If I padded Sebastian on the back, so would Rob, and every time I told Sebastian I loved him, Rob would tell him he loved him as well. I was getting pissed off and looked at Eva a few times.

Sunday came, and it was time for me to go home. We said our goodbyes, and Eva said I could call Sebastian every week if I wanted to. On Monday, I went and saw my Dad to say hello and told him about my weekend. He was happy for me and drove me to the airport.

"I'm proud of you, Steven," my dad told me as we drove to Logan Airport.

On the flight back to Las Vegas, I had a quiet peace about me. I was content. I looked forward to the next time I would see my son.

When I got back to Las Vegas, I made plans to move out of the Rescue Mission. I had been there a long time. It was time to leave. Pastor Jeff gave me his blessing and said he was proud of me. When I was leaving the Mission that day, I made one of the biggest mistakes of my life, a mistake I believe that I am still paying for now. I was so amped up on Jesus that I didn't think the enemy could hurt me at all. As I was leaving the Mission as a resident that day, I said, "I can take whatever you got, satan. Whatever you think you can throw my way, go right ahead, because you're not strong enough to destroy my life. I DARE YOU TO COME AFTER ME!"

What a very stupid, high, drunk thing to freaking say. But I believed it. I was rocking out so hard for Jesus that I felt untouchable, and in the process, invited the devil into my life with open arms.

I sometimes wonder why I go into such detail as I write. Sometimes I write for you, to give you hope. Sometimes I write for me, for my pain. Then sometimes I just write to get things off my chest. Truth be told, I almost forget what I'm fighting for anymore. My kids? God? Myself? I don't even know what keeps me going right now.

"A book is the only place in which you can examine a fragile thought without breaking it, or explore an explosive idea without fear it will go off in your face. It is one of the few havens remaining where a man's mind can get both provocation and privacy."
(Edward P. Morgan)

I want to kill myself right now. I just really want to die. I am almost to the point of seriously giving up. Why continue to fight?

"The mind of a writer can be a truly terrifying thing. Isolated, neurotic, caffeine-addled, crippled by procrastination, consumed by feelings of panic, self-loathing, and soul-crushing inadequacy. And that's on a good day."

(Robert DeNiro)

I wonder why it's taken me more than ten years to complete this book. At times, it can just be so damn painful. I think I'm almost done though, so I have that to look forward to. I'm still not sure if I am going to kill myself of not when I'm done. I just don't have any hope right now. What happens when it's all done? I don't know the answer to that question yet, but right now, I'm hurting. I never knew that not drinking, not doing drugs, could hurt this much...

I moved into Kathie's Faith House. It was nice for the time being. I knew that I wouldn't stay here forever, and in fact, was already trying to see what was out there, but this was where God wanted me at the moment.

Kathie rented out five rooms and was almost always full. The only requirement she had was that we all had to attend a church service once a week. I really loved Kathie. She was a mother to us all and kicked us in the butt when we needed it. Yes, it's fair to say that she was a great lady. She even held a Bible study at her house on Wednesday nights.

I would attend a couple of classes a week at the Rescue Mission, because Pastor Jeff is an unbelievable teacher. God told me I needed to learn from him. I went to church at Valley Bible Fellowship, as well as attending the Sunday night service at the Rescue Mission. With my child support paid off, I was now saving to get my own apartment.

Things were going well, really well, I might add. I worked hard and was promoted to day shift, as well as given a nice raise. I flew to Boston every three months to see Sebastian for long weekends. Eva had only supervised the first couple of visits and then let me have my son whenever I came out. I had to give Eva a lot of credit for that. She had broken up with her boyfriend. I guess Rob had told her he didn't want me in Sebastian's life, because Sebastian didn't look at Rob as his father anymore. Eva told me that Rob had said, "He's taking Sebastian away from me."

"He's not your son Rob. Steve is Sebastian's real father." She told him.

I think Eva enjoyed the fact that I was being a real father for once. I was enjoying being a father to Sebastian as well. Like I said, things were looking up.

The following summer, Eva let me have Sebastian in Las Vegas for a week. I took him all over and did so much with him. I even took him to meet my boss, Lisa Marks, since she knew my struggles. I took him to church with me at VBF and to the Sunday night service at the Mission. Following that service, I went up to pray with Pastor Jeff over the restoration of my relationship with Sebastian. Later on, I found out that the Rescue Mission staff took a picture of Pastor Jeff praying over Sebastian and me, then used that picture on the front of the Las Vegas Rescue Mission leaflet.

My week with Sebastian was finally at an end. I met up with Eva and took them both to the airport. I said goodbye to Sebastian and headed home. On my way home, I got a text from a number I didn't know. I flipped open my phone to see:

-Luke 22:31-
And the LORD said, "Simon, Simon! Indeed, Satan has asked for you, that he may sift you wheat;"
(NKJV)

I had a very uneasy feeling as I read that text. I contemplated trying to call the number back, but decided not to. I thought about that text all the way home. When I got to my room, I prayed hard and opened my Bible. I was bothered. I laid down and tried to think about God but eventually fell asleep. I woke up the next morning thinking about the text from the previous night and prayed. I got into the Word and started to feel better.

I was volunteering at the Rescue Mission one Sunday and met this couple, Mike and Lynn Tomlan, who held a Bible study at their house on Saturday nights. I asked if I could attend, and they said I could. Mike and Lynn are a picture-perfect couple. Lynn is a very beautiful older woman, and Mike is a man's man. Together, they serve the Lord. FYI, Lynn Tomlan is the best cook EVER! It was at this Bible study that I became friends with Sabrina.

I first met Sabrina at a Jeremy Camp concert with a group from our church, then got to know her a little bit while serving at the Rescue Mission. I was mesmerized by Sabrina. There was something about her that I couldn't take my eyes off of. She was a beautiful woman who loved God more than anything in the world. She reminded me of a younger black version of Lynn, except Sabrina couldn't cook at all.

I come from a racist background, but I didn't see color in her. Sabrina was the good girl, and I had a troubled history. I wanted to show her that God had changed my life. Sabrina was an angel in my eyes. I wanted to show her that I could treat her the way God wanted her to be treated. She was smoking hot and loved Jesus. Of all the great qualities that Sabrina had, when I looked at her, there was a quiet sadness about her. I couldn't read her all that well, and reading people is something I have always been good at. Still though, the sadness I saw in her intrigued me.

"I think the saddest people always try their hardest to make people happy because they know what it's like to feel absolutely worthless and they don't want anyone else to feel like that."
(Robin Williams)

I soon became stagnant, and I couldn't understand why. I was doing everything I was doing before, but just felt empty inside. I figured I was just missing Sebastian. On my next trip to Boston, I was on the way to the airport when I got a text from that same number with the same verse.

-Luke 22:31-

And The LORD said, "Simon, Simon! Indeed, Satan has asked for you, that he may sift you wheat;"
(NKJV)

Now I was upset. I did not want it to ruin my trip, so I made a mental note to call the number when I got back home.

Like always, I had a great time with Sebastian. Eva even let me stay at her house on the couch. When the weekend was over, Eva was driving me to the airport when I realized that I forgot a bag of t-shirts I bought. I was in the back seat with Sebastian when I told Eva about the bag I left on her kitchen table. She was quiet and didn't say anything, so I told her again that I forgot the bag. She still didn't say anything but made a hard U-turn in the middle of traffic and drove like a maniac back to her house. She went in, grabbed my bag, threw it at me, and drove off like a bat out of hell. Then she just started yelling at me at the top of her lungs. I didn't say or do anything for a while as she laid into me, hard! I couldn't believe it. I didn't know what it was that I did. She continued to yell at me for at least ten minutes straight before I yelled back at her, "Don't treat me like a freaking child!"

She shut her mouth and didn't say another word all the way into Boston. At the airport, we said goodbye, and I told Sebastian I would call him the next weekend.

"I love you, Sebastian."

"I love you too, Daddy," he said.

I got on my plane and headed back to Vegas. When I got off the plane, I turned my phone on and a text popped up.

-Luke 22:31-
And The LORD said, "Simon, Simon! Indeed, Satan
has asked for you, that he may sift you wheat;"
<u>(NKJV)</u>

I wanted to call the number but was stressed over what happened with Eva, so I put it out of my mind for the time being. For the next two weeks, I called Sebastian repeatedly, with no luck. I was mad at first and then became worried that something was wrong. Then my phone rang and it was Eva's number. Thank God!

"Hello?" I said.

"Steve, this is Eva. I didn't like the way you yelled at me when you were here. I'm changing my number, and I don't want you in Sebastian's life right now."

"WHAT?! You can't do that!"

"Maybe in a year or so you can see him, but not right now. Goodbye." And with that, she hung up.

I called her right back, but it rang until her voicemail came on. I continued to call her back, each time getting her voicemail. By the fourth or fifth time, a message came on that said her number had been changed. I could not believe what had just happened. She was yelling at me, and all I did was react by yelling back. I was at a loss for words. I knew I didn't do anything wrong. I knew she didn't have a right to do what she just did.

I had a little saved, so the following morning I looked for probate lawyers in the Boston area and found one in Salem. Her name was Linda Holland. I explained the situation to Linda, telling her everything that happened leading up to me getting back into Sebastian's life. I sent her her required retainer, then I had to sit and wait for Eva to be served and a court date to be set. Talk about a long wait. I sent Linda all the copies I had from all the classes I took in rehab, plus letters of recommendation from Pastor Jeff and my boss at Haycock Petroleum. I tried my hardest and continued to praise God through it all. I never stopped going to Bible studies, church, or serving at the Rescue Mission. I really did stay strong. I got deeper into His Word because of the emptiness I was feeling. I couldn't understand why she was doing this. I was going through a hard time, and it felt like God was pulling away from me.

I finally heard back from Linda: a court date was set. I couldn't wait to get to Salem to fight for my son. I got the necessary time off from work, flew to Boston for my court date, and my Dad came with me. I met up with my lawyer, and we all went into the courthouse and waited for our turn. Eva was there with her father with a smug look on her face. I felt good though. I had God in my life, Jesus was my Lord and Savior, and I wasn't behind on child support. I was dumping thousands on a lawyer. I was in a new suit and held a respectable job. I was ready.

Finally, my name was called. Some guy led me, my dad, and my lawyer into a small room. I was wondering why Eva was not in here as well.

"Steven Frederick Gray II?" some guy behind me said.

I turned to see two detectives standing there.

"Yeah, I'm Steve Gray."

"Mr. Gray, you're under arrest. You have four outstanding warrants from 1996: two misdemeanors and two felonies. Put your hands behind your back, please."

Man, I could not believe this crap. The warrants were more than ten years old and I had no clue that they existed. This sucked. I was going to lose my job, my apartment, everything I had fought so hard for. I was led out of the room in handcuffs and there was Eva, smiling. I didn't get mad. I just put my head down and went to jail. Once in my jail cell, I prayed the following prayer:

"LORD, thank You for what You have done for me. If You want me to lose my job, then that's okay. If You want me to lose my apartment, I praise you. I'm not mad at You, LORD. I need to clean up my past, and if You want me here in jail, then thank You. In Jesus' name I pray. Amen."

Right then, I heard my name called.

"Steven Gray. Get up and let's go. You have to see the judge."

I was taken to court in my new suite and handcuffs.

"Mr. Gray?" The Judge said.

Just then, my lawyer came running into the courtroom with my dad. She explained to the judge what was going on, that the warrants were eleven years old, and I was involved in a visitation dispute in probate court. To my surprise, the judge released me into the custody of my lawyer, pending I promise to go make new court dates in all four counties I had warrants in. Wow! My dad, my lawyer, and I drove all over Massachusetts that day clearing up all my warrants and making new court dates. I cleared everything up except one warrant, because I had to make my flight back to Vegas. I had to go to work the next day, but I flew back to Boston the following month to clear that warrant also.

For the next six months, I flew back and forth to Boston so I could make all my court dates. I used all my vacation time, and the bills just kept coming in. Lawyers' fees and all the fines were killing me. I had no savings left. I was living week to week, but I was making headway and doing the right thing. Money had gotten so tight that I didn't have any money to buy food.

Sabrina and I had been spending a lot of time together, and one day she came over to my house with a carload full of groceries. I'm pretty sure it was that very moment I fell in love with Sabrina Renee Jones. A week later, though, she told me she spent money that she didn't have and needed some gas money. I didn't have the money for gas to give her, so I told her I couldn't. Now I was upset that she bought me the food and then said she shouldn't have. This is why I hate good deeds from people. I knew she did it out of love, but it made me mad when she turned around and said she spent money she didn't have. It made me feel like garbage. Then she said that she had been wasting her gas coming to see me, and because of that, I should give her some gas money. Now I was pissed. I took her to the gas station and filled her tank with my rent money. I knew she needed the gas. It was just the way she came at me about it that was all wrong. Between that and the food, I just really felt like an idiot. When she left, I threw away all the food she bought me. I would rather be hungry than someone say they bought me food because I was broke and hungry. I didn't need someone to do something "out of the goodness of their heart" only to turn around and say they shouldn't have, then expect something back from me in return, something I couldn't afford to give due to my legal fees. I was broke and fighting for Sebastian. No, I would either be able to feed myself or go hungry. I've been hungry before. It sucks, but sometimes that's just the way life works. I don't feel you can truly be satisfied with a full stomach from a great meal until you've been so hungry that your stomach hurts because of the lack thereof.

"The problem is not the problem; the problem is your attitude about the problem."
(Capitan Jack Sparrow)

As I sit here in this sober house, the manager, Jack, is smoking weed in his room. Real nice! We all smell it, and most of us are upset by it. What makes me even more mad is that some of the same people who are here would get pissed at someone else for using, but they kiss Jack's butt, even though he's getting high in his room, because he's the manager! This is so wrong. I have no respect for Jack now. He stays in his room, gets high, and tries to push his weight around. I have to praise God though. I just want to give up. I hate my life, and I hate my situation. I keep thinking, "Why can't I just get high and have things go well?"

Well, soon enough I had all my warrants taken care of, got my legal life in order, and took Eva to court, again. This time I got what I wanted. The family court judge in Salem did not listen to any of Eva's garbage. God knew, and that was all I needed. Eva was mad, and looking at her and her dad gave me some satisfaction. I got unlimited visitation with Sebastian for as long as I wanted as long as I gave Eva two weeks' notice. I didn't even have to ask Eva if I could see Sebastian, I only had to tell her I was coming. My lawyer even called me to tell me that Eva requested that she not be present at the final hearing. When all was said and done, I had my rights back. I was in a big hole financially, but I felt as if I accomplished something huge.

I was still feeling this separation from God though, and I couldn't understand it. It was more than just not feeling God in my life. It felt as if I could feel Him pulling away. It scared me, but I just kept praying and got deeper into His Word. My faith was slipping away, but I couldn't see that.

Sabrina and I made plans to get married. We set a date of July 16, 2008, and it was early January. I truly loved her. I wanted to be the man that she dreamed God would give her.

One Saturday night, after Bible study at Mike and Lynn's house, this guy, Mark Gabriel, offered me a ride home. I lived out on Craig and Las Vegas Blvd., and Mike and Lynn lived on Flamingo and Buffalo. It would take me two to three hours each way on a bus, depending on traffic, so I took Mark up on the ride. We were about to get on the highway when he turned to me and said, "Do you want to smoke a joint?"

What? I couldn't believe he just asked me that. I was silent for a few seconds and really thought about it.

"No, I'm good, Mark. Thanks anyway."

I just wanted to get out of his car right then. We made small talk the rest of the way to my complex until he dropped me off. I said goodbye and started walking to my apartment. I got to my door and just stood there thinking. I turned around, walked to 7-11, and bought a six-pack of Budweiser. It happened that quick. I was clean and sober for about three years at that point.

-Isaiah 59:2-
But your iniquities have separated you
from your God; and your sins have hidden

His face from you, so that He will not hear.
(NKJV)

It was time to meet Sabrina's family now, and I was nervous. We drove to Sabrina's mom and stepdad's house. Both of her sisters, her mom, stepdad, grandmother, and aunt were there, as well as big-Billy-bad-butt. Everyone seemed to be in a good enough mood. I was standing next to Sabrina in the kitchen, not really knowing what to say, when her mother came up to me and said, "You should have asked me to marry my daughter." Then she walked away. Sabrina would later deny this happened, but she knows the truth. So do I. So does God.

Her grandmother and aunt were nice, but they didn't stay long. As soon as they left, Sabrina's mother said that it was time to go into the living room so we could all "talk." Then everyone laid into me, except for her stepdad. He stayed quiet and didn't say much. Her sister Nichole, who, when I was done getting my butt ripped open, came up to me and said, "Welcome to the family."

Her mother, her other sister, Elise, and her husband, Billy, all had nothing but garbage to say to me. This wasn't a conversation about Sabrina and I getting married. I wasn't talked to; I was talked AT! As soon as it started, I tuned it all out. None of the three had anything good to say to me. I just stood there, didn't talk back, and waited for it to be over. Sabrina and I left as soon as they were done. I didn't even say goodbye, I just waved my hand. When we got to the gate and waited for it to open, Sabrina

473

turned to me, grabbed my hand, squeezed it, and said, "You're a real man, Steve."

I really don't think I loved her any more than I did at that moment. She didn't cry, but she had tears in her eyes. I just shook my head, and we drove to my house in silence. She spent the night that evening and I enjoyed holding her in my arms. Another thing I loved about Sabrina was that she wouldn't have sex with me until we got married. She was the one for me, and God showed me exactly that.

I was struggling with my drinking now. A couple times a week I bought a six-pack after work. I still went to church, read my Bible, and prayed, but it was only because I felt I had to, not because I wanted to. I think I was getting mad at God for pulling away from me. I was just going through the motions and started falling out of love with Jesus. I didn't know it was even happening. Sabrina noticed and questioned me. I told her it was just a few beers a night a couple times a week.

"When you think it's a problem, just tell me, and I'll stop," I told her.

The following week, I was buying a six-pack and Sabrina said, "Steve, it's a problem. Please, stop drinking. Please."

I shrugged it off and told her I was fine and that she didn't know what she was talking about. Over the next few months, my drinking became heavy. I was downing a twelve-pack a night, peeing all over my rug and bathroom floor in my apartment. Sabrina would get mad, and we would fight. In fact, we started fighting all the time now, and it wasn't good. I had given her a key to my apartment. I was trying hard to quit smoking and drinking. She dropped me off one night at my house, and I wanted a cigarette bad. So I went on my patio, smoked a cigarette, and went to bed. She came in while I was trying to go to sleep, smelled the smoke, and yelled at me. I blew up, and as the door closed behind her, I said aloud, "I'm going to regret marrying her." And I would...

"There's a difference between remorse and repentance. Remorse is being sorry for being caught. Repentance is being sorry enough to stop."
<u>*(Greg Laurie)*</u>

I knew where I was headed and truly did not want to end up there. The smoking was one thing. I wasn't going to stop smoking now. She would just have to deal with that for a while. But I had to stop drinking. I was more determined than ever to stop. After I cried out, I could truly feel God again. And as I read my Bible, I felt His presence. When I prayed, I could hear God again. He was the only One that could help me. Things got a little better between Sabrina and me. It wasn't great, but it was better.

One of the greatest moments I ever had with Sabrina was this: she was giving me a ride to work one morning when it was really cold out. Her car had no heat, and while I was waiting for her to open the door, I farted. I tried to make it a soft one, but it came out louder than I had expected. I waved it off with my hand and got into the passenger seat. As soon as she drove off, her car smelled from my fart. I felt so ashamed and was so embarrassed, but she never said anything. It was freezing cold out and she just rolled down her window and drove me to work. Once there, she kissed me and told me she loved me, never saying a word about my smelly fart.

After talking and deciding that we wanted to learn more about each other, we bought the books *All About Me* and *All About Us*. We were supposed to fill them out and ask each other questions. It was supposed to be fun. I asked her a question about something she wrote down, but she became offended when I asked her. She told me she didn't want to talk about it and to just leave it alone. She was so adamant about me not asking her that now I felt she was hiding something. She felt I was wrong for asking. I felt she was wrong for not answering. After all, we were supposed to talk about our answers. That's what the damn books were meant for.

I believed it then, and I believe it now: Sabrina and I were never supposed to get divorced. God wanted us to live, and fight through, this situation. You can sit there and say it wasn't supposed to happen, but it did, because of me, or her, or us. What I mean is this: God, in no way gave Sabrina permission or His "blessing" to divorce me. Doug Loman of Valley Bible Fellowship gave

Sabrina the church's blessing to file for divorce over something she told him, which never happened.

———————————

While waiting for our wedding date to arrive, I had entered a county baseball league. Baseball is my favorite sport, and I'm a huge Red Sox fan. To me, I'm the best baseball player there is, but our team was bad, really bad. As a matter of fact, the only game we won was a game when the other team didn't show up. How awesome is that? During that twelve-game season, I pulled my left groin muscle. A couple months later we were about to start a second twelve-game season, and Sabrina did not want me playing. She said that it was too close to the wedding and was genuinely worried about me getting hurt again. I ignored her and signed up anyway. With baseball and our wedding coming up, I had pretty much ceased all other activities. I went to Bible study, but my heart wasn't in it. I wasn't reading my Bible or praying like I should have been. Actually, I wasn't reading my Bible at all. I woke up one morning and saw that same text, from the same number:

-Luke 22:31-
And the LORD said, "Simon, Simon! Indeed, Satan has asked for you, that he may sift you wheat;"
(NKJV)

Now I was irate. I had been through so much crap these last eight months that now I knew someone was messing with me. This was the fourth time in five or six months, and it was messing with my head. I hit call sender; it rang one time and said that the number was not in service. I was freaked out.

Our team was finally ready for our first game of the second season. It would be different this time. This time, our team would win. I was first up and hit a single. The next two batters hit singles as well, which put me at third base. The next batter hit a home run, but the guy covering centerfield made this ridiculous, over-the-fence, one-handed catch that only someone in Major League Baseball could have done. I had already tagged home plate, celebrating the run I scored, when I realized I had to run back to third base before being called out. I was watching where the ball was instead of paying attention to the base, and when I slid into third, I hit the base wrong with my foot. It was only seven weeks until my wedding, and I just broke my foot, ankle, and leg, which required two surgeries to insert screws.

The first surgery was the following week to put the screws in and pull my ankle back out. My doctor gave me two prescriptions for pain medication: one for that surgery and the prescription for the following surgery. I had forty Percocet and forty Lortab. They were gone within three days. I didn't control taking them like I should have, and now I had no meds for after my second surgery. I was in a lot of pain, so I started drinking on and off again.

Two days before my second surgery, I had my bachelor party— not a good night. I don't even remember it. All I know is that we went to a strip club, and I got hammered. Sabrina was not happy and said that we would not be getting married because she said that going to a strip club was technically cheating on her. I said okay but that she had to cancel the wedding. After a few days, she calmed down enough and took me to my second surgery. I told my doctor I didn't have any pain meds left, so he gave me another prescription and said that's all I was getting. Those, like the others, were soon gone. Now I was popping ibuprofen like candy.

The day before my wedding, we had the rehearsal at Sabrina's mother's house. It was hard for me, because I was in so much pain. I literally could not walk. I had to use a cane to get around and was determined not to drink. All of a sudden, things felt better. I realized that I was about to marry the love of my life the next day. I asked God to help me. I just wanted to be a real man for Sabrina. I looked at her that night, and my heart melted for her. Sabrina was worth me giving her my best, and that's what I was going to do. I was going to give her my best! After the rehearsal, I thanked her mother and stepfather, Eugene, kissed Sabrina, and went home. I tried to relax as much as possible, but I had the jitters. I couldn't really sleep all that well. I was on my balcony smoking a cigarette when my phone rang.

"Hello?" I said.

"Hi, Steve. It's Deidre." It was Sabrina's mother.

"Hi, Deidre."

"I wanted to talk to you about something," she said.

"Okay, what's up?"

"You know, you really disrespected Eugene tonight. This is his house, and you never thanked him for letting you have your wedding here." She went on to blast and disrespect me as well as flat out lie. I just sat and listened to it, and when she was almost done, she said, "Sabrina doesn't need to know about this. I don't want to ruin her wedding day."

"Okay." I hung up the phone and stood there pissed off, looking up at the sky.

It was okay to ruin my wedding day though, right? I called Sabrina and told her what her mother had just done. Looking back on it now, I realize I shouldn't have, but I was just so mad. I was mad because I did thank Eugene. I KNOW I did! I even remembered where I was standing when I thanked him. I stood on my balcony for a while and wound up going to bed mad.

The next morning was a little better. I woke up in a good enough mood and called Sabrina to tell her I loved her. I had some running around to do that day before the wedding. All my ushers showed up on time, and we made our way to Sabrina's parents' house. Pastor Jeff showed up but forgot to bring the wedding song. I was worried, but Sabrina picked a song that made her feel happy. I was standing there when she came walking out with her mother. (Her real father had refused to come and give her away!)

To this day, I have never seen anything more beautiful in my life than Sabrina did as she came walking down the grass in the backyard to marry me. I tried to hold it together, but I broke down, the tears rolling down my face. Everything went pretty smooth, except of course, for me not being able to walk. We were finally married.

Her mother tried signing the marriage certificate when she knew that my best man, Bob, was going to sign it. She was making me angry again, and this time, I had to raise my voice a little to make her understand that Bob was signing it. It just really seemed like her mother wanted to make this day as miserable as she could for me. I had not one family member of mine willing to come to my wedding, so I just didn't want to put up with her mother's crap as well.

-1 Corinthians 13:13-
And now abide faith, hope, love, these
three; but the greatest of these is love.
(NKJV)

I have to give Sabrina all the credit in the world, because she took everything in stride. She did not let anything bother her, and she just kept telling me that she loved me. She seemed determined to not let anyone ruin her day, and when Pastor Jeff introduced us as Mr. & Mrs. Steven F. Gray II, it was one of the happiest days of my life. The day was July 16th, 2008!

Chapter Nineteen

-2 Timothy 3:2-6-
For men will be lovers of themselves, lovers of money,
boasters, proud, blasphemers, disobedient to parents,
unthankful, unholy, unloving, unforgiving, slanderers,
without self-control, brutal, despisers of good, traitors,
headstrong, haughty, lovers of pleasure rather than lovers of
God, having a form of godliness but denying its power. And
from such people turn away! For of this sort are those who
creep into households and make captives of gullible women
loaded down with sins, led away by various lusts.
(NKJV)

The honeymoon was tough for me. I was in a lot of pain and couldn't walk without the use of my cane. I was trying to curb my smoking for Sabrina, so I was ecstatic when she said we should get a couple of drinks. I drank the entire honeymoon. I didn't get sloppy, but I caught a buzz and kept it. I felt bad because Sabrina wanted to do more, but I was limited because of my leg. I remember thinking that she deserved better. To top it off, because my leg was in a cast for eight weeks, I wound up getting third-degree sunburn on my entire shin. It blistered badly, and by the time we got back home to Las Vegas, my leg was twice its regular size. When I took my sock off, a layer of skin came off with it. Fantastic! That was my wedding and honeymoon.

Sabrina and I came back from our honeymoon but weren't living like husband and wife. I just couldn't shake the funk I was in spiritually. I was also in an extreme amount of pain, couldn't walk, and now I had a third-degree sunburn on my right leg.

The problem started with me. I was headed straight back into my addiction. I wasn't using drugs yet, but I was on my way. I was drinking heavily and steadily. We had close to ten cases of wine left over from the wedding, and as soon as we got back from our honeymoon, I started drinking it. I tried to hide it as best I could, but she knew.

Everything was aggravating me. I thought about going to see one of the pastors at Valley Bible, but felt as if my church was losing its focus, and that didn't help. All Pastors Ron and Jim talked about anymore was Brian "Head" Welch, and it never seemed to end. Brian Welch is the guitarist from the rock band Korn. He quit the band to follow Jesus Christ, and it just so happened that he was a part of Valley Bible Fellowship, and that's all our pastors talked about. It was always:

"Brian this!"

"Brian that!"

"We just had 13,000 people at the church in Bakersfield because of Brian!"

"God's doing this for Brian!"

"Brian donated this!"

Brian's daughter goes to school at the campus in Bakersfield." And the list would go on... I wanted to yell out, "WOULD YOU ALL JUST SHUT UP ABOUT BRIAN AND KORN?!" I no longer felt loved, or cared for, by my church because I couldn't produce the kind of attention Brian could.

Sabrina and I bickered non-stop. I could see she was trying hard to be a good wife. She tried to be understanding and pray for me, but I just wasn't connected to God like I once was. I was dead inside. The only reason I still went to church and Bible study was because my church was just down the street.

I was promoted at work and was now the Plant Manager. It was a big job and there was always a lot to do, but I was handling it all just fine. I was responsible for the two plants in Las Vegas. I was working crazy hours and didn't have time for much of anything else. When the arguing increased, I drowned myself in my work. My bosses loved my work, but my private life was suffering.

I got up for work at 1:00 in the morning every day and left the house by 1:30. I had to walk a couple miles to the bus stop on Charleston and Durango to catch the first bus. I would get off on Charleston and Las Vegas Boulevard. Then I had to wait for another bus to take me to the Downtown Transportation Center. Once there, I waited for another bus to take me to Craig and Las Vegas Boulevard. Then I had to walk three to four miles to be at work on time. It usually took me around three hours or so, sometimes a little more. More often than not though, I was at work by 4:30 in the morning. Going home was hard. There was more traffic, so it usually took an average of five hours or more. I wouldn't get home until after 7:00 at the earliest. I would have to take a shower, eat, and try to watch a little Sports Center before I went to bed, then try to relax enough to fall asleep, because Sabrina and I were always fighting. When I did fall asleep, it was four hours max, and then it was time to do it all over again.

Two months after the wedding, Sabrina and I were sleeping in different rooms. One reason was because she kept it way too hot in the house. The main reason, though, was that I just could not deal with her waking me up in the middle of the night to have sex. I would try to have sex with her when I got home, but she never wanted to. Like clockwork though, she would wake me up most nights around 11:00 for sex. I didn't feel as if she had any compassion with how long it took me to go to work and back. I got very little sleep, because it was too much for her to drive me to work. In her defense, I told her when we decided to move here that I would take the bus to work, but I just did not realize how long it would actually take, and it was really starting to drain me. I woke up late one morning and was scared that I might not make it to work on time. I woke her up, and she just flat out refused to take me. It was raining outside, and I was about to be an hour and a half late. I started yelling at her, telling her what a witch she was. It took about twenty minutes to get her out of bed, but she finally got up. I thought she was going to drive me to work, but she only took me down the street to catch my first bus. I couldn't believe it. She told me that she was afraid of falling asleep behind the wheel on the way back. I felt like she was being unreasonable, didn't care, and was unwilling to compromise even a little. I was on a bus for over seven hours a day, and she just did not give a crap. The oil plant was thirty miles away. I lost a lot of respect for Sabrina at that point.

Our fighting only got worse. We didn't talk that much, and when we did, neither one of us had anything good to say to the other. I was tired of the fighting. I was tired of being married to her. During one of our many arguments, Sabrina was laying into me about something, and I yelled a racial slur at her. I won't write what I said, but she's black, I'm white, and I used to be skinhead. I think you can figure out what I called her. Sabrina stopped, looked at me, but didn't say anything. I felt like a scumbag for saying it. I really did.

When we would argue, she would talk down to me and tell me how I'm not doing this right, that right, and how I wasn't a real man. I was sick and tired of the belittling. She wanted to be a good wife and stand by me; she just didn't know how to. She had no clue how to be a wife or how to talk to me. When I feel like you are backing me into a corner, I have no boundaries. So many of our fights could have been settled through prayer and talking, but after feeling as if I was being made out to be less than nothing, I would say the most vile, hurtful, and disrespectful things I could think of. I would be as hurtful as I could possibly be. I began to hurt her before she could ever have a chance to hurt me.

One of the biggest things that bothered me was every time Sabrina and I had an argument, she would tell her sister, Elise. Elise would then tell her girlfriends from church. Her girlfriends would then tell their husbands, and by the time I got to church on Sunday, everyone knew what fights we had and what was going on. At one point, her sister Elise was the biggest stay-at-home-mom-gossip-queen known to mankind. Sabrina would also always call our friends, Mike and Lynn, and tell them what I did wrong that day and how I wasn't living up to God's standards, or hers. Sabrina complained about everything I did.

Soon enough, Sabrina was pregnant. We were both happy about that. We were trying to understand how to be married to each other and were now looking forward to raising a child. I got extremely upset at her, though, because she felt that it was okay to tell her sister Elise, of course, first, before telling me that she was pregnant. I thought that was pretty crappy. I should have been the first to know. I guess I should have known that she would tell her family first. With Sabrina, her family always came first, never me.

Not long after she became pregnant, we had a huge fight about something and were both yelling at each other at the top of our lungs. As she was walking away, she threatened that she was going to move out and file for divorce, and then she yelled, "I'll never let you see you daughter!" We had literally just found out that we were having a girl.

When she yelled that at me, all I saw was red. It was as if Colleen was yelling at me all over again. I calmly walked to the kitchen, grabbed a steak knife, followed her to the bedroom, threw her on the bed, put my hand on her throat, held the knife to her stomach, and said, "If you ever try to hold me from seeing my daughter, I will cut your freaking heart out!" Then I threw a baseball against the wall and walked out.

She ran out of the house and called our friends Mike and Lynn, again, then called the cops. I was done worrying about who she was going to say what to. She was going to tell everything I did to the world anyway, so I figured I would give her a story to tell. The cops came, talked to Sabrina outside, then came to our apartment and talked to me. Of course, I lied to the cops and said I didn't do anything. The next day when I came home from work, Sabrina was gone. She moved in with her sister Elise, of course. Here I was, not married six months yet, and looking at divorce. I called Sabrina that night while she was at her sister's house, and she told me that she was filing for divorce.

What Sabrina never realized throughout our marriage, was that every time I told her to go file for divorce, it all came back to this very moment. She was very quick to throw out the word divorce as if it was going to scare me. I don't play games like that. You don't use that word as a toy, tool, or device to try to get someone to do something you want. She would always blame me for saying it, but it was a direct reaction of this moment in time. I knew she would divorce me eventually. It was always me, never her. She never saw the pain and trouble she caused me. I never cared about hers.

Looking back on my marriage to Sabrina makes me so mad, even sad at times. We could have been a power couple that was devoted to God. We could have made a difference, but we were baby Christians. Neither one of us really knew what we were doing when we got married, except for the fact that God told us to do so. She didn't know how to be a Godly wife. I didn't know how to lead her the way God had wanted me to. I didn't fight hard enough. I could sit here and pinpoint different things and say this part was because of Sabrina, that part was because of me, but it just all boils down to me not being man enough. I was so used to failing at different things in my life that I guess I had expected to lose this marriage anyway. Later on in our marriage, Sabrina would always say that I kept threatening her with divorce, but the truth is that it was a defense mechanism, because she was always moving out. There are men who fight for God to control their marriages and those who don't. I was one that did not. I gave up on my marriage the very first time she moved out.

I tried calling Sabrina over and over, but she wouldn't communicate with me except to tell me that she was filing for divorce, as well as filing for a restraining order. I spent the next two to three months in an alcohol-fueled rage. I would go to work, then drink my sorrows away at night, drinking until I passed out. Also, since Sabrina was filing for divorce, I decided to have sex with hookers on Craigslist.

After a couple of months, Sabrina and I sought counseling to try to save our marriage. Little by little it was working. It wasn't great, but it helped, and she soon moved back home. Although I wasn't drinking, I still had an attitude about a lot of things, but I was trying. One of my biggest issues was that Sabrina expected change to happen overnight, but that's just not a realistic expectation, especially with people like myself who have lived a life filled with drugs, abuse, and living on the street. It's a gradual process. I could be doing most everything right at the time, but when I did something just a little wrong, she would lay into me and continue to talk down to me.

This next part is difficult to admit to, but I'm not going to leave it out and pretend it didn't happen. After Sabrina moved back in, there were three times that I hit her. The first time was when she was yelling at me for something, and she hit me in my chest. As soon as she hit me, I saw red and hit her right back. Of course, everyone at church found out via gossip-queen-extraordinaire, Elise, as did everyone else we knew. I was now labeled a woman beater. I don't condone hitting women at all. I really don't. But when someone hits me, I don't see male or female. I see red. I never understood why it's okay for women to hit men, but not okay for a man to hit a woman. I'm not saying it's okay. I feel it should be just as detestable when a woman hits a man as it is when a man hits a woman. It's wrong for anyone to hit anybody, regardless of gender, at any time, under any circumstances.

The first two times I hit Sabrina, she hit me first. The third time I laid hands on her was when we were having an argument about something and her phone rang. I thought she just ignored the phone as we continued to fight, but then she holds her phone up to me and says, "You're so f'ing stupid!"

I looked and it was Sebastian, my oldest son. She answered the call and let him hear us fighting. I lost it and hit her. I was wrong for hitting her all three times. It doesn't matter how it happened. A real man that follows Christ would have never done what I did.

I am a very jealous person who has extremely low self-esteem. I don't like it when the woman I am with has male friends and has phone conversations with them. I've never been able to handle that very well. Sabrina was friends with this guy Richard she worked with. They would always talk on the phone and text each other. I didn't like it one bit. Richards's dad was a pastor, and Sabrina told me that his mother told her that she wanted her and Richard to get married. And she expects me to be okay with their friendship after telling me this? Are you freaking serious?

I walked into the kitchen one day and saw Sabrina try to hide her phone. Before she could get it completely behind her back, I saw that it had a picture of Richard's face on it. I tried grabbing her phone so I could call Richard and give him a piece of my mind, but we got into a pushing and shoving match over her phone. She was hell-bent on me not seeing her phone, and that made me want it even more. She had her car keys in her hand, and while she was punching me in my back, she accidentally stabbed me with her car keys. So I pushed her up against the wall. She said that she was going to call the cops and tell them that I had hit her again, but I really hadn't. I walked out of the house and waited for the cops to come. I was wrong for pushing her against the wall, but I did not hit her. My back hurt and I could feel the blood starting to drip out. When the cops showed up, I showed them my back, lied, and said that she bit me instead of stabbing me with her car keys. So they arrested her. Little did I know, she would have been arrested anyway for stabbing me with her keys. She was walked from the house to the back of a police car in handcuffs while she was seven months pregnant and crying. I felt like the biggest loser in the world.

-Isaiah 10:25-
"For yet a very little while and the indignation
will cease, as will My anger in their destruction."
(NKJV)

With that, after almost five years of not doing so, I said screw it and started smoking crack again. I let our apartment go after that. Sabrina came and took what was hers while I was at work. I moved into my own apartment, a small one bedroom in the ghetto not far from my job. I worked, smoked crack, and had no real hope that God would do, or even try, to fix anything. My relationship with my son Sebastian was in trouble as well. I was only flying to Boston to visit him once a year, which wasn't enough. I was still calling him every other week, but I could tell that he was starting to drift away from me. I wasn't making Sebastian a priority in my life as I should have.

To my surprise, Sabrina still wanted me in her life. She would come by now and then to talk a little. And when she would leave, I would drink and smoke crack. She wanted me to fight for our family, but she wouldn't commit to anything, so neither would I.

Sabrina was living with her mother and stepdad. It really pained me that things were the way they were. The night she went into labor, she came to pick me up so I could be with her. I had just had a couple of beers, so she wouldn't let me drive. After she was admitted, we sat in the hospital room and talked most of the night as I began to wonder if we could ever make it as a family. Her mother and sisters stopped by the next day and stayed till Sabrina gave birth. That afternoon, on July 11th, 2009, Sabrina gave birth to my second child: the most beautiful girl in the world, my daughter, Rhesa Elise Gray.

Rhesa was so beautiful. I have never to this day seen such a beautiful girl. I was the happiest I had ever been since my son Sebastian was born. I wanted to give up all the drugs and alcohol for Rhesa.

When we left the hospital, Sabrina came home with me and I was loving it. I wanted her to stay and move in. She kept telling me that we would one day be a family again, but she went back to her mother's after a week. It was killing me not seeing Rhesa every day. I could not wrap my head around how Sabrina wanted to make it work, but live apart. It messed with my head big time. I'm not saying that she was right or wrong. I'm just saying that it messed with my head something fierce. Instead of thinking about how I could get my family back, I dwelled on how I wasn't seeing them every day. I decided to get deep into crack cocaine to numb my life.

Every once in a while, Sabrina would come and stay for a few days, then leave again. When she was at my house, I loved being a dad to my daughter, but as soon as she left, the depression kicked in. I would rather die than feel this pain. Sabrina had this power over my mind, the power Colleen had over me when I was a child, so I just did more drugs and was soon fired from the oil company due to my drug use. For five years I worked there, worked my way up to plant manager, and then threw it all away. Even still, Sabrina stood by me. She kept telling me that we should get together to pray, that this was the time for us to call upon God, together. Instead of thinking how great it would be to get together to pray and spend time with my family, all I thought about was when she would leave again. Don't get me wrong, I wanted her to come over with my daughter, but I worried about her saying, "Well, time to go back to Mommy's house."

In my mind, married couples don't work on these issues while they're separated; they work them out together. Her leaving to go to her mother's with my daughter so I couldn't spend time with my child far outweighed the good I could feel. The enemy was winning.

I was soon out of control, drinking and drugging daily. I needed help, and again went back to the Las Vegas Rescue Mission to do their drug program. Once there, I got back into the Word. I wanted God back in my life. I wanted the feeling I had when I first accepted Jesus as my LORD and Savior and was surprised how easy it was to rededicate my life to Him once again. It only took making the time to pray and get into His Word on a regular basis. I needed to put God at the forefront of my life again.

I was talking to Sabrina on the phone one day, she told me she was pregnant again, and of course, told her sister first, again! I was upset for a couple weeks. Just one time I wanted her to be pregnant and for me to be the first to know, but I realized that would never happen. Married or not, I was always second to her family, no matter what the situation was.

I didn't stay at the Mission long this time. I was only there about four months or so. Sabrina's mother and stepdad let me move in with them so I could look for a job. I needed to provide for my family. I hit it hard and soon got a job managing a warehouse for Nike. The pay was decent, the benefits excellent. We were able to move out and into our own place with my second paycheck.

Things were looking up. I was clean and sober. Sabrina was able to give birth to our son in our own home. We were both looking forward to it. I was doing what God wanted me to do. On August 24th, 2010, our son, Asher James Gray, was born. He was so beautiful and handsome! Things were great. I had my family, and I was able to provide for them with God leading the way. I was going to church, prayer group, Bible study, men's ministry, Christian 12-step at the church, and working. It still felt like none of what I was doing was good enough for Sabrina though. It never did. It never was. It just seemed that every little thing I did, she would nitpick. She was literally always on my case about something. I felt like she could give everyone else all the grace in the world, but if I farted the wrong way, crap would hit the fan, and I wasn't even using at the time. When I was clean and sober, she treated me the same way as if I was getting high. I just couldn't win with her.

It was okay that her sister Elise smoked weed and gossiped about the world. It was okay her other sister, Nicole, worked as a stripper, prostitute, high-class escort, and was arrested for stealing more than $5,000 from one of her "clients." It was okay her brother-in-law, Billy, treated his family like crap and almost got divorced. It was okay that her best friend, Chelsea, got pregnant before her wedding and had to change her wedding date. (Chelsea told Sabrina that she was practicing celibacy.) It was okay that her dad, John, screwed her on her car payments after telling her that he would pay for her car. It was okay that her own dad wouldn't give her away at our wedding. It was okay to give her blood relations, and her best friend, forgiveness and grace, but it wasn't okay if I farted the wrong way. I felt like she was weighing me down and treated me as if I was less than freaking zero! Why not just get high and at least give her something real to be pissed at me for. Back to drugs I went.

It was the same cycle all over again. Sabrina moved out. I quit my job. Drugs were more important than life. I would use then get sober for a couple months. Use again, get sober again. I just would not stay sober for long. When I would use, Sabrina would move out. When I was clean, she moved back in and constantly remind me how much of a man I was not. I was enraged at how Sabrina could treat me, but no one noticed. It didn't matter though. I was failing again as a husband and father.

My church, Valley Bible Fellowship, got me into this drug and alcohol program called Teen Challenge in Bakersfield, California. They bought me a bus ticket to get me there while Sabrina was again forced to move back in with her mother. On the bus ride, all I thought about was wanting to be a good father to my kids. I really didn't like what I was doing. I didn't want my kids to go through what I went through. Even through heart-felt prayer and crying out to God for His will, I just could not seem to break this damn cycle.

I got to Teen Challenge just fine and began their program. It was way out in the boondocks on a farm in the middle of the country. My job was working the chicken coop. I did not like it there. I am in no way a country boy. I'm a city boy. This wasn't for me, so, after two short weeks, I took a bus back to Vegas and went back to the Mission. I felt like an idiot who continued to foul up his life. I hated it, but to save my family, this was the only way. This wasn't fair to Sabrina. It wasn't fair to my kids.

———————

As I look at what I'm writing, it sickens me as to how many times I just couldn't hold on to God through the hard times. It sickens me how many times I put Sabrina and my children in danger with my drug use. I want to cry. When do I just hold on to Christ and not let go?

———————

So now, I'm back at the Mission and things were going somewhat okay. I'm focusing on God, and things with Sabrina and I are getting a little better as we try to work through our crap. I learned to play bass guitar, started a Christian band, and called the band SEED. I went to GED classes and got my GED at the community college. After sixteen years with a suspended license, it was reinstated. It seemed like when I would follow God, everything in my life would fall into place, except for my marriage. I could not, for the life of me, understand why.

One day while I was with Sabrina and my kids on a day pass, we got into other fight. I hated fighting in front of my children. I told Sabrina to stop, but she just continued. She was about to drop me back off at the Mission and was yelling at me for things that I'm not doing right. I could not understand it. I really couldn't. I played bass in a Christian rock band, got my GED, got my driver's license reinstated, was praising God, had people looking up to me, yet couldn't get my wife to love me the way I was when I was sober. I just did not understand. No matter how close I was to Christ, she would call me a cheater, liar, a sorry excuse for a man, a low life, bad father, false prophet, loser, woman beater, drug addict, tyrant, as well as a slew of other names. As she was kicking me out of the car, I got upset and threw my middle finger in her face. Just as I did that, she turned towards me, and I accidentally hit her in the face. I didn't mean to. It was honestly an accident. She just turned at the wrong time. To this day, she says I did it on purpose. I did not! That was a Saturday afternoon.

The following day, my band was setting up our gear at the Mission, because we were playing the service that night. After setting up, I bumped into Doug Loman, the associate pastor from Valley Bible Fellowship. He asked me how I was doing, and I said fine. I didn't want to talk to him about Sabrina. Doug and I talked for about two or three minutes. He smiled at me, shook my hand, wished me well with my band, and walked away. He never said anything to me about my family or asked how they were doing.

Later that night, after we played and packed up our gear, I called Sabrina to see how she was doing and to apologize about our fight the day before.

"I'm filing for divorce," she said.

"What?!"

"I'm filing for a divorce, Steve."

"Sabrina, you can't do that. Please, do not do that. Let's talk to the pastors first before you do that."

"I already did."

"What? Who?"

"Pastor Doug, this morning at church. I told him what you did, and he told me that it's gone too far now and that the church is behind me in the divorce."

I was enraged. Sabrina wanted a divorce, plain and simple. She would look for any situation to bring to a pastor until she got the answer she was looking for, thinking it would be justified because a pastor said so. When you look for a certain answer, no matter what answer you're looking for, eventually you'll find what you're seeking, right or wrong. She decided to leave me when I was clean and sober, not when I was in the middle of my addiction. And Doug Loman? That dude had the guts to look at me, smile, shake my hand, ask me how I was, wish me well, and not tell me that earlier that morning he gave my (now ex-) wife, the church's blessing to divorce me. I was at a loss for words.

I went on the church's Facebook and blew up at Doug. I talked crap about him and his son's baseball careers. I was rude, vile, abusive, and let the curse words flow freely on the church's account. Now I was kicked out of the church that I called home for seven years. Ever since that happened, I have prayed constantly this: that if God did not give

Doug permission for Sabrina to divorce me, if he did not seek God first, that his son Seth would never receive a call-up to the majors. None of that mattered though. Sabrina got the answer she searched for for four years. She was dead set on divorcing me.

> ### *"If you're absent during my struggle, don't expect to be present during my success."*
> #### *(Will Smith)*

A month later, I was served divorce papers. I knew God was against this. God did not give Sabrina permission to divorce me. For that reason, any relationship that Miss Jones enters for the rest of her life will be considered adultery in the eyes of God. I know this in my heart...

> *-Jeremiah 29:11-*
> *For I know the thoughts that I think toward you, says the LORD, thoughts of peace and not of evil, to give you a future and a hope.*
> *(NKJV)*

A couple years later, I went through the proper channels, got ahold of Pastor Jim, and asked if I could start attending the church again. Doug responded via email, and told me I was still no longer welcome at Valley Bible Fellowship. I lost the church I loved. The church I grew with the LORD in was gone.

I moved into a sober house that I didn't like, but was cheap. I was collecting unemployment and couldn't afford much. I still played bass in my band and was involved in a ministry called The Gospel Strike Force, run by Pastor Jeff. Things weren't great, but God was getting me through it. After a few months, Mike called me and told me that I could move into his Christian sober house. I moved in the next day.

I was very confused about my life and wondered what God was doing and if He was even there. I was clean and trying to put the pieces of my shattered reality back together. I got a job driving a cab, and things went well at first. I worked twelve-hour shifts and didn't really have time to play in my band anymore. My drummer, Joel, and I never saw eye to eye on much anyway. My guitarist hired him without consulting me or Ashley, our singer, so Ashley and I quit. Sabrina was "allowing" me see my kids. And Ashley and I soon started a relationship that we should not have been in.

I was seeing my kids on my days off until Sabrina decided she didn't like one of the guys who lived in the house with me. Then I was not "allowed" to see my kids until I moved. So I moved in with Ashley. I had never seen Sabrina so livid in my life. I was getting tired of her games. She would have sex with me when I went to see my kids, but said she was still going through with the divorce. I couldn't wrap my head around it. I did not understand her thought process. She said she still had hopes for us to get back together. So then why was she still going through with the divorce? I was in a relationship with Ashley and still having sex with my wife. Of course, Sabrina found out, and now she wouldn't "allow" me to see my kids again. The back and forth with Sabrina had gotten me so upset that I questioned God on why He would do this to me while I was clean and sober. I got high one night, then drug tested the very next day at work. I couldn't believe it. I got fired, and Sabrina found out the truth. She said I couldn't see my kids as long as I was getting high and living with Ashley. The getting high thing I understood, but the Ashley thing bothered me. She filed for divorce. Why does she care who I'm with. Ashley was a good girl who really just cared about the LORD.

I was able to put the drugs down, but Sabrina still wouldn't let me see my kids. I went back to the Rescue Mission until I got a job at Lucky Cab. I soon moved into my own place, and Sabrina finally "allowed" me to see my kids again. I was trying to kiss her butt. Whenever we would fight, she would not "allow" me see my kids. When we did not fight, she would "allow" me visitation. I was tired of the back and forth.

One day I got a letter from Child Support saying that my license was to be suspended for non-payment of child support. I gave Sabrina a check every other week. I went to the Child Support office and told them that she was lying, but they didn't care. They said that I had to show them proof. I went to my bank to get copies of all my cancelled child support checks and brought them to their office. Here is the really super part: Child Support Of Nevada said that all my checks, which all said child support on them, which were all signed, deposited, and cashed by Sabrina, was not enough proof that they were child support payments. Can you freaking believe that? They said Sabrina had to give me credit for them as child support and had thirty days to respond. On day thirty-one I called them back, and they said Sabrina had not responded and that my license was probably going to be suspended the following week. I blew up, because I knew I was right and Sabrina was lying. I drove to the Child Support office, waited in line, asked for my officer, and told her straight out, "If you suspend my license after I gave you all my checks that say child support in the note area, and Sabrina has not responded back in the time YOU gave her to contact you, I swear to Christ, I am going to sue you, and you WILL lose this one, and you know it. I drive a cab, and I WILL get punitive damages from you a-holes!"

They did not suspend my driver's license. In most cases, women have all the rights, and it's very tough for men to catch a break.

I was getting my kids every week on my days off now. I was clean, sober, and doing the right things again. I was paying child support to two ex-wives, but was making good money. I was even able to buy a new car. I was so happy. I didn't have much money left over, but I was getting by just fine. I was being a good father. I was able to take Rhesa and Asher places and actually do things. I made their breakfast, lunch, and dinner. I gave them baths and read them stories. I loved them, and they loved me. For some reason though, no matter how well I was doing, no matter how hard I tried, no matter how close to God I was, no matter how much like Jesus I strived to be, Sabrina just seemed to have it in for me. I lived in the ghetto, because it was cheap. She kept telling me that she didn't like where I lived and didn't want "her" kids there. She even went so far as to tell me that if I didn't move to a better area soon, that she wasn't sure if she would "allow" me to continue to see my children. It never stopped with her.

I got a call from Welfare one fine day, and they told me I owed them over $5,000 for food stamps and medical that my kids were receiving because I wasn't paying child support. I was appalled. This woman was going to stop at nothing to make sure my life was hell. I told Welfare to go screw themselves and that Sabrina was lying to them, because my paycheck had been garnished for months now. I asked Sabrina about this and, of course, she denied it. When Sabrina was offered medical insurance through her employment, for some reason, she didn't cover Rhesa and Asher. (Great, freaking, parenting, Miss Jones! SUPERB!) This was mind boggling to me, as well as extremely stupid. I wasn't even so much as offered medical insurance at the cab company. She knew this, yet she still refused to cover my children when she was given the opportunity.

Today is Sabrina's thirtieth birthday. I wonder if she had a good time with my kids. I think about Rhesa and Asher giving her presents, being so happy that it was their Mommy's birthday. I think about how Sabrina's face must have lit up when my kids told her, "Happy Birthday, Mommy!"

I sit here and wonder what she told my kids when all this crap started. I wonder why she took the picture of me down that was in their room. I wonder what my kids think happened to me, what they were told, or what they do on May 12th every year when it's my birthday.

Happy Birthday, Sabrina! I hope you had a great day with "our" children!

Things went well for a short time. I was getting my kids on my days off, and things seemed to be falling into place. I still had issues with Sabrina, but I learned to just ignore her and her garbage. She didn't want me dressing my kids up for Halloween and going trick or treating with them. She said it wasn't Christian, but she seemed to forget getting the kids dressed up in costumes for the church's Trunk- or-Treat. Christmas was another issue for her. I was teaching Rhesa and Asher about Santa Clause, just a fantasy thing, even telling them that he's not real. She kept telling me not to do either one of those things, because it's not right.

"So you want to raise our kids by lying to them?" she said.

I kind of blew up and told her that I am a good father, that when she decided to divorce me, she had no say on how I raise my kids when I have them. I wasn't hurting them, and I still feel that way today. She had issues with every aspect of how I raised my kids when I had them.

Every week when I had Rhesa & Asher, I cooked breakfast, made lunch, prayed with them, read the Bible to them, gave them baths, watched movies, cooked dinner, and spent real quality time with them. I still have one hundred and twenty-six videos on my old phone of the three of us just having a good time. Every single night, without fail, I had them call Sabrina to say goodnight. Every single morning, without fail, I had them call Sabrina to say good morning. I did this even when they didn't want to, because it was the right thing to do. Not once, though, did I ever receive a call from my kids when I didn't have them. Not. One. Time.

Rhesa's birthday was coming soon and I asked Sabrina if she was having a party for her.

"No," she said.

"Why not?" I asked.

"I don't know. I'm just not."

She said she didn't want to deal with throwing a party. I felt it was wrong. Every kid deserves a birthday party. But if she didn't want to have one, I wasn't about to start a fight. I told Rhesa that I would have a small party for her and Asher the first week of August, because it was between both their birthdays.

In the meantime, I noticed Asher had a new racecar bed that he loved. I asked Sabrina about Asher's new bed and she said, "A guy I know got it for Asher." Cool, I thought. A couple of weeks later,

I was talking to our friend, Mike Tomlan, about something. We were just hanging out and talking, and he mentioned Asher's new bed.

"Yeah, well when I was at Sabrina's house for Rhesa's birthday party, I noticed Asher still slept in his crib. I told her I could get a racecar bed for him."

"Sabrina had a birthday party for Rhesa?!" I was freaking livid!

I wasn't drinking or doing drugs. I was clean for some time then. I asked Sabrina about it, and she had nothing to say. She refused to look me in the eye or respond in any way. She didn't even say, "I'm sorry." I was at a loss for words. I didn't care what she thought about me, not one bit, but I was clean, and she lied to me about my daughter's birthday. It's like I said before, I could live clean and sober and she would just spit in my face. She lied to me about my daughter's birthday party. The "friend" that she said got the racecar bed for Asher was our closest friend while we were married. It didn't matter to her.

As promised, I threw Rhesa and Asher a birthday party together the first weekend of August. It was fun. I got them each a few things, we laughed, and ate cake and ice cream. I took several videos of the small party and sent them to Sabrina. I invited her, but she didn't come. On Asher's birthday, she called me in the early evening and asked me if I wanted to come by for cake and ice cream. Absolutely no one else would be there. Just her, Rhesa, and Asher. I felt bad because Asher got screwed out of a birthday party that year. I felt it was wrong for her to throw a party for Rhesa, but not Asher. It's crazy because a lot of women do these messed up crazy things when it comes to their ex's kids, and they and the courts wonder why we as the fathers snap. The kids lose in the end.

It was stressful dealing with Sabrina. She knew exactly how to push my buttons. She just would not stop and seemed hell-bent on making my life miserable. I never saw this side of her before. I got so sick and tired of her messing with my relationship with my children, her mind games, and her holier-than-thou attitude towards me, that instead of continuing to do the right things, I decided to get high, thus giving her the ammunition she so desired. I gift wrapped it for her.

I made a mistake, a very huge mistake. I didn't go on a runner this time. I quickly stopped and tried calling my kids, but she would not let me talk to them. She said if I wanted to see my kids, then I would have to take her to court.

I had a legal right, per my divorce decree, to have visitation with Rhesa and Asher. I kept driving to her house, but neither she nor my kids were ever home. I would call nonstop, but she wouldn't answer the phone. At one point, she told me she got a restraining order and that I would be arrested if I tried to contact her. I called the cops and they said there was no restraining order on file. This was the first week of November 2013.

I looked into what my rights were, filed a motion with the family court, and then paid to have the hearing fast tracked. Twice a week, every week, on my days off, I drove to her house and called the cops. They told me that they cannot enforce a civil matter, but that they could give me an event number for court, because it was within my rights to see my children. I did this until one day Sabrina moved out. I couldn't believe it. I was lost and had this empty feeling in my stomach! Have you ever seen the Discovery Channel and see what happens when you mess with a lions cubs? It's not good.

I was pulling out of Sabrina's apartment complex one day when she came driving in. I stopped and told her that I wanted to see my kids.

"Nope! Not till we go to court. And right now I'm calling the cops," she said, laughing.

"Good. Because I'm calling the cops too, you freaking witch." All I got was another event number. I was never arrested, because there was no restraining order. Just seeing her, watching how cocky she was, made me want to snap her neck right there. She tried having me arrested, but the cops told her that there was no restraining order. She was allowed to drive away, and I had to go back home. When I got home, I was steaming mad. I couldn't control my emotions. I blamed God.

The following week on my day off from work, I drove out the Primm Nevada Outlets, where Sabrina worked, found her car, parked one aisle over and waited five hours for her to come out and drive away. I pulled out, got directly behind her, and followed her back into Vegas to her sister Elise's house. I got out of my car, and the look on her face was one of complete shock. My kids were outside

510

and ran right up to me, "Daddy! Daddy!" Rhesa and Asher both said. I picked them both up and hugged them so hard. They were both happy to see me.

"Where you been, Daddy?" Rhesa asked me.

It was so good to see them both I almost started to cry. Sabrina called for the kids to get in the house, but I grabbed them and hugged them both so tight.

"I love you, Daddy," Asher whispered in my ear. "I miss you."

"I love you too, buddy."

I told them to listen to Mommy, and they went into the house. I drove down the street, parked, and called the cops. Just after I called the cops, Sabrina put the kids in her car and drove off. I explained everything to the 911 operator and was told to stay put and wait. At that time, her sister's husband, Big-Billy-Bad-Butt, came walking down the street with two of his friends and a baseball bat, telling me he was going to beat my face in with it. I stood and waited for him, because Tiny-Billy is, and always has been, one of those all-talk guys anyway. Just as I expected, he wound up walking away when the cops showed up. I was explaining the situation to the police when Sabrina drove up. My kids were in the car and I said, "Can I see my kids?"

The cops made Sabrina walk away so I could see them. Asher was sleeping, so I grabbed Rhesa. She held me tight, asked me not to go, started crying, and asked me what was happening.

"I love you, Rhesa!" I said through tears. "Don't ever forget me, okay? Please, Rhesa. Don't ever forget me." I knew in my heart that I wouldn't see Rhesa or Asher for a very long time.

"I love you, Daddy," Rhesa said while she was crying

"Don't forget me, Rhesa."

"I won't, Daddy. I won't never forget you, never." Those were the last words I've ever heard my daughter speak.

Then I had to leave. Asher was still sleeping in his car seat, so I picked him up, gave him a kiss on his head, hugged him, put him back down, buckled him back in his car seat, whispered in his ear, "I love you, Asher. Don't forget me. I'm coming back for you one day." I walked to my car and drove off in tears. I was madder than I'd ever been. I felt my heart ripped right out of my fucking chest.

-Jeremiah 18:12-
And they said, "That is hopeless! So we will walk according to our own plans, and we will every one obey the dictates of his evil heart."
(NKJV)

I was lost and empty. I missed my kids so much more than words can tell you. I hadn't received my letter yet from the court telling me when my court date was scheduled, so for the time being, I was in limbo. The following week was Thanksgiving, and I couldn't see my kids. I was hurting, and instead of running to God for His help and comfort, I was blaming Him. I had three days off from work for the holidays and decided to drink and drug to numb the pain.

I couldn't do this again. I was going to flush everything that I had worked so hard for down the toilet, so I stopped. I flushed the rest of the dope down the toilet and tried to pray and read my Bible. I made up my mind that I would at least try to let God handle it.

The next Monday I got home from work and got my letter from the family court saying that my hearing was scheduled for the middle of December. I gathered everything I had from Sabrina telling her lies, my divorce decree, her false statements to Child Support, the false paperwork she filed with Welfare, and all the event numbers from the police. The judge didn't want to hear it.

"I don't care if you're showing me the gospel. It doesn't make it true!" the less-than-nothing Judge Matthew Harter said.

Sabrina told him I used to be in rehab.

"So, you're a drug addict!" Judge Matthew Harter said.

When I was finally able to tell him about Sabrina moving and not letting me see my kids per my divorce decree, he told her, "You cannot do that, Sabrina. That's child abduction!" And then took all my rights away pending a drug test and set a new court date for the next week.

I went and took my drug test and was scared. I figured the dope would be out of my system in a few days, so I just prayed. The following week when we went back to court, I lost all my rights because my test came back positive. I was both mad at myself and at Sabrina. I don't blame her for my

using; it was my choice, not hers. I will tell you this
though: I believe in my heart of hearts that she knew
if she pulled this crap long enough, I would go out
and get high. I believe in my heart, the entire time
she was messing with my mind and my relationship
with Rhesa and Asher that she knew exactly what
she was doing. She wanted me to use. She knew if
she leaned on me hard enough that this is what I
would do, and I did. There is nothing anyone can say
that'll make me think different. I believe this was her
plan. I believe she wanted it to happen the way it did.
Everything else aside, it all boiled down to me not
being man enough to hold on to Christ during a
difficult time. I could have chosen differently. I did
not.

The judge told me that to see my kids I had to
go to this place called Options, get a sweat patch put
on to detect drugs in my system, and do counseling
once a week. I was to do this for nine months. After
three months, I could see my kids. I didn't have any
other choice, so this is what I had to do.

I went to Options the following week, and
they told me to come back the first week of January
so none of the dope I did on Thanksgiving would
come up. So, I went home and waited.

Christmas came, and I sat on my couch
crying, missing my kids. I had all their presents
wrapped up and waiting for them. I bought them all
kinds of stuff and even bought them their first bikes.
I looked at their gifts all day long and asked God
how this all happened. I missed Rhesa and Asher so
much. I started drinking, and by nighttime, was

hammered. I was blaming Sabrina for playing her games the last year and a half, so I started calling and texting her. I left her messages telling her that I was going to kill her, her family, and called her racial slurs. I did this nonstop until I passed out in my bed crying.

I woke up to the cops at my door. I was arrested for felony aggravated stalking. That was my Christmas 2013. I could not understand how I could work so hard to get where I was, have Sabrina tell all these lies, and lose it all. I felt as if she could do all this garbage and have no consequences, but it takes me forever to build up what I had, make a stupid mistake, and lose it all. Nothing mattered at that point though. I was in handcuffs and on my way to jail.

Chapter Twenty

-Ephesians 2:8-9-
For by grace you have been saved through
faith; and that not of yourselves; it is the gift
of God, not of works, lest anyone should boast.
(NKJV)

I want to be surprised at how things are going right now, but I'm not. I still haven't found a job and almost got kicked out of this sober house the other day. I was roommates with Ron, the manager's brother, and we got into an argument. Ron comes home drunk, passes out, and Jack just lets it slide. It fits, because Jack stays in his room and smokes pot. I don't understand what's going on. I just cannot explain it. I have nowhere to go and can't find a job. I have an interview tomorrow morning at nine, but I'm not real excited about it. I've been on a million interviews and it's always the same outcome. I don't get the job because of my background. I just need a break and feel as if God keeps telling me to finish this book. I don't understand why He wants that either. I feel like a failure, even when I know I'm doing what God wants me to do.

I was in jail for about a week, I think. I just laid on my bed every day, wondering what the heck just happened. I sat on my bunk for New Year's Eve watching an empty road as the New Year rang in. I knew I had reacted wrong, but I was just so sick and tired of how Sabrina was allowed to run her games and lie, while nothing ever seemed to happen to her. I snapped. I lost it.

A week later I was released and walked to the Golden Nugget, where I caught a cab home. I walked in my house, sat down, opened my Bible, and read for a while. I wish I could tell you that I had this big revelation, but that didn't happen. I didn't even feel like God was talking to me. I had probably lost my job and had to go see them the following morning.

Within a week of getting out of jail, Sabrina took me to family court to have me put back in jail for violating the restraining order. This woman was stopping at nothing to keep me from my kids.

The following morning, I went to Lucky Cab to talk to my bosses, Steve and Desiree, about my job. I had all my paperwork from the jail, and they were not happy about it. They knew I was going through a hard time, and both had bent over backwards to help me. Desiree was concerned about having a driver not in his right frame of mind driving a cab. She was right. To my surprise, they gave me my job back with the stipulation that I had to keep a level head. Steve tried talking to me about what he went through with his ex-wife, and Desiree truly cared about how I was going to handle things. To be honest, I think they were both a little on edge, but they gave me a chance anyway.

I started thinking about how I was going to deal with all of this. The District Attorney's offer was one to five years in prison, and he wouldn't budge. So I decided to fight. In the meantime, I started going to church again, prayerfully reading my Bible, began a heartfelt prayer life, and went to get my drug patch put on so I could see my kids again. I did my best to have a positive attitude and looked forward to seeing Rhesa and Asher again.

Every week, my patch was changed, and I was doing everything I was supposed to be doing. I never missed a church service, worked my butt off, tithed, read my Bible, and truly sought the LORD with all my heart. During the eleventh week, I filed my paperwork to see my kids with the family court, because it takes a week to process everything. I was excited to see my children again and could finally see the light at the end of the tunnel. I went to get my patch changed on the twelfth week. I checked in at the window and the lady said to me, "Um, we have a problem."

"What problem?" I asked.

"You came up positive for methamphetamine."

"What?!"

She went on to explain that the cut off was .10, and I tested positive at .14. I was four one-hundredths over the limit. The problem was that I was not using at all! I could not understand it. Meth isn't even my thing. I don't like meth. She said that they give a cut off because even cops test positive when they are dealing with drug addicts. I even had a surprise drug test that same week at Lucky Cab and came up clean. I went to court the next week and lost all my rights, again. I didn't understand what was happening. Very few times in my life was I ever right, but this was one of them. I looked up the drug patch online and found out that when you do a line, you test positive in the thousands. If you smoke a bowl, you're in the high hundreds. I was only four one-hundredths over, not enough to have gotten high. This was the EXACT moment I lost every single ounce of faith I had in Christ. The date was April 8th, 2014.

Driving home after that appointment, I was in a complete daze and contemplated suicide like never before. I hated God! Christ was a joke! I started to cry and heard, loud and clear, a voice speak this verse:

-Luke 22:31-
And the LORD said, "Simon, Simon! Indeed, satan has asked for you, that he may sift you as wheat."
<u>(NKJV)</u>

"I hate You God! How can You do this to me? You know I wasn't using! You freaking know it! I have been doing everything I was supposed to be doing. You have taken my kids away, AGAIN! If I do the wrong things, You give me crap! When I do the right things, You give me MORE crap! Why try to live for You when You freaking HATE me?! I hate You! I HATE YOU! STAY OUT OF MY FUCKING LIFE!"

I couldn't understand why this was happening at the time. I don't even care if you all believe me or not, because it's one-hundred percent truth! God knows I'm telling the truth. Since I just lost everything again when I wasn't even getting high, why not just drink and drug until my heart stops? This was now my plan: suicide…

Not long after this, The Las Vegas Taxi Cab Authority notified me to let me know that they were not going to renew my permit to drive a cab. In Las Vegas, you can't get licensed to drive a cab with a felony arrest or conviction within the previous five years so as to protect the tourists. Now I was jobless to go along with my fresh felony arrest. And the hits just – keep – coming. Fantastic!

"Trials should not surprise us, or cause us to doubt God's faithfulness. Rather, we should actually be glad for them."
(Edmund Clowney)

I had a hard time seeing it this way. To me, God was just playing with my life and having fun watching me writhe in pain.

It was time to die. Job-hunting was useless with my background, although I did try at first. I was trying to save the things I had by paying all my bills with credit cards, but this proved to be just as useless. I just sat there and watched as God allowed everything I had to be taken away. Now I lived in my car. I had no job and nothing to eat. I stole food from local Wal-Marts when I was hungry. I lived like this for a couple months until I decided to go to The Rescue Mission again for help. I wasn't using, and I didn't need the program. I just needed somewhere to sleep.

They let me stay there, and I quickly got a job. The pay was okay, but the job was also dependent on me getting this charge dropped to a misdemeanor, so I hoped and prayed hard for God to help me out in this.

One week before Christmas of 2014 was when my restraining order ran out, so I called Sabrina to see if I could see my kids, or at least talk to them. I gave her my address and both of my work addresses. (I had a second job delivering pizzas at night.) I called once a day to say hi to my kids and sent them a video message once a day as well. Sabrina took me to court for another restraining order. She lied and said I was being cocky, but I have all the videos saved on my phone for Rhesa and Asher to see. She hadn't seen me in over a year and still didn't want me to see my kids. The judge gave her the order, and I was again blocked from seeing my kids.

The following month I lost my job because I copped out to the felony. I didn't want to, but I felt like I had no choice. My lawyer had the video from the family court of the judge telling Sabrina she committed child abduction. He had the paperwork where she lied to Child Support about me not paying child support; the paperwork from Welfare where she lied, again, about me not paying child support; and all my event numbers and 911 calls from Sabrina not letting me see my kids when I had a legal right to see them. None of this mattered. I either had to take the one-to-five suspended and do three years parole or go to trial. I asked my lawyer, "What about all the stuff she did?"

"You still broke the law, and that's what they'll prove," he responded back.

If I lost at trial, I was looking at ten years, so I took the plea, and in doing that, I lost my job, and, because I lost that job, I soon lost my job delivering pizza, because I couldn't afford my car insurance, car payments, and child support. I lost everything. This is why men snap!

That's where the house I'm living in now comes in. I haven't done a drug since September 14th, 2014. I get drug tested every month at my parole check in. I have nothing. I have no job and no way to pay rent. I live in a sober house where the manager smokes pot and lets his brother drink. I look around me and see a place where people use this house for free food and cheap rent. I don't even know what keeps me clean. I don't know what God wants. I miss my Rhesa and my Asher so much it hurts. I think of them every single day! I read my Bible every day! I pray every day! I'm clean! My car is gone, and my license is suspended, because I can't pay my child support. So badly, I want to talk with Pastor Jeff to ask him what to do. He would point me to Jesus, but my spirit is vexed. I feel like I have nothing left to give to Jesus. I'm mad at Him. I feel as if He failed me. I just want to talk to Pastor Jeff again!

"Are you okay?" He asks me.

"No! Not at all, damn it!" I responded.

"Why?"

"Because my entire life is filled with crap. That's why!" I tried my hardest to fight the tears, but couldn't.

"Why?" he asks.

"God hates me. That's why. If I do wrong, He punishes me. When I do right, He still punishes me. I don't get it."

"Give Me an example."

"When I tested positive on my drug patch, I wasn't using. I lost everything. I lost my faith at that point."

"Why?"

"Because I felt like He was against me. From that point on, I knew He didn't love me."

"I've NEVER not loved you, Steven!"

I couldn't speak.

"I said, 'I've NEVER not loved you, Steven!'"

"God?"

"Who else do you think has been holding you this entire time?

I couldn't speak.

"One of the greatest things about you, Steven, has been watching you get back up to try again. No matter how many times I've allowed you to be knocked down, you got back up again. Over, and over, and over, and over, and over again you continued to get back up to fight. After all your yelling and blaming Me, you get back up to fight. That's been one of My greatest joys about watching you. Explain something for Me: If you lost all your faith in Me, why do you continue to get back up and fight? Why do you still believe that getting back up to fight might just be worth the pain? Why do you continue to pray? Why do you continue to read My Word? If you have no faith in Me, why, then, do you continue to seek Me?"

I had no answer.

"It's not about you, Steven. My reasons for bringing you through so much is not just about you. My plans for you are so much greater than you realize. Not many people would have gotten back up after so much. So many couldn't. But I knew you would. You are a very stubborn child. I know everything about you. Every time you were on the ground, you cried out to Me. That is what I love about you the most. That is why you love the Rocky movies so much. You, Steven, are the underdog whom no one believes in. Guess what though: that's one of the things I do best. I take the broken, defeated, crushed, unlovable, dirty, rotten people the world laughs at and use them for My glory. Every time I knocked you down, or allowed you to be knocked down, you got back up trying to prove Me wrong. What you never realized, though, was every time you got back up to fight, you were proving Me RIGHT, which I always am. I needed no one to believe in you so My power would shine the brightest. I'm going to use you in ways you can't even fathom. I'm going to use you in ways that show My power. I am going to shine through you!"

"What about my kids?"

-Matthew 10:37-
... And he who loves son or daughter

524

more than Me is not worthy of Me.
(NKJV)

"Keep your focus on Me. I had to touch your life where it would hurt you the most. I need you to understand this. I need you to love nothing more than Me. You'll see Rhesa and Asher again. I promise! They'll know the truth. It broke my heart every time you said you hated Me, but I still love you. It didn't have to take you this long, Steven, but it did. And you're here now."

"I'm empty inside," I said as the waterfalls continued to flow out of my eyes.

"It's like I told you through Pastor Jeff that time: there's a difference between believing in Me, and believing IN Me! You've been crawling to me ever since Officer Dancer introduced you to Me at the Chemung County Jail in 1994."

"I have nothing left."

"That was kind of the point, little dude! You're going to change lives, Steven! By Me working through you, you will change lives. Do you believe that?"

"I don't know."

"You don't have to know how right now. Just trust Me. Do what I tell you to do. Enjoy the simple things in life I give you! Everyday doesn't have to be Christmas morning, Steven. Now just sit back and enjoy the ride."

———

-Acts 4:10-
let it be known to you all, and to all the people of Israel, that by the name of Jesus Christ of Nazareth,

whom you crucified, whom God raised from the
dead, by Him this man stands here before you whole.
(NKJV)

I don't know what tomorrow holds, dear reader, but:

-Joshua 24:15-
"And if it seems evil to you to serve The LORD, choose for
yourselves this day whom you will serve, whether the gods
which your fathers served that were on the other side of the
River, or the gods of the Amorites, in whose land you dwell.
But as for me and my house, we will serve the LORD."
(NKJV)

If there is one thing I can tell you, it's please do what God tells you to do, how He tells you to do it, when He tells you to.

―――――――

"I'm scared," I said.

"Imagine Me on the cross: brutally beaten, slapped, punched, spit on, then dying for you. Could you possibly compare what you have gone through to what I did for you? I still get rejected! Pray and believe, Steven. Then believe in what you are praying. Love!"

"I loved my children more than I loved You, Jesus. I'm sorry."

"Now you're starting to understand. Now go. My Father has plans for you," Jesus said as He starts to walk away.

"Can I ask You a question, please?"

"You'll find out if there's baseball in heaven when you get there, Steven," he says with a smile.

"Do You like baseball, Jesus?"

"Yes! This Lion of the tribe of Judah loves baseball!"

"Who's your favorite team?"

He looks at me with a smile and says, "Well, Steven, I'm a Red Sox fan, of course!" Jesus says.

"I KNEW IT!"

"But Dad's a Yankees fan."

"What?! Dude, I thought He was supposed to be perfect!"

So how does it feel to live a lifetime filled with hate? I don't know. I couldn't tell you because I'm not filled with hate any longer! My life is far from perfect. In fact, my life hurts a lot right now, but I have Jesus Christ. That's all that matters.

-2 Corinthians 11:24-27-
From the Jews five times I received forty stripes minus one. Three times I was beaten with rods; once I was stoned; three times I was shipwrecked; a night and a day I have been in the deep; in journeys often, in perils of water, in perils of robbers, in perils of my own countrymen, in perils of the Gentiles, in perils in the city, in perils in the wilderness, in perils in the sea, in perils among false brethren; in weariness and toil, in sleeplessness often, in hunger and thirst, in fastings often, in cold and nakedness –
(NKJV)

All of my life, I crawled, and didn't even have to. God is on the throne! Jesus is LORD! HE WILL RESTORE! I'm done crawling..., crawling to God!

5

Epilogue

-Psalm 45:1-
My heart is overflowing with a good theme;
I recite my composition concerning the King;
My tongue is the pen of a ready writer.
(NKJV)

So, this is where I am supposed to catch you up on what is happening now. This is the part where in most books you learn that everything has turned out just the way it was supposed to: the bad guy loses, good guy wins, justice is served…, but that is just not the case.

The date today is August 6th, 2019, and I still haven't seen my kids. It's been five years, eight months, three week, and three days to be exact, and I still have zero clue as to when I will see them again. I never realized how it's possible to lose everything, and for everything to stay gone, when you're truly trying to do the right things. All I know is that God keeps telling me to, "Be still."

I currently live in California. I moved here the day after Christmas in 2017. I was in jail for not being able to afford my child support and really felt as if God told me to move. I was scared, didn't know what I was going to do, or where I was going to go, but I knew for certain that God was telling me to move. When I got out of jail, I got a bus ticket to Los Angeles and stayed in a homeless shelter until I found a job. Long story short, it's a year and eight months later, and I have a job. I'm paying my child support and have a place to live. I'm only renting a room, but it's a place to go home to.

I've done so much thinking this past year and have also done some priceless soul-searching with Christ. Just about every issue, or so-called injustice that you've read about in my book, could have all been avoided had I just called on the LORD and decided to become the man that He intended me to be, or at least tried. But I didn't do those things. My reactions to everything were all wrong. My attitude was wrong. My anger was misdirected, misplaced. I wasn't a good husband. I wasn't a man. I was a bad father.

Not long after I became settled in and got my routine down, I started to become aware of idols in my life. I loved Rhesa and Asher more than I loved God. All the force I was putting into trying to see my children should have been energy put into furthering my relationship with Jesus Christ. I would do more for Rhesa and Asher than I would for the LORD. That's just wrong. Everything in my life centered on my feelings towards Rhesa and Asher. It has taken a very long time for me to understand that my feelings, my love, and my life must be dedicated to Him. Jesus Christ needs to be paramount in my life. Nothing else. Not even my children. Learning this has been the single hardest life lesson I have ever had to learn. I miss home. California has been great, but I miss home. When my book is completed and published, I will be moving back to Las Vegas to make contact with Rhesa and Asher.

One morning when I got home from work, three days after Christmas of 2018, I received a call from none other than Sabrina. She told me there was something medically wrong with one of my children, but refused to tell me what. I kept asking her to tell me, but all she did was scream at me at the top of her lungs while swearing at me, belittling me, and name-calling. No matter what I tried to say, she would not tell me what was wrong with my kids and would continue to tell me to shut the (expletive) up. When I tried to talk, she would laugh at me and continue to scream. I would hang up, and she would call back. I don't get it. She really doesn't think that I've recorded every phone conversation I've had with her since 2013? Does she really not think I am going to show Rhesa and Asher everything? Then, her boyfriend, Seven-Eleven, continues to call and threaten me, calling me a 'M-F'n Cracka,' as well as sends numerous threatening texts, most of which I forwarded to Sabrina. I've saved it all. Maybe they were trying to get a reaction or something, but I just don't react to things the way I used to. Not being on drugs probably helps as well. It was very hard getting through the holidays this year, the hardest so far. And getting those calls and texts from Sabrina and her wanna-be thug boyfriend didn't help much.

It's an amazing thing when God tells you to "be still" when you're in the middle of a war, and all He wants you to do is to stand there, bullets flying, bombs exploding:

> learning to give up self,
> learning to listen,

learning to obey,
learning to love.

His name is Jesus Christ! He's my God! He is on the throne!

-Psalm 49:22-23-
"Now consider this, you who forget God, lest I tear you in pieces,
and there be none to deliver: Whoever offers praise glorifies Me;
and to him who orders his conduct aright I will show the salvation of God."
(NKJV)

"Hypocrisy desires to seem good, rather than be so; honesty desires to be good, rather than seem so."
(Arthur Warwick)

Placing hope and confidence in anything, or anyone, aside from the LORD Jesus Christ, will ultimately leave you feeling broken and defeated. The best use of life is love. The best expression of love is time. The best time to love is now!

Sabrina-

I've never known you to lie until you decided to not tell people, including Rhesa & Asher, the entire truth. You know what I'm talking about. More than that, though, God knows. You know He knows. Let me explain something to you Sabrina…

-Psalm 118:13-
You pushed me violently, that I might
fall, but The LORD helped me.
(NKJV)

Then, while continuing to not tell people the entire truth, as well as flat out lying, you let another man tell me that he is my voice to Rhesa & Asher! I have tried for years to contact Rhesa & Asher and get back into their lives. Have I not? Try to lie again, Sabrina. I have saved everything. EVERYTHING! You have done your best to keep me away, but…

-Psalm 118:5-6-
I called on the LORD in distress; the LORD
answered me and set me in a broad place. The LORD
is on my side; I will not fear. What can man do to me?
(NKJV)

When your storm comes, and it will come, Sabrina, and it pushes you violently, just remember:

-2 Samuel 1:14-
"How was it you were not afraid to put forth
your hand to destroy the LORD's anointed?"
(NKJV)

In the same way I told you that God told me your sister would give birth to a girl two years before she even got pregnant, I tell you now, God is going to take you through a VIOLENT storm. Why? You lied to my children about me. You relied on your own feelings about me without seeking Him! Vengeance belongs to the LORD, Sabrina! He will repay you, not me! When your storm comes, hold on to Christ and don't let go.

Today I am forty-three years old. My storm started when I was three. For 40 years I have been in the middle of a storm, Sabrina. My storm turned violent in 2012 and stayed violent until today, August 6th, 2019. I was 7 years in a violent storm. I tried everything to get out of it. Nothing worked. Not until I decided to listen to Christ and STAND STILL in the thunder to receive my allotted storm. I've done that. It was hard! It was painful! It was Earthshattering and faith-shaking! My storm is over now, though. I have a peace you'll never understand. Why? Simply because I love Rhesa & Asher so much that they will ALWAYS come second in my life to Jesus Christ. I love them so much that it must be this way.

Sabrina, I was hard-pressed on every side, yet not crushed; I was perplexed, but not in despair; persecuted, but not forsaken; struck down, but not destroyed. Sound familiar? My time is now. I'm done going through you to see my kids. Now I go to them.

-Steve

Steven,

You cannot withstand the storm!

-satan

satan,

I AM THE STORM!

-Steve

Steven,

-2 Samuel 18:31-
"There is good news,….
For the LORD has avenged you this
day of all those who rose against you."
<u>(NKJV)</u>

-Isaiah 55:11-
So shall My word be that goes forth from My
mouth; it shall not return to Me void, but it
shall accomplish what I please, and it shall
prosper in the thing for which I sent it.
<u>(NKJV)</u>

-1 Kings 2:2-
"I go the way of all the earth; be strong,
therefore, and prove yourself a man."
<u>(NKJV)</u>

Today is the first day of the rest of your life! Make it count!

I love you
-**God**

The Beginning!

Steven F. Gray II spent his life in a living Hell. Being abused, rejected, and imprisoned multiple times instilled in him an unquenchable rage that came within inches of destroying him and everyone he had ever loved. For years, God stood at the door and knocked, but it wasn't until he was completely desperate and ready to die that he answered and let in Jesus Christ. Steven lived through the nightmare of drug and alcohol addiction, and a series of unholy and sometimes violent romance relationships. He was imprisoned several times for a gamut of crimes. But now, Steven is overjoyed to find that Jesus Christ is everything that the addictions promised, but could never deliver. Now he knows that his horrific past was necessary to give him the life he has today, having walked away from everything he ever was and ever owned to gain Christ (Phil. 3:8). By the power of total surrender, Steven is finally free, finally not trying to tell God how to do His job, and living his life in the center of God's will. Trusting God to give him back who and what He wants him to have, Steven has totally surrendered.

Extra Special Thanks To;

(Joe Panico)

Joe, you never judged me! Your constant communication throughout these past seven years has meant more to me than you will ever know. I never understood how powerful just a few words of encouragement could help someone. Just when I was at the brink of life, feeling as if continuing to move forward was pointless, ready to give up, and contemplating suicide, my phone would go off with your never-ending, and sometimes AGGRAVATING, phone calls. You'll never understand how God used you to keep me from taking my own life. Thank you for the aggravation Joe!

Made in the USA
Las Vegas, NV
27 March 2024

87849674R00302